Chartered Banker

STUDY TEXT
Retail Banking

In this 2014/15 edition

- A **user-friendly format** for easy navigation
- **Updated** on recent developments
- A **chapter review** at the end of each chapter
- A full **index**

Chartered Banker

Leading financial professionalism

BPP LEARNING MEDIA

Published July 2014

ISBN 978 1 4727 0501 3

British Library Cataloguing-in-Publication Data
A catalogue record for this book
is available from the British Library

Published by

BPP Learning Media Ltd
BPP House, Aldine Place
London W12 8AA

www.bpp.com/learningmedia

Printed in the United Kingdom by Ricoh UK Limited

Unit 2
Wells Place
Merstham
RH1 3LG

Your learning materials, published by BPP Learning Media Ltd, are printed on paper obtained from traceable sustainable sources.

BPP
LEARNING MEDIA

CONTENTS

INTRODUCTION

The aim of this module is to provide an extensive, detailed and critical knowledge and understanding of the legal, practical and philosophical aspects of the retail banking environment and develop the practitioner's skills and ability to synthesise complex issues, evaluate information, apply principles and techniques, and make professional judgements and informed decisions in relevant work situations.

Learning outcomes

The main learning outcomes associated with this module should be able to:

- Critically analyse what differentiates retail banking from other types of banking and examine the factors that contribute to the success of a retail bank

- Evaluate the significance of a client-centred approach to retail banking and identify a range of factors that would contribute to the success of a client-centred approach

- Examine the challenges of managing delivery through diverse distribution channels in a retail banking environment and assess the impact of technology on a retail banking operation and its customers

- Assess the significance of the processes and relationships between customer-facing and support roles in a retail banking operation and explain how this impacts on delivery of service to the customer

- Recognise and discuss the factors that contribute to the effective leadership and management of a retail banking operation

- Critically review the scope and examine the impact of the current UK and international regulatory environment on the retail banking sector

Assessment structure

Your online extended response examination will be worth 70% of your overall result and your summative assignment will make up the remaining 30%. Continuous formative assessment will be provided in the form of feedback on a draft assignment.

Introduction to your study text

The aim of this study text is to give you a broad understanding of the legal, practical and philosophical aspects of the retail banking environment in the early 21st century. As you work through the book, you will see that the materials are a blend of both hard and soft factors. For example, the types of products and services offered by retail banks are explained in a very factual manner. However, you will also know that one of the ways in which banks seek to compete with one another is through the quality and expertise of their staff. Because of this, there is also material describing people management, which is a far more subjective field.

The book begins by looking at what we mean by a retail bank and how it can be differentiated from other financial institutions. In any line of work, it is important that we are aware of how the current organisations and activities have evolved, therefore part of the first chapter will consider the history and development of retail banks. We also need to be clear about how these banks operate, serve their customers and contribute to the global economy.

In the second chapter, our attention is turned to the customer as we discuss the client-centred approach. This puts the customer at the heart of the organisation, as we consider not only the products and services offered by most retail banks, but also the ways in which these products can be used to meet the needs of the customer. Certain legal aspects are also included in this chapter surrounding the banker-customer relationship.

The changing ways in which banks and their customers engage and interact are considered in Chapter 3 when we discuss the distribution channels used by banks in order to get their offerings to the market. Whilst this information is up to date at the time of writing, the pace of change is so rapid that you may well be aware of more recent developments and you should take steps to keep abreast of these.

The retail arm of an organisation will never exist in a vacuum, so the next chapter discusses themes around people, processes and risk. This chapter will discuss not only the support functions that are provided internally by other parts of the organisation, but also those that may have been outsourced to third party providers.

As discussed earlier, an organisation is only as good as the people who work in it, so in the penultimate chapter we focus on management and leadership. This section of the course will consider ways in which we can work with colleagues to bring out the best in them.

The book ends considering the topic of regulation. If you have previously studied the Professionalism, Ethics and Regulation course, then you will be aware that much of this material has been imported from this area. The reason for this is the vital importance of this subject for all professional bankers. Part of the fall-out from the banking crisis that started in 2007 was a call for a change in the role of financial services regulation and this is discussed towards the end of the course.

You will be aware of the dynamic environment that retail banks are currently operating in. This landscape has changed dramatically since the banking crisis and the fall out from the events associated with the crisis is reflected in the text. Regulation is changing, ownership has changed and the organisational structure of banks will change. The reputational damage to both banks and bankers is still being felt and it will take a long time for the public's perception of bankers to be repaired. However, you should also be aware that circumstances are continuing to change at the time of writing and, by the time you come to sit the exam, further changes will have occurred. One of the challenges facing you is to keep abreast of these developments and relate them to the materials in the text.

chapter 1

RETAIL BANKING

Contents

Learning outcomes

On completion of this chapter you should be able to:

- Identify the various types of banking and critically analyse how retail banking differs from these
- Examine the factors that contribute to the success of a retail bank
- Explain how retail banking has evolved and, based on current trends, create a vision of how it may continue to evolve in the future
- Identify those factors that contribute to the profitability of a retail bank and explain the measures used to analyse its financial health and operational efficiency
- Explain how a retail bank contributes to the world economy

Introduction

Welcome to the first chapter of the Retail Banking Operations and Regulation course! This chapter will lay the foundations for what is to follow in your studies. The chapter commences with a discussion of what we mean by a retail bank and in what ways is it different from other banks in the economy. You should be well aware of the banking crisis that commenced in 2007. One of the responses to this was the establishment of the Independent Commission on Banking and the outcome of their deliberations will be discussed next. The chapter moves on to discuss the work of the central bank in the UK – the Bank of England, before we look at some other financial institutions – building societies, National Savings and investments, Credit Unions and merchant/investment banks. We conclude the chapter with an explanation of the basic conundrum of banking – the need for banks to balance their need to generate profits through lending out funds to borrowers.

1 What is a retail bank?

QUICK QUESTION

We are all familiar with banks and use them every day. However, it can be challenging to summarise this knowledge in a working definition. Reflect upon this for a few minutes, and then write down your definition of a bank

How easy did you find this task? Possibly it was more difficult than you first thought!

Write your answer here before reading on.

Here are a couple of dictionary definitions of a bank:

> A bank is an organisation where people and business can invest or borrow money, change for other currencies *(Cambridge Dictionary)*.
>
> A bank is an organisation offering financial services, especially the safekeeping of customers' money until required as well as making loans at interest *(Oxford Dictionary)*.

Looking at the second definition in particular, we can see that a fundamental purpose of a bank is to act as a conduit – or go-between – between two groups of people in society. These are those people who after satisfying their economic needs have too much money (i.e. savers) and those in society who cannot meet all of their economic needs from current and available income (i.e. borrowers). The name given to this function is **financial intermediation**. However, before we get too concerned with what banks do in the twenty first century, we will consider the evolution of banking.

Banking began back in ancient Mesopotamia as far back as the 18th Century BC. It was subsequently developed and expanded in ancient Greece, Rome and medieval Italy. The word bank comes from the Italian word 'banco' meaning a bench or a table at which Italian money lenders used to conduct business in the Middle Ages (1200-1500 AD). This Italian connection continues as the oldest bank still in business today is Monte dei Paschi di Diena in Italy, founded in 1472. There is a connection between this and the development of the word bankruptcy. Bankruptcy stems from the Latin 'bancus' (a bench or table), and 'ruptus' (broken). As you now know, the word bank originally referred to a bench, which the first bankers had in the public places, in markets, fairs, etc. on which they offered their services. When a banker failed and so ceased to trade, he broke his bank (bench), to advertise to the public that the person to whom the bank belonged was no longer in a condition to continue his business. As this practice was very frequent in Italy, it is thought that the term bankrupt is derived from the Italian 'banca rotta', or broken bank.

Coming back to the discussion above, a bank is a place or organisation which provides a link between those with surplus funds who wish to place them for safekeeping and those who are short of funds and wish to borrow them. Banks also effect the payment of orders, such as cheques, online transactions or automated payments drawn on it by their customers or indeed authorised on some way by these customers.

2 How do we differentiate between banks?

When most people think of a bank they think about the banks that they see on the High Street or deal with over the phone or online. However, banking is a much wider area than this. Given the diverse nature of banks operating in the country it is sometimes helpful to classify them into broad categories. One technique is to classify institutions according to the products and services they offer. The problem with this classification is that many institutions do not rigidly specialise but instead offer a range of services to their customers. Another way to differentiate is to consider the size of an institution's typical transactions and then decide whether it is involved in retail or wholesale operations.

QUICK QUESTION

How do you think we could make this distinction between retail and wholesale banks?

Write your answer here before reading on.

The way in which we may make this differentiation is:

- Retail banks operate large branch networks and are prepared to deal in small and large sums of money.

- Wholesale banks usually do not operate branch networks; they deal in large sums of money often raised in the London money markets.

Another way to classify banks is on the basis of their balance sheets according to the kind of deposits they accept. This divides banks into **primary banks** and **secondary banks**:

- Primary banks operate the payments mechanism system within the country and offer a system for transferring money by means of current accounts (sometimes called money transmission accounts).
- Secondary banks do not form part of the payments mechanism or take part in the clearing system.

2.1 Other financial institutions within the economy

Primary and secondary banks are not the only financial institutions to accept deposits from the public. Some finance houses are authorised by the Financial Conduct Authority (FCA) to accept deposits. Others such as building societies, credit unions and National Savings and Investments are covered by separate Acts of Parliament which authorise their acceptance of deposits from the public. A feature of most of these institutions is that they accept deposits for small sums of money from large numbers of personal customers.

2.2 Other financial institutions

A final group of financial institutions comprises those which do not accept deposits from the public; instead they provide facilities for long term saving and investment.

This group consists of:

- Investment trusts/unit trusts
- Insurance companies
- Pension funds

Having considered the broad categories of banks, we will now turn our attention to the evolution of banking in the UK. As this development has been different in Scotland as opposed to England, it makes sense to consider the evolution of banking in these countries separately.

2.3 The development of banking in the UK

English banking

In the early 19th century, English private banks were restricted to six partners due to an Act in 1708 which gave the Bank of England a monopoly in joint stock banking (this means a bank with a large number of shareholders) in England. Most banks were small, local and unregulated. In 1825 over 60 private banks failed in England, the outcome of which was the *Country Bankers Act 1826*. This Act represented a milestone in the development of English banking. It broke the Bank of England's monopoly and permitted the creation of joint stock banks outside a 65 mile radius of London with the right to issue notes. New banks were able to raise more capital than the old ones were, to open branches and thus lend to a variety of industries, thereby spreading their risks.

The Bank Charter Act 1833 authorised joint stock banks to open branches within the 65 mile radius provided they did not issue notes. In 1834 the London and Westminster Bank was established; ultimately through mergers it became the National Westminster Bank plc, which in turn became part of what is now known as the RBS Group. The number of joint stock banks increased during the next few decades while the number of private banks diminished through mergers and takeovers. Barclays Bank grew out of a series of mergers by private banks from 1896 onwards.

The period 1890 – 1918 witnessed the increased concentration of banking in England whereby a few banks dominated deposit taking and lending business. This trend was encouraged by the public's greater confidence in large banks, a view also held by the authorities. Bank mergers were seen as strengthening the financial system.

In 1918 a Treasury Committee was set up to examine bank mergers as fears began to be expressed about the size and influence of large banks. A proposed legal ban on mergers was dropped, but the banks did agree to consult the authorities before proceeding with any further amalgamations. For the next 50 years the pattern of English banking remained stable. Five banks dominated the banking scene – Barclays, Lloyds, Midland, National Provincial, Westminster – plus six smaller joint stock banks. A strong argument for bank mergers in the 1960s was that English clearing banks faced increased competition from both home and abroad, from finance houses, building societies and foreign banks. In 1968 Barclays merged with Martins Bank while the National Provincial, District and Westminster Banks became the National Westminster Bank.

These retail bank mergers resulted in three major benefits:

- Strengthened bank balance sheets and thereby greater lending capacity
- Cost savings via branch mergers and reduced staff requirements
- More funds available for investment in new technology available at that time

Scottish banking

The Scottish banks are proud of their history which is quite separate to that of banking south of the border. The Bank of Scotland was established in 1695 to meet the needs of commerce and it began by issuing notes and making loans. In 1727 the Royal Bank of Scotland was set up; thus Scotland gained two joint stock banks to England's one. Both were legal corporations with limited liability for their shareholders. Fierce competition ensued over the issue and presentation of notes until both realised the mutually destructive nature of such competition.

As time passed, more banks were set up in Scotland to meet the needs of expanding industry and commerce. The prohibition of having more than six partners did not exist in Scotland and thus by the 19th century most major Scottish towns and cities had joint stock banks issuing their own notes. For example Clydesdale Bank was set up in Glasgow in 1838. Similar to the situation in England, a process of amalgamations took place which reduced the number of Scottish banks to eight by 1907. The 1950s and 1960s witnessed further mergers until there was only the Bank of Scotland, Royal Bank of Scotland and Clydesdale Bank.

Innovations that came from the Scottish banking system include:

Overdrafts – The overdraft developed from the cash credit introduced by the Royal Bank of Scotland in 1728. Under this system, the bank agreed to honour claims against a person's account up to an agreed amount. The sum was debited against the customer's account and interest was charged on the outstanding balance.

Branch banking – Scotland developed a network of branches which added to the stability of the banking system. It allowed banks to tap a wider source of funds and spread risks associated with lending over a wider geographical area.

Joint stock banking – This form of banking meant that shareholders in a bank were protected from personal liability for the bank's debts should it fail. Limited liability encouraged a greater number of people to become investors in banks, thus providing them with a larger capital base.

The clearing house – In 1771 the Scottish banks introduced a note exchange in Edinburgh which meant that each bank's notes were more acceptable to the public. This example of interbank cooperation encouraged the concept of a clearing house for cheques.

The Chartered Banker Institute – Established in 1875, the Institute was the world's first professional body for practising bankers. It dedicated itself, as it does today, to the training and educating of bankers and other financial services practitioners both in Scotland and globally.

2.4 UK banking in the 21st century

In recent years, the UK banks have been embroiled in the global financial crisis. However, before we discuss this, we will look at the quieter early years on the twenty first century.

The UK clearing banks are among a number of deposit taking institutions which, in the eyes of most people, are very similar. All have deposits with a fixed monetary value – they do not appreciate nor depreciate like equities or bonds, and depositors are aware that there is little risk of loss, whether they deposit with a bank, a building society, National Savings and Investments or some other regulated institution. This was seen in the banking crisis that started in 2008 when although UK banks faced severe financial difficulty, depositors' funds were still safe. Whilst depositors' funds are safeguarded to a specified limit by the Financial Services Compensation Scheme, during the banking crisis the UK government stated that they would offer further protection for depositors in an attempt to maintain a degree of confidence in the banking system. Customers' funds deposited with the bank are repayable on demand or after an agreed interval of time, and interest is paid, or a range of services given in lieu of interest.

One of the huge commercial pressures faced by modern day banks is that the public regard the products offered by banks as close substitutes for each other, which can make it very challenging when banks seek to win customers from one another. This public perception has recently come even closer to reality, as the old differences between clearing banks and building societies have now largely disappeared. All now provide a range of payment facilities including money transmission, cash dispensers, automated paying in facilities, direct banking and credit cards as well as lending facilities which, although they are not identical, do overlap, particularly in personal lending and mortgages. This operating environment has resulted in intense competition between deposit taking institutions where much of the focus has been on attempts to personalise the service offered by a bank.

The UK clearing banks are mostly involved in retail banking. Retail banking implies a large number of customers generating volume business on standard terms and conditions. The interest rates payable on the different varieties of deposits will normally be advertised and thus be widely known. Rates to borrowers are not advertised, although base (or reference) rates are widely publicised and rates to borrowers will be based on these.

QUICK QUESTION

In what ways do clearing banks and other deposit takers compete?

Write your answer here before reading on.

Competition among clearing banks and between them and other deposit taking institutions takes the form of:

- The range of services available online and contact centres
- The extent and location of branch networks
- The interest rates charged on loans and paid on deposits
- The fees charged for arranging loans
- The range and quality of additional services provided
- The perceived stability, trustworthiness and personalisation of the services provided by the organisation

The clearing banks are all examples of primary banks which operate the payments mechanism. Although they vary considerably in size, to some extent they all enjoy economies of scale. The particular advantages deriving from these are that:

- The branch network, internet and contact centres make the clearing banks accessible to a wide range of customers.
- Offer a comprehensive direct banking service.

- Risk is spread over a range of sectors of the economy and parts of the country (a bank is much more vulnerable to losses when it is involved with only a few customers or industry sectors).

- A larger bank can afford to employ experts and have specialist departments and services. Alternatively they have the financial resources to be able to afford to outsource some operations.

- Larger banks require proportionally lower levels of liquid assets as risk of unexpected withdrawals is spread more widely.

- Larger banks can make fullest use of modern technology.

A clearing bank's cash inflow will consist of customers' deposits and loan repayments (including interest) while cash outflow will be customers' withdrawals and new loans granted. The amount of loan repayments will be fixed at any given time, dependent on the amount of lending in previous periods, but the inflow of deposits and the amount of lending and withdrawal of deposits will depend on current interest rates and other conditions attached to deposits and loans. These rates and terms can be varied, consequently varying the level of inflows and outflows. As clearing banks are very similar in the range of services offered, altering interest rates would appear to be the main variable they have, but interest rates on products can be quite similar from one bank to another.

They do not operate an interest rate cartel, although the tendency to simultaneously adjust of interest rates might suggest otherwise. This apparent coordination of rate adjustments, the banks would claim, derives from them all operating in the same money markets and thus being subject to precisely the same market forces.

Interest rates on loans and deposits are adjusted to give each bank a desired level of liquidity – a balance between inflows and outflows. They will not normally be keen to alter these rates relative to each other, unless the existing balance appears to have been permanently upset – an abundance or shortage of liquidity within a bank.

One final point is that the distinction between retail and wholesale banking has become blurred in recent years. Most of the UK clearing banks are now banking groups which provide through subsidiaries a wide range of services, such as deposit taking, share issues, leasing, etc. However, as you will read later in this chapter, one of the outcomes of the Independent Commission on Banking was to have a clear distinction between a bank's retail and its riskier wholesale activities.

The key distinction of clearing banks from other deposit taking institutions is that they play a major role in money transmission services and hold a high proportion of demand deposits in the economy.

2.5 The banking crisis

The period since 2007 has been extremely turbulent for the UK banking sector. It was characterised by a tightening of credit conditions brought about largely by international factors, most notably triggered by the credit crisis in the US, the deteriorating situation within the Eurozone and the global economic recession. At the start of the crisis, several banking institutions have had to seek government support and some were taken either wholly or partly into public ownership. There was also a significant rationalisation in the UK financial services sector.

The crisis had a major impact on all organisations that depended to any extent on the wholesale markets and, as many UK-based financial institutions were heavily reliant on wholesale funds from the US, deteriorating conditions in the US economy quickly had an impact on the UK financial services sector.

Until 2007, the housing market in the USA had enjoyed a period of sustained growth, fuelled by low interest rates and readily available funds, including buoyant inflows from Asian economies and oil producing countries. Much of the growth was based on the belief that mortgage assets were generally safe. Many US lenders leveraged their growth by issuing mortgage-based securities, which raised funding based on the perceived quality of existing mortgage assets. In addition to the burgeoning mortgage market, demand for other types of loan such as credit cards and car finance was extremely strong. Most economists agreed that the UK credit market peaked in late 2006.

The US economy inevitably overheated. Default rates started to rise and lenders became increasingly nervous. The costs of funding started to increase. As recession loomed the banks in the US became reluctant to make wholesale funds available. Alarmingly, the five largest investment banks in the US – major players in the wholesale and derivatives markets – all ran into difficulties. Lehman Brothers collapsed in September 2008. Goldman Sachs and Morgan Stanley became commercial banks. Bear Sterns and Merrill Lynch were bought out. Also in 2008, the Federal National Housing Association (Fannie Mae) and the Federal Loan Mortgage Corporation (Freddie Mac) were placed into conservatorship of the Federal Housing Finance Agency.

All of these developments put pressure on many of the larger banks in the UK, who had to make their lending products competitive but could not secure funding at the right price.

The crisis in UK banking was triggered by fundamental problems affecting many of the players in the market.

CASE STUDY

Northern Rock

In July 2007, Northern Rock announced a set of upbeat results and stated that the outlook for their business is 'very positive'. However, within a month of this announcement, the Governor of the Bank of England was made aware by the FSA (the UK financial services regulator at the time) and the Treasury that the developing global credit squeeze was having an effect on Northern Rock. Within a month of this, the Governor announced that the Bank of England would be willing to provide funds to any bank that encountered short-term difficulties as a result of temporary market conditions. On the following day, the BBC announced that Northern Rock had received funding from the Bank of England in the Bank's role as lender of last resort (this role will be discussed later in this chapter). On the next day, Northern Rock announced that the 'extreme conditions' on the financial markets had forced it to turn to the Bank of England for assistance and a statement was issued by Northern Rock, the Bank of England and the Treasury to the effect that Northern Rock was solvent. However, this cut little ice with many customers who formed queues outside the bank looking to withdraw their deposits. Over the next few days, the queues continued and the bank's share price continued to plunge, causing the Chancellor of the Exchequer to guarantee all of the bank's deposit – even those in excess of the Financial Services Compensation Scheme limit – this move seemed to appease depositors.

One week later, the bank cancelled its proposed dividend and stated that it has commenced talks with parties interested in buying all or part of the business.

In the weeks and months that followed, Northern Rock was rarely out of the news as others sought to buy the bank, before it was eventually nationalised and the FSA was heavily criticised for its part in the process.

On 1st January 2012, Northern Rock was acquired by Virgin Money.

However for most people, the abiding memory of the Northern Rock story is television pictures of customers queuing to get their savings out of the bank.

Other financial institutions soon found out that they too needed government support. In the autumn of 2008, several of the larger banks, including the Royal Bank of Scotland, the Lloyds Banking Group and HBoS, were supported by public funds when the government decided to take shares in these banks in return for capital injections. Further funds were provided by the government in spring 2009.

These measures, which amounted to part nationalisation, were intended to be temporary, in that the capital will eventually be repaid to the government.

The government also sought to increase confidence in the financial system by reinforcing the compensation available to the customers of failed organisations – with effect from 31st December 2010, the amount of protection for individual (personal) customers deposits was increased to £85,000.

CASE STUDY

The international dimensions of the crisis were brought home by the collapse of the Icelandic banking system, and in particular the failure of Landsbanki. This bank had offered attractive interest rates for depositors through its subsidiary, Icesave, which provided easy access, on-line retail banking services to retail customers in the UK and the Netherlands.

In October 2008, Icesave stopped processing withdrawals. Initially the government of Iceland announced that it would only protect domestic depositors, causing diplomatic tension between the UK and Iceland. Eventually in October 2009, the Icelandic government announced that it would make compensation available to personal non-resident account holders.

Some banking organisations took the more conventional route of seeking merger partners and were effectively bought over. Some of the former building societies that had become plc's during the 1980s and 1990s including Abbey, Alliance and Leicester and Bradford and Bingley, had some of their business taken over by other financial institutions. These three organisations have all become members of the Santander group.

Ironically, in a sector in which size had become important, some of the smaller institutions with less dependence on wholesale markets were less seriously affected by the crisis. Some observers have commented that none of the former building societies that relinquished their mutual status to become plc's survive as independent institutions. By contrast, few of the building societies were seriously affected by the crisis, although there has inevitably been some rationalisation. In addition to this, the only mutual bank in the country – Airdrie Savings Bank saw an expansion from its traditional base in industrial Lanarkshire with the opening of a new branch in Falkirk.

The crisis has led to an inevitable restructuring of the financial sector, with several mergers and acquisitions as well as the total demise of some companies. Recovery from the economic recession was slow to take hold and it was only in the second half of 2013 that more sustained growth occurred in the UK economy.

These recent events have put the spotlight on the way that many financial services organisations conduct themselves, with a re-evaluation of corporate governance, values and ethics. The regulatory landscape of the UK financial services sector was fundamentally altered and this will be discussed later.

As a result, banking institutions are faced with new compliance challenges, and they will also have to consider the extent to which their corporate social responsibility policies go further than simply obeying the letter of the law. In building their business models for the future, the larger organisations have to undergo a period of consolidation and possibly fundamental restructuring of the ways in which they do business in order to compete with new challenges, including the new players that enter the market.

A significant outcome of the crisis is the re-inforcement of the view that some organisations are 'too big to fail'. The financial services sector in the UK did much to generate the wealth in the 25 years that followed the end of World War 2, giving successive governments the confidence to deregulate and permit banking institutions to compete with one another, largely free on external interference.

This led to greater innovation and a wider choice for the consumer, but perhaps also to complacency that if and when things did go wrong, then the industry would be able to deal with any issues as and when they arose. The fact that many financial institutions came to rely on the government – and thus the taxpayer – supporting them financially is a timely reminder that the essence of banking is risk.

3 Independent Commission on Banking

In June 2010, the Chancellor of the Exchequer announced the creation of an Independent Commission on Banking (ICB), chaired by Sir John Vickers. The ICB was asked to consider structural and related non-structural reforms to the UK banking sector to promote banking stability and competition.

3.1 Report and recommendations – September 2011

This outlined the ICB's current and provisional views on possible reforms to improve stability and competition in UK banking.

With regard to stability, the ICB stated that making the banking system safer required a combined approach that:

- Makes banks better able to absorb losses
- Makes it easier and less costly to sort out banks that get into trouble
- Curbs incentives for excessive risk taking

The two ways to make banks safer were firstly by increasing their ability to bear losses, by requiring them to hold a great deal more capital (even than that laid down by the Basel requirements); and secondly to alter their structure. It was recommended that this would be done by splitting retail from wholesale and investment banking with these functions being carried out by separate banks. This would aim to isolate retail banking and the taxpayer from the risks of global wholesale and investment banking.

In December 2011 the Chancellor announced that the government would accept these recommendations.

Regarding competition, the IBC stated that UK retail banking needs to be more competitive and that the damage done by the financial crisis will not be remedied by the selling off of the RBS and Lloyd's bank branches as required by the European Commission (EC).

Their view is that the following opportunities should be seized:

1. The number of Lloyd's branch sell-offs could be increased beyond the EC requirement of 600 branches to create a more effective challenger to the incumbent banks.

2. The ability of customers to switch banks could be greatly improved.

The reform of the UK regulatory institutions must ensure that effective competition can be a central force in UK financial regulation.

The changes brought about by the ICB and the Parliamentary Commission on Banking Standards came into effect through the Financial Services (Banking Reform) Act 2013.

3.2 The major function of UK retail/clearing banks

Note issue

As you will probably know, a distinctive feature of Scottish (and indeed Northern Irish) banking is the right of these banks to issue their own notes. London/English-based banks are not allowed to issue notes. *The Bank Charter Act 1844*, which gave the Bank of England an eventual monopoly of the note issue in England and Wales, did not apply to Scotland. Thus the Scottish joint stock banks retained the right to issue their own notes after 1844.

Under the *Bank Notes (Scotland) Act 1845* each bank was granted an authorised circulation based on its average circulation for 1844; thereafter any notes issued above this figure were backed by gold. Today that privilege appears very small for the three Scottish banks which issue their own notes, as only £3m out of over £2,000m in circulation does not need to be covered at the Bank of England. Scottish clearing banks must meet the cost of printing and security for their own notes. However, the banks appreciate the prestige, advertising and appeal to Scottish patriotism of issuing their own notes. Any public discussion regarding the cessation of the Scottish note issue has always been met with disapproval in Scotland.

There are also sound financial benefits from maintaining the separate Scottish note issue. These stem from the fact that Scottish notes do not need to be covered until in circulation with the public; this reduces the cost of till money. If the Scottish note issue were abolished, Scottish banks would have the expense of holding all their till money in the form of Bank of England notes for which a fee is payable.

Accept deposits

The retail banks offer a variety of deposit facilities. Money transmission account facilities form the principal means of payment in the country. The banks also offer numerous deposit/savings account facilities.

Agents for payments

Although the UK Payments Administration has opened the money transmission system to foreign and smaller banks and building societies, the payments mechanism is still dominated by the traditional clearing banks.

Grant loans

Much of their lending is to personal customers; this includes overdrafts, personal loans, instalment credit (either directly or through a subsidiary company), bridging loans (although these are becoming less popular) and loans through credit cards. The clearing banks also provide house mortgages. There is also substantial lending to companies – sometimes referred to as corporate business. In the past the emphasis was on short term lending through overdrafts, but there is now more lending by term loans, leasing and factoring.

The credit function within banks is quite specialised. Within the retail divisions most lending decisions are automated and made through some type of automated credit scoring system. Business customers could also be subject to credit scoring, but will be more likely to have any lending requests scrutinised by a lending official in the bank. Once this assessment has been made, the final decision will be communicated to the customer. This type of credit decision making is called manual underwriting. Depending upon the size of the organisation looking for credit and the amount of credit involved, then the customer will tend to deal with a commercial or corporate lending department which will be staffed by members of staff with substantial credit experience.

Other services

The clearing banks offer a wide variety of other services both to individuals and organisations, including:

- Investment management
- Insurance
- Income tax advice
- Trustee and executorships
- Keeping companies' share registers
- Foreign business

4 The role of the central bank

Fundamental to the operation of retail banks in any economy is the central bank – so it is to this organisation that we will now turn our attention to.

QUICK QUESTION

What is the name of the UK's central bank?

Write your answer here before reading on.

The central bank in the UK is the Bank of England. The Bank was established by Royal Charter in 1694 and was promoted by a Scot, William Paterson, who believed that a large joint stock bank with its greater capital would have a considerable advantage over the then existing banks, which were actually goldsmiths who also provided banking services.

The original intention was to operate as an ordinary commercial bank on a larger scale; only gradually did the Bank assume the functions now associated with central banking. Under its Charter the Bank of England was authorised to:

- Accept deposits and make loans
- Discount bills
- Issue notes

In return for its Charter the Bank made a loan to the government of £1.2 million at 8% which was added to Britain's National Debt. The loan took the form of notes issued by the Bank. The Bank thus issued notes; it made a profit by making loans in the form of bank notes which it persuaded the public to accept and to hold. In this respect the Bank of England was similar to the other banks of the time. For its part the Bank tried to get a monopoly of the right to issue notes. At various times its Charter required to be renewed which provided opportunities for the government to increase its borrowing and for the Bank to strengthen its position.

Although the Bank of England was founded as a commercial bank, it differed from other banks in a number of ways:

A joint stock company

The Bank of England was established as a joint stock company and its capital was raised by public subscription which gave the Bank an advantage over the existing private banks which were restricted to six partners and so limited in potential size. An Act in 1708 made the Bank the only joint stock bank allowed to issue notes in England. The Bank did not operate in Scotland and by 1746 Scotland had three joint stock banking companies issuing notes (Bank of Scotland, Royal Bank of Scotland, British Linen Company).

Limited liability

The Bank of England was given the privilege of limited liability which limited the shareholders' liability for the Bank's debts in the event of failure to the amount they had paid for their shares. This reduced the risk of investing in the Bank and so made its shares more attractive.

The government's banker

By granting a loan to the government the Bank of England established a special relationship which developed over the years as the Bank undertook new responsibilities such as the circulation of Exchequer bills and the issue of government securities. In 1751 the Bank undertook the administration of the National Debt. Despite the competition that the Bank posed, private bankers in London found it convenient to keep an account with it for their surplus funds, thus the Bank took a step nearer to becoming a central bank by acting not only as the government's banker but also as the bankers' bank.

4.1 The Bank Charter Act 1844

The principal aim of the 1844 Act was to control the money supply by regulating note issue. This was achieved by placing a limit on the Bank of England's ability to issue notes unbacked by gold and by the gradual phasing out of private bank note issues in England and Wales.

To ensure the proper operation of the note issue, the Bank was reorganised into two departments:

- An Issue Department solely concerned with the note issue
- A Banking Department to carry out the Bank's normal commercial activities

The Bank was required to redeem its notes for gold at a fixed price (£3.87 per ounce of gold), thus linking the pound sterling to gold.

4.2 The bank and financial crises

During the 19th century the Bank assumed another function of central banking by acting as the lender of last resort which involved the Bank in providing support to the banking/financial system when major financial panics occurred. In many instances this support resulted in the Bank discounting bills or extending loans against bills offered by banks in need of liquidity. This function of the Bank of England was seen in more recent times during the banking crisis of 2008 – reflect back to the Northern Rock Case Study earlier in the chapter for an illustration of how the Bank of England acts as Lender of Last Resort to UK banks that are experiencing liquidity problems.

4.3 Nationalisation

In 1946 the Bank of England was nationalised and thus passed into public ownership. The Bank's shareholders were compensated with government stock. Public ownership was the culmination of years of close cooperation between the Bank and government. The Bank often appeared to be as much the government's agent as an independent bank. With the government playing a much greater role in the management of the economy after 1945 it seemed inappropriate that the Bank should remain in private ownership.

4.4 The organisation and structure of the Bank of England

The Court of Directors

Ultimate responsibility for the work of the Bank lies with the Court of Directors which consists of the Governor, two Deputy Governors (both appointed for a term of five years) and sixteen non-executive members (three-year term) appointed for their expertise and drawn widely from industry, commerce and finance. The non-executive members' main role is to review the performance of the Bank as a whole, including the work of the Monetary Policy Committee (which sets base rate).

The Bank is managed on a day-to-day basis by the Governor and the two Deputy Governors – one deputy works with the Governor on monetary stability and the other on financial stability. The Governor keeps a close liaison with the City – financial institutions and markets – and represents the Bank at international financial and monetary meetings.

Similar to many organisations, the Bank of England has a mission statement which identifies its goal:

> **'As the central bank of the United Kingdom, we are committed to promoting the public good by maintaining a stable and efficient monetary framework as our contribution to a healthy economy.'**

In pursuing this goal, the Bank identifies three core purposes:

- Maintaining the integrity and value of the currency
- Maintaining the stability of the financial system, both domestic and international
- Seeking to ensure the effectiveness of the United Kingdom's financial services

The Bank's accountability is ensured by the fact that the decision-making process is fully transparent and by the government's overall accountability to Parliament for economic policy, including the setting of the inflation target. The Bank makes reports and gives evidence to the House of Commons through the Treasury Select Committee.

Part of the functions of the Bank of England will be altered with the new regulatory landscape that is evolving in the UK. This will be discussed further in the Regulation chapter of this course.

Offices and staff

In addition to its head office, a branch is maintained in Leeds to assist in the distribution of bank notes in the north of England. Agencies also operate in twelve major cities such as Birmingham, Glasgow and Manchester in order to gather economic intelligence and assess economic developments in the whole country which assists the Monetary Policy Committee decision-making process on interest rates.

4.5 The functions of the Bank of England

As the UK's central bank the Bank undertakes a number of important domestic and external functions on behalf of the government and other financial institutions. Its main functions are:

The government's banker

The Bank of England keeps the government's bank accounts. The main government account is the **Exchequer Account** into which nearly all government receipts are paid and out of which nearly all payments originate. The Bank also keeps the accounts of government departments.

Revenue flows very unevenly into the Exchequer and on occasions is inadequate to meet current government expenditure. The Treasury has then to make arrangements to bridge the gulf between the inflow of revenue and the outflow of expenditure by advances from the Bank or by the issue of Treasury bills.

The Bank provides temporary finance at market interest rates to the government by **ways and means advances**. These advances are often not very large and are provided as an overnight facility.

The Bank advises the government on economic, financial and monetary matters.

The bankers' bank

The main clearing banks find it convenient to keep part of their cash reserves in operational accounts at the Bank of England. These banks constantly need to make and receive payment from one another due to the operation of the clearing system and these payments are made through the banks' accounts with the Bank of England. The banks need to keep these balances large enough to cover their needs and are expected not to overdraw.

Issue of notes

The Bank is the sole bank of note issue for England and Wales. As discussed, Scottish and Northern Ireland banks issue their own notes under strict regulation and once in circulation, these must be covered by Bank of England notes.

There is now no gold backing of notes issued which means that the UK note issue is a fiduciary one – called thus as the note issue is based purely on faith that notes will be acceptable to UK residents in settlement of debts at all times. Notes cannot be exchanged at the Bank of England for gold coins or bullion. As to be expected with inflation, the note issue has increased over the years.

Lender of last resort

As discussed earlier, the Bank occasionally acts as a lender of last resort to individual banks or the banking system which generally involves the provision of liquidity, sometimes at a penal interest rate, secured by first class bills and securities. By undertaking this role, the Bank endeavours to stabilise the banking and financial system and thereby prevent financial panics and depositor runs on banks.

BPP
LEARNING MEDIA

International relations

The Bank cooperates with the principal central banks of the world, such as US Federal Reserve Board, European Central Bank and others, and takes part in the work of the International Monetary Fund, Bank for International Settlements and the World Bank. It also provides services (gold and foreign exchange business) for the central banks of some Commonwealth countries. The Bank can arrange loans from overseas when necessary in order to add to the UK's foreign currency reserves and thereby confidence in sterling on the world's foreign exchange markets.

Manages the Exchange Equalisation Account (EEA)

The EEA was established in 1932 to stabilise the pound's exchange rate in relation to other currencies. It consists of the UK's gold and foreign currency reserves (US dollars, euros and Japanese yen) which technically belong to the Treasury. The EEA is managed on behalf of the Treasury by the Bank.

If there is a temporary fall in the pound's exchange rate, the Bank will buy pounds using its foreign currency reserves on the foreign exchange market to bid up the pound. When the pound is too high, the Bank sells pounds for foreign currencies and so forces down sterling's exchange value. This process is known as official intervention in the foreign exchange market.

Regulatory role

Since the introduction of the new regulatory system, the Bank of England has once again become involved in the regulation of the UK financial services sector. The Bank's Financial Policy Committee (FPC) identifies, monitors and acts to remove or reduce risks that are deemed to be a threat to the banking system in the UK. The FPC also makes recommendations and gives direction to the Prudential Regulation Authority (PRA) and the Financial Conduct Authority (FCA).

The PRA is a subsidiary of the Bank and its role is to carry out the prudential regulation and supervision of banks, building societies, credit unions, insurers and major investment firms.

We will return to this theme of regulation in the final chapter of this Study Text.

Private banking

The Bank does have about 8,000 old established private banking customers plus staff members and pensioners, but the general public cannot now open accounts at the Bank.

4.6 The Bank of England Act 1998

The main provisions of this Act are:

- The monetary policy objectives of the Bank as set out in statutory form are to maintain price stability and support the Government's economic policy.
- It established a Monetary Policy Committee which has responsibility for formulating monetary policy within the Bank.
- It put in place a new accountability framework for the Bank based on its statutory duties. It also created the need for greater transparency in the Bank's operations.
- The transfer to the Financial Services Authority (FSA) of the Bank's function in relation to the supervision of UK banks – although this has now been changed in light of the banking crisis.

These were quite sweeping changes and marked a fundamental shift in the Bank's operational and supervisory roles from the position it took prior to this Act. Apart from the Bank's new statutory responsibility for monetary policy, the most significant step was the transfer to the FSA of responsibility for bank supervision, although this has now changed.

4.7 Quantitative easing

The banking crisis led to the tightening of credit conditions. In addition, there was a rise in global commodity prices which had the impact of squeezing real incomes and this combination pushed many advanced economies, including the UK's, into recession – the most severe since the Great Depression of the 1930s.

The conventional way for the Bank of England's Monetary Policy Committee to use monetary policy to inflate the economy is to reduce interest rates. Such action boosts spending (as the cost of borrowing has been reduced), and thus demand (and inflation), by deterring saving and encouraging borrowing. However, with UK interest rates already at 0.5%, the Government authorised the Bank of England to create a new fund, the Asset Purchase Facility.

Known as **quantitative easing**, the objective is to inject money directly into the economy, not by printing more banknotes, but by the Bank of England buying assets from private sector institutions, i.e. insurance companies, pension funds, banks or non-financial firms. The aim is to take financial assets out of the economy and exchange them for money which can then be spent on the purchase of other assets, thus pushing up overall asset prices and wealth. Alternatively, increased cash in the hands of banks can be lent to companies and individuals to boost spending.

5 Other providers of financial services

Having looked at how we differentiate between types of banks and considered how banking in the UK has developed, we will now turn our attention to those organisations that provide banking services, but do not necessarily spring immediately to mind when we hear the word 'bank'. The organisations we will consider are:

- Building Societies
- National Savings and Investments
- Credit Unions
- Merchant and Investment Banks

5.1 Building societies

Building societies originated in the late 18th century among working people who wished to build their own homes. The oldest society for which records survive was Keltey's Building Society founded in Birmingham in 1775. Others were to follow. By 1800 there were 23 building societies.

It was in the Midlands and the North of England, in the rapidly expanding towns of the industrial revolution, that the new movement took root and prospered. The names of the towns or regions where the societies began are still to be seen in the titles of today's societies such as the Skipton or the Yorkshire. Building societies were first legally recognised under the *Friendly Societies Acts*. In 1836 an Act applying specifically to building societies regulated their management and vested their property in trustees. Compared with today's financial giants, the early societies were simple in the extreme – probably more akin to the Credit Unions of today in many ways. A group of working men would pool their financial resources to purchase some land and build houses for themselves and their families. Each member paid a regular subscription to the society. As each house was completed, lots would be drawn to decide the member to whom it should be allocated. When every member was housed, any loans repaid and all other expenses met, the society would be dissolved. For this reason the early societies were known as terminating societies.

Modern building societies are permanent societies which means they are not dissolved once their founding members are housed, but have a continuing existence. The first permanent society was established in 1845. By 1873 there were 540. This development opened up membership to those who wished to save rather than to build or buy a house.

These new societies were very much in tune with the self-help ethic of Victorian Britain and their position was secured by the *Building Societies Act 1874* which made building societies into corporate bodies with full legal powers similar to limited companies and provided the legal basis for their activities over the next 100 years. Local societies were established in many parts of the country and the movement continued to increase its strength – by 1900 over 2,000 separate societies existed.

5.2 The inter-war period

The 20th century saw the growth of the building society movement, particularly in the inter-war period. In 1920 total building society assets were £87 million and by 1940 they stood at £756 million. Even the economic depression of the 1930s failed to halt this expansion; indeed, the building societies were able to benefit from the prevailing low interest rates. This depression was predominantly a regional problem hitting the traditional heavy industries of the north of England, south Wales and central Scotland. The new consumer goods industries were concentrated in the south and Midlands of England.

For those in work, real incomes grew as did the volume of savings and the demand for home mortgages. This period of substantial growth ended with the outbreak of war in 1939.

5.3 The post-war period

When the war ended in 1945, the immediate problems were reconstruction and repairing wartime damage. Government housing policy concentrated on building public sector houses to let which offered little scope for the building societies.

In the 1950s, the emphasis switched back to the private sector and there was a rapid increase in the number of houses built for owner occupiers. This began a new period of growth for the building societies.

5.4 Later 20th century

As building societies increased in importance, so they became subject to greater public scrutiny and political comment which tended to concentrate on questions of house prices, mortgage queues and interest rates, the latter tending to fluctuate more frequently as interest rates in general became more volatile. Governments were particularly sensitive to the political consequences of a rise in mortgage rates and gave the building societies favoured treatment to keep rates down.

At times of rapidly rising house prices, building societies were blamed for overgenerous lending policies. In 1988, the societies were criticised as house prices increased at an annual rate of 34%. On other occasions, when funds were limited, societies were accused of being too cautious and keeping too high a liquidity ratio.

The number of building societies has reduced since the start of the 20th century.

QUICK QUESTION

Why do you think that this has happened?

Write your answer here before reading on.

Underlying this decline are the following factors:

- The closure of some of the very small permanent societies

- The process of amalgamation by mergers has reduced the number of societies. Whilst this has occurred over a number of years, you will be aware that some of the smaller societies merged with some larger ones as a consequence of the banking crisis. For example, the Derbyshire Building Society and the Cheshire Building Society both merged with the Nationwide on 31st December 2008.

- Under the Building Societies Act 1986, a building society has the right to convert from mutual to company status. The Abbey National converted in July 1989, other major societies – Halifax, Woolwich, Alliance & Leicester, – converted in 1997. Once company status is achieved, the building society is reclassified as a bank (or mortgage bank). This trend has reduced further the number of building societies and their share of personal sector financial assets and mortgages.

5.5 Building societies in Scotland

The development of Building Societies in Scotland was quite different to that south of the border.

Although there were building societies in Scotland in the early 19th century, they have always done proportionately less business in Scotland than in the rest of the United Kingdom. None of the larger societies originated in Scotland. This lack of a major Scottish-based building society may be explained by a number of interrelated factors.

- The dominance of other savings institutions – commercial banks/savings banks – may have retarded the development of an indigenous building society movement.

- The relative poverty of the working class and lower middle class in the past may have made house purchase an unrealistic aspiration for most people.

- The former availability of council houses with subsidised rents that bore no relation to actual interest cost associated with their construction.

- The Scottish tradition, up until the 1980s, of renting rather than purchasing a home. In the early 1990s about 55% of Scottish homes were owner-occupied compared with almost 70% in England.

- A previously inadequate stock of suitable houses in Scotland for purchase or acceptance as security for advances by building societies.

The 1980s and 1990s witnessed increased home ownership in Scotland, encouraged in part by the sale of council houses from local authorities to tenants, the near cessation of new council house building and higher council house rents. Mortgage business generated by this trend transferred largely to building societies and mortgage banks based in England. At the same time, the main building societies, such as Nationwide and the Yorkshire, have branches in Scotland's cities and main towns, the savings deposits of which have partly financed their mortgage operations north of the border.

5.6 The Building Societies Acts 1986 and 1997

Building societies are mutual organisations owned by and run for the benefit of their members. A member is anybody who holds a share in or borrows from a society. As mutual societies they have only their customers to consider and have no shareholders to whom they need to pay dividends. Generally, this means that mutual building societies can probably offer more competitive interest rates on mortgage and savings products.

The *Building Societies Act 1986* provided an entirely new legal framework for the building society movement and replaced all earlier building society legalisation. It removed many of the restrictions which had limited their activities and gave them a much broader remit to enable them to extend their range of financial services. The Act was part of the wider move towards deregulation/liberalisation which affected all financial institutions in Britain in the 1980s. Since 1986 the Act has been amended and revised by the *Building Societies Act 1997* and the *Financial Services and Markets Act 2000*, but the main provisions of the 1986 Act relating to the constitution, governance and principal purpose of building societies remain in place.

The principal (but no longer the sole) purpose of building societies remains that of raising funds from personal savers to lend out for house purchase to owner occupiers. To this was added a range of new services such as money transmission services, house purchase services, non-mortgage lending and other financial services – for example, share dealing.

5.7 Retail shares and deposits

The most popular form of personal investment in a building society is through a share account, although there are many variants on this. Building society share accounts are very similar to bank accounts except that when a person places money in a building society account, he or she becomes a member of the society and a shareholder. In some ways this is like holding shares in a public limited company since a member must receive a copy of the society's annual accounts and is entitled to attend and vote at the annual general meeting. However, there are important differences. A member of a building society has only one vote no matter how large the sum invested, whereas the voting power of a shareholder in a company depends on the number of shares held. Building society shares are not negotiable and so cannot be traded on the Stock Exchange, nor do they vary in value. Instead, building society shares can be cashed in at par (cashed in at their face value) together with any accrued interest in the same way that bank deposits can be withdrawn from a bank account. Another difference is that building societies are non-profit making organisations, so only the shareholders, i.e. customers, have direct claim over the surplus income and reserves of a building society.

Building societies offer a variety of share accounts, as well as deposit accounts.

QUICK QUESTION

What do you think is the difference between a share account and a deposit account?

Write your answer here before reading on.

Deposit accounts differ from share accounts in that deposit account holders are creditors, not members, of a building society. As such, in the unlikely event of a society going into liquidation, the depositors would have a prior claim over the society's assets. Such deposit account holders receive a lower rate of return than investors holding share accounts and are not entitled to vote on the society's affairs.

6 National Savings and Investments (NS&I)

The idea of a national savings bank operating through the post office was proposed as long ago as 1807, but it was not until 1861 that the Post Office Savings Bank (POSB) was established. The POSB had a number of advantages over retail and trustee savings banks:

- It was able to provide national coverage through an established network of post offices.

- Deposits and interest of 2.5% per annum at the POSB were guaranteed by the state so there was no risk of default.

- All deposits were placed in an account at the Bank of England and subsequently invested in government securities.

These perceived advantages encouraged the closure of small local savings banks in the south of England as customers transferred their accounts to the POSB. The POSB continued its expansion in the first half of the 20th century, reaching a peak of £1,982 million deposits in 1946. Various improvements were made to the service such as the payment of small sums on demand, payment by crossed warrant through a bank, a method of making periodic payments and the sale of savings stamps. The basic service, however, remained essentially unchanged. The Bank accepted deposits at 2.5% and reinvested the funds in government securities.

The subsequent decline in the POSB's popularity in the 1950s and 1960s may be explained by:

- The reluctance to provide competitive services – at a time when other savings institutions were broadening their range of services, the POSB continued to offer its one basic account; the management showed no enthusiasm for introducing a payments system such as a giro, nor was the management prepared to offer an investment account.

- An uncompetitive interest rate – in the 1930s and 1940s the 2.5% offered by the POSB was competitive; with rising/fluctuating interest rates from the mid-1950s onwards, the POSB steadily lost ground to its more aggressive competitors which offered higher interest rates.

6.1 Reform and revival

In the 1960s a number of developments took place:

- The POSB headquarters were shifted from London to Cowglen, near Glasgow in 1966.

- Also in 1966, investment accounts were introduced offering higher interest rates to long term savers.

- In 1969 the POSB changed its name to the National Savings Bank (NSB) although it continued to operate through post offices.

The investment account reversed the overall decline of funds held in the NSB. All the funds raised by the NSB were made available to the UK Treasury.

At the turn of the century, NSB was absorbed into the National Savings and Investments (NS & I) department of the UK Treasury. NS & I raises funds for the government by offering a broad range of savings products to the general public. This includes fixed interest savings certificates, index-linked savings certificates, capital bonds ISAs and retirement bonds, etc. Some of the facilities on offer provide various tax concessions or exemptions for personal savers. The NS & I also offers two types of bank accounts for use by the general public.

The NSB staff of about 4,000 was transferred to Siemens Business Services as part of a ten-year public private partnership agreement which gave the NS & I access to new technology and expertise.

In 2004 the ordinary account facilities were terminated, customers were asked to transfer their business to a more flexible savings account. At this time 13 million people had ordinary accounts but many of these accounts were inactive. The interest rate was only 1/4% per annum and more than 4 million accounts had a balance of less than £10. It was this situation that encouraged the NS & I to introduce a new, easy access savings account and continue to provide an investment account.

7 Credit unions

In the UK credit unions are relatively new entrant to the financial services market although they have been around in some countries for a long time. Credit union services are extremely popular in North America. About 25% of Americans bank with credit unions which offer a wide range of banking and financial services. In the United Kingdom the movement was established first in Northern Ireland. Irish and West Indian people who were already familiar with its benefits brought it to mainland Britain. Credit unions are mutual savings and loan societies providing a basic low cost banking service. Members finance their personal borrowing from their own combined resources.

As mentioned earlier, credit unions are quite similar to the early building societies although there is no longer the provision that members must share some common bond. The common bond could be that members attend the same church, live in the same locality or worked for the same employer. It was possible for a firm to support a credit union for its staff and deduct its employees' savings automatically from their salary.

Each credit union is a self-governing club owned by the members themselves and run on co-operative principles. Administration is through a board of directors, a credit committee and a supervisory committee elected by and from the members. Officials are all unpaid, although they may employ people. Members must be regular savers and can apply for small loans at moderate rates of interest to meet such expenses as holidays, weddings or even, in the winter, high fuel bills. Borrowers must continue to save while repaying their loans. Loan requests are treated in confidence and dealt with by the credit committee.

Part of the strength of credit unions is their lack of size, although some credit unions are now large enough to invest in credit scoring systems. Managers and members should be known to each other and loans can be granted on the basis of personal knowledge of the borrower. This is important for low income families with no financial assets to offer as security. It is also important for those groups whose needs and culture are outside the experience of the established financial institutions.

Unlike building societies, the demutualisation of credit unions into bank public limited companies is not possible under current legislation. The operations of credit unions in the UK are governed by the *Credit Unions Act 1979* as amendments came into force in 2012 and can be summarised thus:

- The need for a common bond amongst members was removed.

- The introduction of a 'field membership' test that allows for all potential members to be served by a credit union.

- Credit unions are now allowed to offer services to community groups, companies and social enterprises, as well as individuals.

- The removal of restrictions on 'non-qualifying' members.

8 Investment and merchant banks

Some **merchant banks** (formerly known as accepting houses) can trace their origin to the overseas trading houses of the 19th century. Banking in many cases developed as a sideline to the main activity of merchant houses which was dealing in commodities. With their knowledge of commodity trading and banking, the merchant houses developed a market for bills of exchange in London.

These bills of exchange are the traditional stock-in-trade of merchant/retail banks and securities houses and as such provide a major source of short term finance to industry and commerce. A bill is drawn by one trader (seller/exporter) and accepted by another trader (purchaser/importer); the latter by signing the bill acknowledges their obligation to pay it on the due date. The purchaser (drawee) returns the signed/accepted bill to the seller (drawer). Ideally a bill of exchange should be self-liquidating, i.e. the completion of the transaction which the bill was intended to finance should coincide with the maturity of the bill and so provide the funds to pay the bill. For example, the purchaser of goods will have sold them and received the funds before the bill is due to be paid. Say the bill is due for payment in 120 days – this means that the purchaser of the goods has 3 months to sell them and receive payment before they must settle with the original supplier.

The bill of exchange provides this short term trade credit. This kind of facility allows companies to borrow by means of bills rather than by borrowing from their banks.

The holder of an accepted bill has three options:

- Hold the bill to maturity and then present it for payment by the acceptor (purchaser).

- Sign the bill over to another party in settlement of a debt.

- Sell the bill to a bank or securities house at a discount, i.e. for a sum of money less than the bill's face value on maturity. The discount rate will reflect prevailing short term interest rates in the money markets.

E X A M P L E

Imagine a bill for £100 payable in three months' time and market interest rates around 10% per annum. The holder of the bill may sell it for, say, £97.50 and the buyer will receive £100 after 90 days. The buyer's profit, therefore, is £2.50 on an outlay of £97.50 = 2.56%, but this is just for three months and expressed as an annual rate the interest rate would be around 10.5%.

A bill of exchange can be compared to a post-dated cheque. For the trader (issuer of the bill) it provides a simple and convenient method of raising short term, self liquidating finance. For the acceptor, the bill provides a credit period in which to sell the goods.

The willingness of banks to discount a bill or other traders to receive a bill in payment of an outstanding debt depends on the confidence they have on the names that appear on the bill of exchange. The more reputable the names, such as ICI or British Aerospace, the more attractive the bill. Lesser-known companies find it easier to finance their trade if they can persuade a merchant bank to add their name to the bill. By doing so, the merchant bank adds its guarantee that the bill will be met – paid – on its maturity date for which it also receives commission.

An accepted bill can be sold (discounted) in the market at a higher price, i.e. lower interest rate, than a normal trade bill which does not have a merchant bank's guarantee. This is to the benefit of the drawee of the bill and makes it worthwhile paying a commission to have the bill accepted. For the merchant bank providing the acceptance, it appears as a contingent (potential) liability in the accounts – a footnote to the balance sheet.

It was through this role of accepting bills and thus providing the means to raise short term finance that merchant houses evolved into the merchant banks (or accepting houses) of the present day. One of the largest and most prestigious merchant banks in the UK is Rothschilds Bank. Others include the merchant/investing banking subsidiaries of the major retail or clearing banks, for example, Barclays Bank owns Barclays Capital. A number of London-based banks opened Scottish offices and a Scottish-based merchant bank – Noble Grossart – was established in Edinburgh in 1969.

8.1 Other functions of merchant banks

Accept deposits

As wholesale bankers, merchant banks deal in large deposits mainly from the corporate sector (industrial and commercial companies) rather than the personal sector. Merchant banks' wholesale activities now predominate. Much of this business is with other banks through the London interbank market and with banks abroad, but lending to corporate customers in both sterling and foreign currencies remains significant. Merchant banks do not operate a chain of retail branches or provide the general public with money transmission accounts. While this saves the expense of a branch network and the cost of administering numerous small accounts, it means that the bulk of a merchant bank's liabilities are market interest rate bearing deposits.

Finance

Apart from accepting trade bills and thereby providing a source of finance to firms, merchant banks often provide their own clients with acceptance credits which enable a customer to issue bills drawn on a merchant bank up to an agreed amount. These bills are then discounted to raise finance. The bank pays these bills on maturity and debits the client's account with the bill's face value. Clients pay merchant banks for the use of such facilities. Merchant banks also provide term loans in sterling and foreign currency to companies and institutions. Like finance houses, they also provide leasing and factoring facilities to their clients, but on a larger scale.

New share issues

If a company is seeking to raise funds, for example to finance an expansion programme, the ycan borrow the money or they may issue new shares to investors. If they choose the latter route, then a merchant bank may be able to help in their role as an issuing house. As issuing houses, merchant banks advise companies on the most economical way to raise capital. If an issue of shares is considered appropriate, most merchant banks will be able to provide the necessary expertise – the issue of share prospectus; compliance with Stock Exchange requirements, etc, to help their corporate client to raise the necessary finance. There are a number of ways that new shares may be issued, but the most usual is known as an offer for sale where the issuing house buys the shares from the company trying to raise finance and offers them for sale to the general public at a higher price. Advising on the price at which to issue the shares is another responsibility of the issuing house which will also arrange underwriting to ensure that all the shares are sold. For a commission, an underwriter undertakes to buy any of the shares not taken up by the public.

Financial advice

An area of merchant banking activity that sometimes receives considerable publicity is their work in mergers, acquisitions and takeovers. Merchant banks advise companies on the tactics and strategy to employ in carrying out a merger or for that matter in resisting an unwanted (sometimes called hostile) takeover bid.

Investment management

Merchant banks provide investment management expertise to a large number of pension funds, investment trusts and unit trusts. Some merchant banks operate their own unit trusts.

Other activities

Merchant banks deal in foreign currencies, gold bullion and other commodities, either on their own account or for clients. Their range of activities is not uniform, dealing only with certain industries or sectors.

It is these last few activities which give rise to the usage of the term investment banks (or securities houses) in most countries with institutions similar to UK merchant banks.

9 Retail banks – liquidity and profitability

In its simplest form, banks can be thought of as money shops. A supermarket makes profits by buying stock from suppliers and then selling it to customers at a higher price, the difference being the profit. Banks are really no different – they buy in money (in the form of deposits) and sell this money (in the form of loans). The rate of interest that they pay to savers is lower than the rate paid to borrowers, with the difference being the profit made by the bank. At the start of this chapter we discussed financial intermediation – this is an example of this in practice.

QUICK QUESTION

In what other ways to banks make money?

Write your answer here before reading on.

In addition to generating profit from the difference (or turn) between the rates of interest paid to savers and borrowers, banks also make profit from the fees and commissions that they charge to customers. For example, when setting up a loan facility, the bank will charge an Arrangement Fee to the customer to cover the expenses incurred by the bank in settling up the loan – for example, staff time, use of technology, etc. Banks will also charge commission for other services – for example, the provision of foreign currency, arranging payments for customers, levying service charge on business and personal accounts, and so on.

In arranging the distribution of their assets, retail banks are pulled in opposite directions – on the one hand towards liquidity (holding enough cash on hand to meet the immediate demands of customers), on the other hand, towards profitability. As operators of the payments system, the clearing banks cannot allow their liquidity to fall too low, even though liquid assets offer a poor return. As mentioned earlier in this chapter, you should remember the news images of customers queuing outside branches of Northern Rock when savers responded to the bank's liquidity crisis by withdrawing their funds. Cash and operational balances at the Bank of England pay no interest. In fact, when we take account of the cost of protecting cash from theft, it can be said to have a negative yield.

Having said that, 70% of deposits are virtually payable on demand (at least in theory) and so the banks must keep enough cash or its equivalent (for example, balances at the Bank of England) to meet all likely withdrawals. This does not mean that banks keep 70% of their deposits in cash. If they did, they would earn very little profit indeed. From experience, banks know that only a small proportion of deposits will actually be withdrawn at any given time. Provided the banks maintain sufficient cash to meet these likely withdrawals and a margin of liquid assets which can be converted into cash rapidly to meet any unexpected demands, they can lend the remainder of their funds for longer periods.

Banks are companies operated for profit on behalf of their shareholders. They earn income from money transmission service charges, investment and insurance fees and loan interest, etc. The more the banks lend the more interest and profits they have the potential to make.

As with any commercial organisation, profit is important to a bank. It provides for future growth and a return for shareholders. A bank considered to be earning inadequate profits could find itself subject to a takeover bid by a competitor. A management unable to earn sufficient profit could well be replaced. This pursuit of profit conflicts with the need for liquidity since the most profitable assets (loans) tend to be the least liquid. The asset structure of a bank is a compromise between the desire for profit and the need for liquidity. Success depends on striking the right balance between the two.

Liquidity thus represents the ability of a bank to convert its assets into cash quickly and without loss. Government securities can be speedily converted into cash via the stock exchange, but the price of these securities fluctuates and thus losses might be incurred if some of these need to be sold at the wrong time.

Advances are slow to realise, because it is not normal practice to call them in and so, perhaps, force the borrower into liquidation or bankruptcy. The usual way of contracting advances is to slow down the granting of new advances while allowing repayment of existing advances to continue, thereby reducing the total amount of advances outstanding. Advances are thus slow to convert into cash for the purpose of repayment.

KEY WORDS

Key words in this chapter are given below. There is space to write your own revision notes and to add any other words or phrases you want to remember.

- Financial intermediation

- Primary banks

- Secondary bank

- Independent Commission on Banking

- Exchequer account

- Ways and means advance

- Lender of last resort

- Quantitative easing

- Building societies

- National Savings and Investments (NS&I)

- Credit unions

- Investment and merchant banks

R E V I E W

Now consider the main learning points that were introduced in this chapter.

Go through them and check you are happy that you fully understand each point.

- Banks act as a link between savers and borrowers in society.

- The development of banking is Scotland and England was quite separate.

- The banking crisis brought about a tightening of credit available to customers.

- The Independent Commission on Banking recommended that banks hold more capital and that their retail and investment departments are separated.

- The major functions of a retail bank are: note issue, accepting deposits, acting as agents for payments and granting loans.

- The central bank in the UK is the Bank of England. Its purpose is to maintain the integrity and value of sterling, to maintain the stability of the UK financial system and to ensure the effectiveness of the UK's financial services.

- The functions of the Bank of England are to act as the bankers' bank and the government's bank, to issue notes, to act as the lender of last resort, to cooperate with other central banks and to maintain the Exchange Equalisation Account.

- Building societies originally existed to allow working people to finance house purchase. Many have now converted to limited companies offering a wide range of financial services.

- National Savings and Investments raises funds for the government by offering savings products to the public.

- Credit unions are mutual organisations offering basic low cost banking services to members.

- Merchant banks offer a range of specialised services including accepting bills of exchange, accepting deposits, arranging share issues and offering financial and investment advice to clients.

- Banks generate part of their profits by paying depositors a lower rate of interest than that they charge to borrowers.

chapter 2

A CLIENT CENTRED APPROACH

Contents

Learning outcomes

On completion of this chapter you should be able to:

- Examine the significance of the contractual relationship between banker and customer and outline the rights and duties incumbent on each party

- Compare and contrast a range of retail banking products and services

- Differentiate between and explain the impact of delivering regulated and unregulated products and services

- Examine the factors that contribute to the successful matching of a retail bank's products and services to meet customer needs

- Identify a customer's retail banking requirements and discuss appropriate products and services that match those needs in a fair, professional and ethical manner

Introduction

Having started to course by examining the definition and development of retail banking, we are now going to bring the focus down to a lower level by considering the more operational functions that you could encounter working in a retail bank. To do this we will examine the concept of the client-centred approach, before considering the technical and legal factors that underpin the banker-customer relationship. We shall then discuss the range of products that are offered by most retail banks in the current market, before concluding by examining how to deal with the more challenging types of customer that you may encounter, as well as those customers who wish to make complaints.

1 A client centred approach

QUICK QUESTION

How would you describe a client centred approach?

Write your answer here before reading on.

As might be expected from the phrase, the client-centred approach puts the client at the heart of everything that an organisation does. As you will be aware, customer service is high on the agenda of all successful organisations.

This approach should be contrasted with the way that banking operated until the mid-1980s. Up until then banks were very reactive organisations. By that, we mean that banks would respond to customer requests, but were organised very much on the banks rather than the customers' terms. For example, banks would open their doors at 9.30 in the morning; close for lunch between 12.30 and 1.30 pm and close of business would be 3.30pm. This was before internet and telephone banking (and even ATMs), so it was very difficult for the customer to access banking services unless they were willing to take time off work.

Allied to this approach was the fact that if a customer made a request, the bank would certainly consider the request, but would not make any effort to go beyond this to meet the needs of the customer. For example, if a customer approached the bank for a personal loan to help with the cost of a holiday, the bank would credit assess the proposal, before going back to the customer a few days later. If the request met with the bank's current lending criteria, the loan would be granted and that would be that.

QUICK QUESTION

If you were talking to this customer today, what other products and services offered by your bank would you consider offering this customer?

Write your answer here before reading on.

There could be quite a range of products you may hove considered, some of which would depend upon your knowledge of this particular customer and your bank's relationship with them. However, obvious products that spring to mind would be:

- Foreign currency and travellers cheques
- Credit card to use abroad
- Advising the customer of the possibility of using their debit card in ATMs abroad – depending on the type of card held and their destination
- Travel insurance

Whilst this may seem second nature to you, before the development of the client-centred approach, the bank would simply react to the immediate need and not take matters further. This was a very unfortunate set of circumstances, as the customer could have a genuine need for the services outlined above, but also, the bank was in a position to meet these needs.

At the centre of this approach is the customer and it has to be said that the banking industry has not always been successful in delivering to customer needs – we only need think back to the PPI Mis-Selling situation to see an example of where banks chose to sell products to meet their needs rather than the customers.

QUICK QUESTION

If an organisation is to embrace the client-centred approach, should it give priority to sales or customer service?

Write your answer here before reading on.

If the client is to be at the heart of an organisation, then excellent customer service must be at the heart of everything that the organisation does. Therefore, before we think about any products that an organisation seeks to offer to its customers, we must examine what is meant by customer service.

1.1 Customer service

 QUICK QUESTION

How would you define customer service?

Write your answer here before reading on.

Customer service covers a multitude of things and it can be difficult to tie it down to a concrete definition of what customer service is. However, we all know when we receive excellent customer service and we certainly all know when we don't receive it.

A working definition to cover what customer service is would cover:

- Providing those products and services that meet a customer's financial needs
- Giving the customer what they want, when they want it
- Providing consistent and ongoing backup to customers. For example, this would include accuracy, reliability and courtesy amongst others

 QUICK QUESTION

Why do you think a client-centred approach is so fundamental in building a successful bank in the early twenty first century?

Write your answer here before reading on.

Whilst the products offered by most banks are very similar, the staff in each organisation and the levels of service that staff provide can be a key differentiator.

Staff have a large amount of influence over service levels. Individual members of staff who deal with customers day in and day out do not have any influence over what rate of interest the organisation decide to apply to a mortgage account. However, they do have influence over how they greet customers, how accurately they process transactions and their telephone technique. These things all comprise customer service.

There are a number reasons why service is so important, which include:

- The better the customer service a bank provides, then the more satisfied their customers will be. Satisfied and happy customers are far easier and more enjoyable for the banks employees to deal with.

- It is quicker for staff to deal with a satisfied customer, rather than one who is making a complaint.

- Satisfied customers are an important source of referral business for the bank. This is a far more effective way for the organisation to build their business as opposed to prospecting and winning new customers.

- Satisfied customers will keep their business with their bank. It can cost 4 – 5 times as much to win business from a potential customer than it does to gain further business from an existing customer.

QUICK QUESTION

Reflect back to a negative experience you have had as a customer.

What were the factors that made this experience negative?

Write your answer here before reading on.

There could be a myriad of reasons why your experience was bad, but you may well have encountered the following.

- Miserable looking staff

- Untidy/dirty premises

- Lack of stock

- Staff made commitments that they did not follow through on

- Rude staff

- Having to wait in a long queue

- Having to wait for staff to stop chatting to one another before they would serve you

- Staff tried to sell you products that you didn't need – just to meet their sales targets

QUICK QUESTION

Now reflect on a positive experience that you have had as a customer.

Again, write down what it was about this experience which made it memorable.

Write your answer here before reading on.

As with the last example, you could have a variety of reasons why you had this good experience, but it is likely that some of the following played a part:

- Pleasant and helpful staff
- Attentive and efficient staff
- Staff were interested in what your needs were
- You got the products/services that met your needs at a price that was reasonable
- Well laid out premises
- You were dealt with quickly and efficiently

From completing this simple exercise you can see what a huge effect individual members of staff can have on the customer experience and how influential they are in maintaining the client-centred approach.

QUICK QUESTION

What other factors do you think comprise customer service?

Write your answer here before reading on.

There are probably more things covered than you first thought.

The areas that we will look at in the rest of this section are:

- **Queue management**
- Greeting the customer/smile/use the customer's name
- Treating the customer courteously
- Thanking the customer at the end of the transaction

All of these are things that should be covered in routine, day to day transactions. We will also look at the following items that should be provided beyond the transaction:

- Providing privacy and confidentiality to the customer
- Image and presentation of the organisation
- Telephone technique
- Informing the customer of the most suitable way to conduct their transactions

2 Queue management

Everybody hates queuing – whether it is to get into the cinema, onto a train, or to be served in our bank. You can rest assured that if we don't like having to wait, then neither do your customers. Your customers don't just have to queue if they are waiting in a traditional bank branch. Queuing also occurs when they have to wait to have their telephone call answered – whether calling their branch or a contact centre.

Whilst customers get frustrated at having to queue, it helps if the person serving them apologises for the wait once they do serve them.

QUICK QUESTION

What can be done to reduce the time a customer has to queue?

Write your answer here before reading on.

There are a number of things that you and your colleagues could do to reduce queuing. These include:

- During busy periods having staff who normally work in the back office able to come onto the counter to serve – assuming that they are trained to do this – there are a number of banks who now train staff in a very narrow range of skills, so this option is not always feasible.

- Having a member of staff walk the queue. By this we mean that a member of the team approaches each customer to find out what business they would like to transact to see if they actually need to wait in the queue. For example, if a customer is in to pay a credit card bill by cheque, the person walking the queue could take this transaction and either process it later, or process it in the back office.

- Identify if the customer is aware that perhaps they do not need to call into the office. Here you may need to educate the customer in the most suitable delivery channel to suit their needs. For example, this may be that they use the Automated Telling Machine (ATM), use a Drop Box facility, or perhaps use the Internet Banking Service. In many banks, it is now possible for customers to pay bills and make lodgements via an automated service inside the branch. It is common to find that a number of customers are resistant to using this type of service – however, a quick demonstration of how to use this technology will often allay any fears that the customer may have had and results in a quicker service for them.

3 Greeting the customer/smile/use the customer's name

Whilst your customers are well aware that the person they deal with will deal with many other customers in the course of the day, they still like to feel that the person they are dealing with wants to deal with them on a personal level.

The simplest way to do this is by smiling authentically at the customer when we meet them. It is worth keeping in mind that smiling is not something that we need only do when we are face to face with the customer. When talking to a customer over the phone, if you smile, it makes the tone of your voice more pleasant.

What we have looked at so far in this section comes at the start of the transaction – where we greet the customer and smile. By using the customer's name at the start and a couple of times during our conversation with them will serve to personalise the transaction for the customer. Again, this point is as important when we speak to the customer over the phone as it is when we meet them face to face.

Using the customer's name is easy in that the customer will tell us their name when they telephone us. Alternatively, if they call into the office, their name will inevitably be on either the plastic card they hand over to us or on some form of documentation – for example, on the bill they are paying.

To have the greatest impact, the customer's name should be used at the start and at the end of the conversation.

3.1 Treating the customer courteously

We have already started looking at this area in the last section. If you greet the customer, smile at them and use their name during the transaction, you have got your conversation off to a good start and are already treating the customer with courtesy.

There is a large list of other things that we should do to demonstrate courtesy. The ones we are going to look at in this section are:

- Appear attentive

- Give the customer your name

- Don't chat to colleagues unnecessarily when dealing with a customer

- At the end of the conversation, ask the customer if there is anything else you can help them with today

Appear attentive

This can be done simply by:

- Showing you are listening to what they are saying. You can do this by paraphrasing or summarising what the customer has said.

- If you maintain eye contact with the customer as they speak, you make it easier for them to continue the conversation. Also nodding as the customer speaks is an encouraging non-verbal signal you can give the customer.

These points demonstrate **active listening** techniques.

By being attentive, you are showing the customer that you are interested in them and you are demonstrating a client-centred approach. You are also communicating that you genuinely want to be of help to the customer.

Give the customer your name

If you are seeking to use the customer's name during the conversation, then you should reciprocate by giving the customer your own name.

Most organisations insist that staff wear name badges. However, if talking to a customer over the phone, you should seek to tell the customer your name early on in the conversation – indeed, many companies will have included this in the prepared dialogue that staff use at the start of the telephone conversation.

To make it easier for the customer to remember your name, it is useful to repeat it. For example, you could say to the customer 'Good morning, Mr Customer, my name is Peter, Peter Jones, how can I help you today?'

Don't chat to colleagues unnecessarily

Put yourself in the customer's shoes – one of the most infuriating things to happen is when the person serving you breaks off to chat to a colleague. Therefore, you should not do this when dealing with a customer.

There can be occasions when a situation arises when a colleague needs to interrupt you urgently when you are dealing with a customer. If this does occur, you should apologise to your customer and deal with the interruption as quickly as you can.

Similarly, there may be occasions when you need to leave the customer to deal with their enquiry. If you are face to face with the customer, you should explain to them why you need to leave them and let them know approximately how long you should be away for.

Alternatively, if the customer has telephoned, you should do the same thing, but if you expect to be away from the phone for any length of time, you should give the customer the option of having you call them back with the information.

If your researches take longer than expected, you should keep the customer informed of progress and the reason for any delays. This is particularly important if the customer is on the phone.

Ask the customer if there is anything else you can help them with today

At the end of the conversation, simply ask the customer if you can help them with anything else today. By doing this, you are showing concern for their needs and a willingness to help them, rather than just completing the business and moving onto the next customer.

Thank the customer at the end of the transaction

Moving on from the last point, once you have completed the transaction and there is nothing else you can help the customer with, you should thank the customer before they either leave the office or end the call.

3.2 Providing privacy and confidentiality to the customer

When working in a financial services organisation, you are dealing with customers' financial affairs day in, day out. It can therefore be easy to fall into the trap of looking at your customers' financial affairs as being routine. However, customers will rightly expect their financial affairs to be kept confidential. Confidentiality is one of the banker's duties we will consider later in this chapter when we study the banker-customer relationship.

If the customer has called into your office, you need to be particularly aware of your duty to maintain the confidentiality of the information we are giving them. The legal implications of this and the four occasions where the banker may depart from this duty of confidentiality will be discussed later on in this chapter.

If a customer has called into the office to request their account balance, the first thing you need to do is to verify that the customer is actually who they purport to be. Once you have satisfied yourself in this regard, you should print out their balance, fold the slip of paper, and then hand it over to the customer.

Similarly, the customer may request this information over the phone. If it is your organisation's policy to give this information out by phone, you again need to verify the caller's identity before you do so.

You should always be aware that when working in an office that has customers visiting, you must always take steps to ensure than when discussing other customers details either with colleagues or over the phone, that this information cannot be overheard. This is a way in which you can demonstrate your professionalism and it is another component of the client-centred approach.

When you move away from the routine, day to day transactions, you also need to give careful thought about confidentiality. For example, if you are about to conduct an interview with a customer, or obtain more detailed information from them, you may need to take them away from a public office and speak to them in the privacy of an interview room. This helps put the customer at ease, as they know that other customers will not overhear confidential information. It is also useful for you as you are more likely to get more information from the customer – and the more information you have about the customer, then the easier it will be of you to identify their needs and provide the most appropriate products to meet these needs.

The confidentiality of customer information can be maintained by ensuring that confidential information is not left in sight of other customers. This is particularly important if, for example, you are working at a desk that is out in the front office of a branch. Also, if you have been speaking to a customer in an interview area and are about to see another customer, always ensure that the desk is clear of any confidential information before seeing the next customer.

Any paper that has customer information on it should be carefully disposed of – preferably shredded or placed in the confidential waste.

You should also be aware of the requirements of the Data Protection Act – we will look at this in more detail letter on in the course.

It is also vitally important that customers' affairs are not discussed outside the office and we do not discuss anything about customers to anyone outside the organisation. This is another part of a banker's duty of confidentiality that will be discussed later on in this chapter.

4 Image and presentation of the organisation

One of the first and most lasting impressions of any organisation is the condition, tidiness and cleanliness of their premises. This is something that we can all relate to easily as customers. Think about when you have thought about entering a shop and been out off by its untidy appearance.

The smartness and tidiness of a bank is a key way that the organisation can communicate its image to current and potential customers. If a branch office is untidy, with the desks overflowing with paper, then that will suggest to a potential customer that they are dealing with a disorganised and inefficient firm. So an important aspect of the service that is given to customers is the presentation of the office.

If you look back to the earlier exercise when we looked at the items that made for a bad customer experience, one item was dirty and untidy premises.

The factors that can display a positive image for any organisation can be split into these two headings:

External Environment

- The first impression that every current and potential customer has of your office is the external environment. Therefore for this impression to be positive, the outside of the office must be clean, free of graffiti and any illuminated signs should be operational.

Internal Environment

- All publicity material on display should be up to date and smartly presented. Therefore, posters should be hanging straight; leaflet dispensers should be full and neatly stocked.

- The office should be well lit and all light bulbs should be operational.

- There should be adequate stocks of customer stationery and any pens that are for customer use should be working. As with leaflets, customer stationery should be displayed neatly.

- Any signage used should be clear.

- Clocks and calendars should be at the right date/time.

- Any machinery for customer use should be kept clean – for example, ATMs, night safes, non-cash transaction drop boxes, automated pay-in machines, etc.

- The customer area should always be clean and free of litter. It is usually necessary to look over the customer area at various times in the day to ensure that there are no discarded slips or other litter lying on the floor.

- Desks should be tidy, with any excess papers and files stored out of sight.

Telephone technique

Whilst many customer enquiries will be routed through a contact centre, there are still instances where calls can come straight to a branch. This is an area where you can give excellent service to customers and enhance the impression of professionalism that you display.

Any time that a customer telephones your office, you should strive to display a professional and positive attitude. Remember the point that was made earlier about the importance of smiling when greeting the customer – even on the phone.

QUICK QUESTION

What standards should you set when answering an incoming call?

Write your answer here before reading on.

First and foremost, you should answer the call quickly.

Once you have picked up the phone, you should greet the customer with a good morning/afternoon/evening, then give out your organisations name followed by your own name. You should end the greeting by asking the customer how can you help them.

If you need to transfer the call to a colleague, you should explain this to the customer and, where possible, let them know the name of the person that they will be dealing with. You should then give your colleague all of the relevant information that you have so that the customer does not have to repeat this.

Many of the techniques that were discussed earlier regarding face to face communication are equally relevant to telephone communication. These are:

- Smiling when you greet the customer
- Personalising the call by using the customer's name during the conversation
- At the end of the conversation, asking the customer if there is anything else you can help them with

4.1 Inform the customer of the most suitable way to conduct their transactions

The advances in technology in recent years has meant that the there are now a variety of ways in which customers can carry out transactions with their bank. Providers call these **distribution channels** and will be considered in more detail later on in the course.

One of the ways that a bank can provide a client-centred approach is by advising customers of different and more suitable ways for them to carry out business with the organisation. By doing this the bank can make the service offered to the customer more appropriate for that individual.

There are a number of distribution channels to consider, including:

- Standing Orders/Direct Debits/Faster Payments
- ATMs
- Night safes
- Quick Deposit/Drop Boxes/Automated Pay-In Terminals
- Telephone banking
- Internet banking

5 The banker-customer relationship

The banker and customer relationship is, in essence, a contractual one based on common law. The basic principles to keep in mind here are:

- A contract imposes legally binding rights and duties (or obligations) on both parties
- These duties on one party confer corresponding rights on the other
- Non-fulfilment of these duties may result in a civil action being brought by the aggrieved party

The banker-customer relationship creates such rights and duties on banker and customer. It is essential that bankers are aware of what these rights and duties are and the legal position of both banker and customer, so that they can anticipate and resolve any problems which may arise in the course of the relationship.

5.1 Creation of the banker-customer relationship

When a customer deposits money in a bank account, they lend it to the banker, who is bound to repay on demand. The relationship between the banker and customer is, therefore, the contractual relationship of debtor and creditor.

When the customer deposits money with the banker, then the bank is a debtor of the customer (i.e. the banker now owes this money to the customer) and the customer a creditor of the banker (i.e. the customer is now owed their money from the banker). When the customer borrows money from the banker then the bank is a creditor of the customer, and the customer a debtor of the bank.

> The debtor/creditor nature of the relationship along with the added contractual obligation of repayment was stated in the case of *Foley v Hill, 1848.*
>
> 'The money in the custody of a banker is, to all intents and purposes, the money of the banker, to do with as he pleases; he is guilty of no breach of trust in employing it; he is not answerable to the customer if he puts it into jeopardy, if he engages in hazardous speculation; he is not bound to keep it or deal with it as the property of his customer; but he is, of course, answerable for the amount because he was contracted, having received that money, to repay the customer, when demanded, a sum equivalent to that paid into his hands.'

Thus, the relationship between banker and customer is that of debtor and creditor. Money paid in becomes the bank's money to make what profit it can, subject to the contractual liability to repay the money when demanded.

There are, however, other implied contractual duties on the banker. Therefore, it is important to determine when the banker-customer relationship is created since that is the point at which these contractual obligations on banker and customer come into existence.

5.2 When is a person deemed to be a customer of the bank?

In *Great Western Railway Co v London and County Banking Co, 1901* it was held that a person is not a customer unless they has some sort of an account, either a deposit or current account or some similar relation with the bank.

In *Taxation Commissioners v English, Scottish and Australian Bank, 1920*, it was held that a person becomes a customer as soon as the customer opens an account.

Lord Dunedin stated:

'Their Lordships are of the opinion that the word 'customer' signifies a relationship in which duration is not of the essence.

A person whose money has been accepted by the bank on the footing that they undertake to honour cheques up to the amount standing at his credit is, in the view of their Lordships, a customer of the bank ... irrespective of whether his connection is of short or long standing.'

In *Woods v Martins Bank, 1959*, it was held that a person could become a customer even before the account is opened if there was intent to open one and they subsequently did so.

CASE STUDY

Woods v Martin's Bank 1959

The plaintiff – Woods – a young man without business experience was considering an investment in Brocks Refrigeration Ltd, a private company banking with a branch of the defendant bank. He sought the advice of the branch manager and was told that the investment would be a wise one, the company being financially sound. Acting on this advice he invested £5,000 in the company and subsequently, having opened an account at the same branch, he invested further funds on the manager's advice. Unknown to the plaintiff, the company's account was heavily overdrawn throughout this period and the branch manager was under considerable pressure from the District Head Office to get the debt reduced. Eventually, the plaintiff lost nearly £16,000 – a not inconsiderable sum at that time - and brought an action against the bank and the manager for fraud or negligence.

It was held that the manager's advice was grossly negligent but not fraudulent. The bank was liable for the negligent advice given and its plea that it was no part of its business to give investment advice was rejected after examination of its advertisements. The plaintiff had become a customer of the bank from the time the instructions to make the first investment had been accepted although the current account was not opened until nearly one month later.

The banker-customer relationship is deemed to begin:

As regards an account holder

- As soon as the bank opens an account for someone (with the intention that the relationship be permanent). In the *Great Western Railway Co v London and County Bank Co Ltd* it was held that the cashing of cheques over a long period of time for a person who had no account with the bank did not make him a customer – although you should bear in mind that such a service would not now be offered by a bank.

As regards any other banking service

- As soon as the bank agrees to provide that service (e.g. advice on investments as in *Woods v Martin's Bank*).

QUESTION TIME 1

1. What did the case of Foley v Hill state about the banker's obligation to repay?

2. In Woods v Martin's bank:

(a) Why was the bank liable?

(b) At what point was Woods deemed to be a customer of the bank?

Write your answer here then check with the answer at the back of the book.

5.3 The contract between banker and customer

The full terms of the contract between the banker and his customer are rarely found in writing. When a person opens an account at a bank they do not normally sign any document, apart from the simple opening form, setting out the conditions on which his account will be kept.

It has been left to the courts to decide what terms should be applied.

CASE STUDY

In Joachimson v Swiss Bank Corporation, 1921 Lord Atkin said:

'The bank undertakes to receive money and collect bills for its customer's account. The proceeds are not to be held in trust for the customer, but the bank borrows the proceeds and undertakes to repay them. The promise to repay is to repay at the branch of the bank where the account is kept and during banking hours. It includes the promise to repay any part of the amount due against the written order of the customer addressed to the bank at the branch, and, as such written order may be outstanding in the ordinary course of business for two or three days, it is a term of the contract that the bank will not cease to do business with the customer except upon reasonable notice.

The customer, on his part, undertakes to exercise reasonable care in executing his written orders so as not to mislead the bank or facilitate forgery. I think it is necessarily a term of such a contract that the bank is not liable to pay the customer the full amount of his balance until he demands payment from the bank at the branch at which the current account is kept.'

It is clear, therefore, that the contractual relationship between banker and customer creates rights and imposes duties on both parties.

We will now consider the implied rights and duties in the Joachimson case, and the other implied rights and duties which are derived from them.

5.4 Banker and customer rights and duties

The banker's duties are:

1. To receive money and collect cheques for the customer's account

2. To pay customers' cheques on demand provided that adequate funds are available or appropriate overdraft arrangements have been made; they are drawn in the proper form; payment is demanded at the proper place and during business hours

3. In refusing to pay a cheque (also called 'dishonouring'), to act in good faith and without negligence

4. To maintain secrecy regarding all the affairs of his customers

5. To advise the customer of any forgery of his signature

6. To give reasonable notice before closing a credit account, so that the customer can make other arrangements and have outstanding cheques cleared without damage to their reputation

You will see from this that the contract between banker and customer is not restricted to debtor and creditor. The banker will often act as the customer's agent. Historically, banks have acted as agents for their customers when collecting customers' cheques and other instruments; when paying cheques drawn by its customers; and when acting upon a customer's authority in connection with the purchase and sale of stock exchange securities.

As services provided by banks expand, so too will this role of agent increase.

QUICK QUESTION

What do you think are the customer's duties?

Write your answer here before reading on.

The customer's duties are:

1. To exercise reasonable care in drawing cheques. Cheques drawn carelessly may facilitate fraud or forgery and mislead the bank

2. To advise the bank of any forgery of their signature, otherwise they may subsequently be barred from denying the validity of the signature

3. To pay charges

QUICK QUESTION

What do you think are the banker's rights?

Write your answer here before reading on.

The banker's rights are:

1. The right to charge a reasonable commission for services provided. The banker has an implied right to charge a commission for keeping the customer's account and for other banking services. Bank charges may be imposed on certain current account holders as outlined in the Terms and Conditions of the account.

2. The right to interest; for example, on loans. The banker has no implied right to charge interest on money borrowed by a customer – this will normally be decided by express agreement or implied from the usual course of dealings between the banker and his customer. The point is essentially academic nowadays as banks make a point of ensuring that details of interest charged on customers' accounts are advised to customers – in respect of personal customers' overdrafts, this is a requirement that must be adhered to if banks are to continue to benefit from not documenting current account overdrafts under the Consumer Credit Act.

3. The right of **set off**. Where a customer has two accounts, one in credit and one in debit, the banker can, unless otherwise agreed, set off or combine accounts, thus reducing the amount which the customer owes, or vice versa.

4. The right to return unpaid any cheque which would create an unauthorised overdraft or any cheque which would exceed an agreed overdraft limit. Where a customer has signed an automated payment authority, the bank is only liable to check if there is a sufficient balance available on the due date of payment. If there are insufficient funds on the due date the bank is not obliged to continue checking the balance until there is sufficient to allow payment.

The case of *Baines v National Provincial Bank Ltd* illustrates that it is:

The Banker's Duty – To pay cheques on demand provided payment is demanded at the proper place and during business hours

The situation which gave rise to this case is one with which bankers are familiar – a last minute influx of customers just as closing time approaches with the result that the doors are closed before the last person is served.

CASE STUDY

Baines v National Provincial Bank Ltd

On 14 August 1925 at the Harrogate branch of the National Provincial Bank Ltd it was a busy market day and at 3 pm closing time there were still several customers awaiting attention. Among those waiting was a man named Wood with a cheque for £200 drawn by a customer of the bank named Baines. The ink on the cheque could hardly have been dry, since Baines had only issued it shortly before 3 pm, but the cheque was duly cashed some ten minutes after the official closing time.

Baines, a bookmaker, had issued the cheque believing that it would be impossible for it to be presented for payment that day and thus give him time to countermand payment should this prove necessary. It so happened that Baines did decide to do this and sent his son, at opening time next morning, with instructions to stop payment of the cheque. One can imagine his surprise and annoyance when he was told it was too late to countermand payment since the cheque had been paid. The eventual outcome was the case forming the subject matter.

It was held that the bank was not liable to Baines for paying this cheque after hours, at 3.10pm, because a bank is entitled to deal with a cheque within a reasonable business margin after their advertised time of closing, and in cashing the cheque, the bank had acted within their rights.

The Banker's Duty – To act in good faith and without negligence when dishonouring customers' cheques.

The banker must ascertain beyond any doubt that the customer has no funds, or insufficient funds, in the account before refusing payment or returning cheques unpaid. If a bank fails or refuses to honour customers' cheques when presented then they may be liable in damages for breach of contract and injury to credit.

A bank might make this kind of mistake if it has paid a customer's stopped or post-dated cheque, thus leaving insufficient funds for later cheques which the bank then returns unpaid, or the bank fails to credit a customer with a credit paid in or debits him with an item which is not theirs. The customer's balance is thus lower than it should be and this may result in the bank wrongfully dishonouring some of its customer's cheques.

Wrongful dishonour of a cheque is a breach of contract and in addition, the answer that the paying bank places on the cheque, for example insufficient funds or refer to drawer, may give rise to a claim for libel.

CASE STUDY

Davidson v Barclays Bank Ltd, 1940

Davidson, a bookmaker, drew a cheque for £2.15s.8d. on the Kennington branch of Barclays Bank. Owing to the fact that the bank had previously paid in error a cheque which Davidson had countermanded, there were not sufficient funds on the account to meet the later cheque, which was returned marked 'Not sufficient'.

Davidson brought the action claiming that the words meant that he had drawn a cheque knowing that he had insufficient funds, that he was unable to pay £2.15s.8d and that it was unsafe to transact business with him and give him credit.

Barclays pleaded that, amongst other things, the words were published only to the payee who had an interest in knowing why the cheque had not been met, and to whom they were under a duty to communicate that reason: that the words were published in the honest, though mistaken, belief that they were true.

It was held that the bank owed no duty of communication to the payee and that there was common interest between bank and payee calling for communication.

It was further held that Davidson, as a business customer, was entitled to substantial damages of £250 for libel.

The answer in this case 'Not sufficient' was clearly defamatory. It is also unlikely that a bank would succeed in a plea that 'Refer to Drawer' is not defamatory, since the case of *Jayson v Midland Bank Ltd, 1968* considered that 'Refer to Drawer' was likely 'to lower the plaintiff's reputation in the minds of right thinking people.'

QUICK QUESTION

What do you think is the position for a personal customer regarding damages if a cheque is wrongfully dishonoured by a bank?

Write your answer here before reading on.

The following case partially answers this question:

CASE STUDY

Gibbons v Westminster Bank Ltd, 1939

Mrs. Gibbons, who was not a trader, paid into her bank account a sum of money which the bank, in error, credited to another customer's account.

Gibbons then drew a cheque in payment of her rent which the bank dishonoured under the impression that there were insufficient funds to meet it.

It was held that because Gibbons was not a trader and had not proved any special damage, she was entitled to nominal damages only.

For a business customer there had been a long held rule that actual damages need not be alleged or proved by a trader to recover substantial rather than nominal damages in contract for loss of business reputation resulting from a cheque being wrongfully dishonoured by his bank. Until the case of *Kpoharor v Woolwich Building Society, 1995* the rule for customers who are non-traders was that they were only entitled to recover nominal damages for wrongful dishonour of a cheque unless they could prove some special loss.

In the *Kpoharor v Woolwich Building Society* case it was held by the English Court of Appeal that circumstances had changed since the earlier rule had been formulated. History had changed the social factors which moulded the rule in the nineteenth century. It was not only a tradesman of whom it could be said that refusal to meet his cheque was so obviously injurious to his credit that he should recover, without allegations of special damage, reasonable compensation for the injury done to his credit. Credit rating of individuals was as important for their personal transactions, including mortgages and hire purchase as well as banking facilities, as it was for those who were engaged in trade.

In the Court's view there is a presumption of some damage in every case and is not limited to a business or trading context. Lord Justice Evans stated that *Gibbons v Westminster Bank* was not binding authority, so in future cases it is likely that a personal customer whose cheque is wrongfully dishonoured may be able to claim substantial damages in contract without having to prove a special damage which hitherto would have been necessary.

In the Court's view a presumption of some damage arises in every case. Such damages may be additional to substantial damages for libel which could be claimed on the grounds that the answer on the cheque was defamatory.

If the bank is at fault in this way, a letter of apology should be sent to the customer, the account should be corrected, and the payee should be advised that if the cheque is re-presented it will be paid, and that no fault at all lies with the customer. This may help to reduce damages if the customer brings a civil action.

The Banker's Duty – To inform the customer of any forgery of his/her signature

If the customer's signature on cheques is forged, the bank has no mandate to pay and cannot debit the customer's account unless the customer adopts the signature as genuine, or fails to inform the banker when they have discovered a forgery.

In the case of *Tai Hing Cotton Mill Ltd v Liu Chong Hing Bank Ltd, 1985* the hopes of banks – that in modern times they might be entitled to look to their customers for a greater measure of protection when dealing with forged cheques – were shattered.

CASE STUDY

Tai Hing Cotton Mill Ltd v Liu Chong Hing Bank Ltd, 1985

The company was a textile manufacturer in Hong Kong and a customer of three banks with which it maintained current accounts. The banks honoured by payment on presentation some 300 cheques which appeared to have been drawn by the company and to bear the signature of its managing director. The cheques were in fact forgeries but the banks were unaware of this and debited the company's accounts with the amount of the cheques. The forgeries were the work of an employee who was in a position to manipulate the accounts for which he was responsible and the company's system of internal control was such that it was unable either to prevent fraud or to discover it after the event.

Its system of internal financial control was described in court as unsound and inadequate. The issue in the case was upon whom the loss arising from the forgeries was to fall – the company or the banks.

It was accepted that Hong Kong law was the same as English law on this point and the question to be decided was whether English law recognised any duty of care owed by a customer to his bank in the operation of a current account beyond, first, a duty to refrain from drawing a cheque in such a manner as might facilitate fraud or forgery, and second, a duty to inform the bank of any forgery as soon as he became aware of it.

The banks argued that in view of the modern practice of rendering periodic statements of account, a customer owed a further duty to his bank to exercise reasonable care to prevent forged cheques being presented to the bank, or at the very least to check his statements so as to be able to notify the bank of any items which had not been authorised by him.

However, the Privy Council rejected this argument. It did not accept that because the obligations of care placed upon banks in the management of a customer's account by the courts had become, with the development of banking business, more burdensome, they should be met by a reciprocal increase of responsibility imposed on the customer. The business of banking was the business not of the customer but of the bank. Banks offered a service which was to honour their customers' cheques when drawn upon an account in credit or within an agreed overdraft limit. If a bank paid out upon cheques which were not the customer's, it was acting outside its mandate and could not debit his account.

That, said Lord Scarman, was a risk of the service which it was the business of a bank to offer. If banks wished to impose upon their customers an express obligation to examine their monthly statements and to make those statements, in the absence of query, unchallengeable by the customer after expiry of a time limit, the burden of the obligation and of the sanction imposed had to be brought home to the customer. This could only be done by a clear and unambiguous provision introduced into the contract between the bank and the customer.

If banks are to have the protection which they argued for in this case, it can only come about with the consent of the customer or through legislation. Compare the content of this case with:

The Customer's Duty – To inform the bank if he knows his signature is being forged.

If the customer is aware of the forgery, then they have a duty to inform the bank. If they do not, then they cannot contest the validity of the signature at a later date and the bank will not be liable for paying such cheques.

CASE STUDY

Greenwood v Martin's Bank Ltd, 1933

Greenwood had an account with Martin's Bank Ltd. His wife kept the cheque book, and gave Greenwood cheques as and when he wanted them. In October 1929, he asked her for a cheque saying that he wished to withdraw £20, whereupon she told him there was no money in the account – she had drawn it all out to help her sister pay for legal proceedings in which she was involved.

The wife had forged her husband's signature on a number of cheques over a period of time. She pleaded with him not to inform the bank of the fraud. Eight months later, he discovered that the explanation about her sister's legal proceedings was false. The husband told her that he was going to notify the bank, whereupon she committed suicide. Greenwood subsequently sued the bank for the amount paid by them on the forged cheques.

It was held that the customer owed a duty of disclosure to the bank on his first discovery of the fraud, and that as his conduct had deprived them of their right of action against the forger, he was barred from claiming forgery.

Lord Justice Scrutton said:

'There is a continuing duty on either side to act with reasonable care to ensure the proper working of the account. It seems to me that the banker, if a cheque was presented to him which he rejected as forged, would be under a duty to report this to the customer to enable him to enquire into and protect himself against the circumstances of the forgery. This, I think, would involve a corresponding duty on the customer, if he became aware that forged cheques were being presented to the banker, to inform his banker in order that the banker might avoid loss in the future. If this is correct there was in the present case silence, a breach of duty to disclose.'

Given Lord Justice Scrutton's remark in the Greenwood case – 'There is a continuing duty on either side to act with reasonable care to ensure the proper working of the account ...,' it seems appropriate now to consider:

The Customer's Duty – To exercise reasonable care in drawing cheques so as not to facilitate fraud or forgery.

Where the customer's neglect or carelessness in drawing cheques has caused the banker to be misled, for instance, where the amount on a cheque can be easily altered, the banker is entitled to debit his customer with the full amount he has paid on it.

QUICK QUESTION

What do you think are the implications here?

Write your answer here before reading on.

CASE STUDY

London Joint Stock Bank v MacMillan & Arthur, 1918

A person employed as a clerk by MacMillan & Arthur presented a cheque drawn in favour of the firm or bearer to one of the partners for signature. There was no sum in words in the space provided, but the figure 2 was in the space for figures. The partner signed the cheque.

The clerk subsequently added the words One Hundred and Twenty Pounds in the space for words, and inserted the figures 1 and 0 on either side of the 2. The clerk presented the cheque for payment at the firm's bank and obtained payment of £120, which was then debited to the firm's account. The clerk absconded. The firm declined to recognise the debit.

It was held that the account had been properly debited with the amount.

Lord Finlay stated:

'It is beyond dispute that the customer is bound to exercise reasonable care in drawing the cheque to prevent the banker being misled. If he draws the cheque in a manner which facilitates fraud he is guilty of a breach of duty as between himself and the banker and he will be responsible to the banker for any loss sustained by the banker as a natural and direct consequence of this breach of duty ... If the cheque is drawn in such a way as to facilitate or almost to invite an increase in the amount by forgery if the cheque should get into the hands of a dishonest person, forgery is not a remote, but a very natural consequence of negligence of this description.'

QUESTION TIME 2

1. What should the banker ensure before dishonouring cheques?

2. In what way will a bank be liable if it wrongfully dishonours a cheque?

3. In any court action against the bank, for wrongful dishonour of a cheque, does a court distinguish between customers who are in business and those who are not?

4. What should the bank do when it has been guilty of a wrongful dishonour, in order to appease the customer?

5. With what claim was the bank unsuccessful in the Tai Hing Cotton Mill case?

6. Why was the bank not liable for loss caused by the forged signature in *Greenwood v Martins Bank Ltd*?

7. What duty did MacMillan and Arthur fail in?

Write your answer here then check with the answer at the back of the book.

6 The banker's duty of secrecy

This duty is a legal one arising out of the contractual relationship between the banker and the customer. Breach of this duty by the banker gives a claim by the customer for nominal damages or, if injury, say to credit-worthiness, results from the breach, then substantial damages.

The statement of a bank's duty of confidentiality is to be found in the English Court of Appeal's decision in the case of *Tournier v National Provincial and Union Bank of England, 1924*:

> 'The obligation of confidentiality clearly goes beyond the state of the account, that is, whether there is a debit or a credit balance, and the amount of the balance. It must extend at least to all the transactions that go through the account, and to the securities, if any, given in respect of the account; and in respect of such matters it must, I think, extend beyond the period when the account is closed, or ceases to be an active account ... I further think that the obligation extends to information from other sources than the customer's actual account, if the occasion on which the information is obtained arose out of the banking relations of the bank and its customer – for example, with a view to assisting the bank in coming to decisions as to its treatment of its customer ... in this case, however, I should not extend the obligation to information as to the customer obtained after he had ceased to be a customer ... ' (per Lord Justice Atkin).

This duty, however, is not absolute. There are exceptions and disclosure is permitted:

- Under compulsion by law
- If there is a duty to the public to disclose
- With express or implied consent of the customer
- If the interests of the bank require disclosure

These exceptions were laid down by Lord Justice Bankes in the Tournier case:

CASE STUDY

Tournier v National Provincial and Union Bank of England Ltd, 1924

In March 1922 the manager of the Moorgate Street branch of the bank in London came to an agreement with a customer named Tournier concerning repayment of his overdraft. The amount of the overdraft was £9.8s.6d. and the agreement was that, beginning in April, Tournier would clear the debt by weekly payments of £1.

The promise was kept for three weeks and some time then passed with no further transactions. The manager was disturbed and annoyed since he was aware that Tournier was receiving cheques but not lodging them to his account. In particular, one cheque for £45 had been drawn by another of the branch's customers in favour of Tournier, but had not been lodged. Enquiry by the manager revealed that Tournier had negotiated this cheque to a firm of bookmakers. The manager wrote letters to Tournier but received no reply.

In the meantime Tournier had started a new job on a three months contract with a firm called Kenyon & Co. Eventually the manager telephoned the company to enquire about Tournier's address. He had lengthy conversations with two of the directors and in the course of these conversations the manager disclosed that Tournier had an overdraft and commented that he thought Tournier was gambling.

When Tournier's three-month contract expired, the company would not renew it. Tournier alleged that this was because of the disclosures made by the manager and sued the bank for slander and breach of implied contract of secrecy.

The first hearing was in favour of the bank but Tournier appealed and the appeal was upheld.

The effect of such authoritative comment is of considerable importance in banking since it has established general guidelines to bankers concerning disclosures.

The case itself is also a reminder of the need for discretion and the constant care which bankers must exercise to avoid unwarranted disclosure of a customer's affairs. It should also be noted that the information obtained during the lifetime of the account remains confidential even after the account has been closed.

6.1 Disclosure under compulsion of law

The exemption under compulsion by law may be divided into three headings:

1.   Disclosure under compulsion of a Court Order.
2.   Disclosure to an official who is statutorily entitled to compel disclosure.
3.   Disclosure where there is an onus on the bank to disclose information.

The first category includes:

Bankers' Books Evidence Act, 1879

An order under the *Bankers' Books Evidence Act* is probably the most familiar example of disclosure under compulsion by law. The Act was not designed to enforce bankers to give evidence before the courts but to deal with the form in which evidence may be given and to avoid the inconvenience of a bank being deprived of its books during court cases.

QUICK QUESTION

Who do you think is empowered to order bankers to give evidence?

Write your answer here before reading on.

Orders under the Act are usually given by a court and, although they empower the pursuer or defender to take copies of relevant entries in the bank's books, in practice the bank will provide the copies and certify them in terms of the docquet contained in the Act.

A party to legal proceedings can apply to court for leave to inspect and take copies of entries in a banker's books for the purposes of such proceedings. This power applies to an account of a person (or a company) who is also party to the litigation or that of a person closely connected with the litigation. This provision applies to both civil and criminal proceedings, although it has largely been superseded by more recent statutes with regard to criminal investigations.

The power applies to entries in a banker's books (which includes records of the customer's transactions, details of cheques, etc) but does not extend to correspondence between the bank and its customer, or to paid cheques and paying-in slips retained by the bank after the conclusion of any transaction.

There are a number of other statutes relevant to this heading including:

- The Value Added Tax Act 1983
- The Companies Act 1985 as amended by the Companies Act 1989
- The Insurance Companies Act 1982
- The Insolvency Act 1986
- The Taxes Management Act 1986

- The Income and Corporation Taxes Act 1988
- The Criminal Justice Act 1987
- The Pensions Schemes Act 1993
- Criminal Justice (Scotland) Act, 1987 (as amended by the Criminal Justice Act, 1993)
- Prevention of Terrorism (Temporary Provisions) Act, 1989
- Drug Trafficking Act, 1994
- Proceeds of Crime Act 1983
- Terrorism Act 2000 (as amended by the Anti-Terrorism, Crime and Security Act 2001)
- Social Security Fraud Act 2001

If there is a duty to the public to disclose

In the Tournier case it was said that many instances of such a duty might be given, but the judges did not actually give any, except to refer to another case where dangers to the state or public duty may supersede the duty of agent to principal. Thus, where in a time of war the customer's dealings indicated trade with the enemy, a duty to disclose could arise.

However, there is no duty to give information to the police about a customer suspected of a crime, but the bank cannot plead in this way if the end result is to conceal fraud. Banks also have a duty to report suspicions of money laundering – this area will be considered in the final chapter of the course.

It has been established that the police must show they have a real interest in the account, and are not just trawling for information which may or may not help them.

Where it is in the interests of the bank to disclose

Where there is court action between the bank and its customer some disclosure about the customer's affairs will be necessary. Were this not the case, then any court action against a defaulting customer would fall as the bank would not be able to explain its position to the court – as a result, there would be no motivation for a borrowing customer to repay funds lent by the bank as they know that any subsequent court action would fail.

Where disclosure is made with the consent of the customer

Where a customer has given their express consent, there cannot be a breach of secrecy, but this authority should be in writing. For instance, a customer may authorise the bank to furnish his accountant with banking details in order to assist the accountant to complete year end accounts or submit Returns to HMRC on the customer's behalf.

Until the major banks introduced a new status enquiry system with effect from 28 March 1994, it had been a long held view that when a customer entered into a banker-customer relationship with a bank, the banker had the customer's implied authority to respond to enquiries about the customer's status and financial standing provided the enquiry was received from another banker or certain trade protection societies or other organisations. It was not the practice to respond direct to individuals or businesses. The new system introduced certain procedural changes. Individuals or businesses wishing to obtain a banker's opinion now send their request direct to the bank concerned. That bank responds direct to the enquirer rather than channel the reply through the enquirer's bankers. However, reliance is no longer placed on the implied authority of the customer to respond to status enquiries and the bank will only reply to an enquiry with the express consent of the customer who is the subject of the enquiry.

You may have encountered this situation where, for example, you have obtained credit from a finance company, say to assist with the purchase of a car, and they wish to obtain an opinion from your bank.

The banking industry introduced model forms of combined enquiry and consent forms and most banks now charge the enquirer for providing this service. People who submit status enquiries can either pay by means of plastic card, i.e. a Visa or MasterCard, or pay by cheque.

If the enquirer does not understand the reply to his status enquiry, then they are free to ask their own bank to express a view as to the meaning of the response, i.e. through experience and knowledge of how the responses are framed; a bank can usually decode the message.

7 The banker's duty of care

As an integral part of the banker-customer contractual relationship, there exists an implied duty of care owed by the banker to the customer and likewise, an implied duty of care owed by the customer to the banker. This duty of care is tied in with the performance of the specific duties of the banker and customer identified earlier. In addition, there are two other main areas where a duty of care falls on a banker:

- The giving of advice
- The taking and realising of security

The duty of care on a banker when giving advice was set out in *Woods v Martins Bank Ltd, 1959* as you will recall from earlier. It was held that if a customer of a bank requests advice on the merits of a particular transaction and the bank gives it, then a duty of care falls on the bank.

In 1995, there was a widely reported case, *Verity and Spindler v Lloyds Bank*, which, while it did not extend the main principles of a bank's duty of care owed to its customer, highlighted an instance where a bank manager 'overstepped the mark' on the advice given. The judge noted '... if a bank manager undertakes to give financial advice to customers, then ... he must expect to be judged by the same standards as those applicable to other professionals who give financial advice'. The case did confirm that a bank did not adopt an advisory role merely by lending money, although care must be taken to ensure that the marketing material of a bank does not hold out the bank as a source of valuable, expert advice.

There are two cases which, while confirming that there is a duty implied into a bank's contract with its customers to act with reasonable care and skill, it was held in both cases that the bank was not liable because the customer had not sought its advice and was seeking to establish liability merely on the grounds of a failure to advise. These cases are *Schioler v National Westminster Bank, 1970* and *Redmond v Allied Irish Bank, 1987*.

The position on taking and realising of security is less straightforward. There is a line of cases decided by the English courts which deal with many of the issues concerning taking security. *Lloyds Bank v Bundy, 1975* held that when a bank was obtaining a guarantee there was a duty on it to explain the effect of it to the proposed guarantor. This is usually satisfied by ensuring that the guarantor had independent and informed advice.

National Westminster Bank v Morgan, 1985 reviewed the law on **undue influence** in the context of taking security, that is where undue influence can be proved by showing that a person entered into a transaction which was to his disadvantage as a result of the domination by another party.

Normally to avoid a claim of undue influence, it is usual that a third party granting security, for example a guarantor, be afforded independent advice to ensure he is in possession of all the relevant facts. It was held by the House of Lords that unless the wronged party can show that he has suffered 'manifest disadvantage' and the bank exercised undue influence either by its own actions or those of someone acting as the bank's agent, the transaction would not be voidable.

In 1993, on the same day, the House of Lords gave judgement in two cases, both of which dealt with a wife's ability to set aside a transaction with a lender on the basis of undue influence or misrepresentation by her husband.

C A S E   S T U D Y

Barclays Bank v O'Brien, 1993

Both spouses owned their matrimonial home jointly. They gave Barclays a second charge (mortgage) over it, and the wife granted a guarantee to Barclays for the business debts of her husband. Their liability under the second charge could reach £135,000 but the husband had told his wife that the maximum extent of the liability was £60,000. The wife signed the charge without reading it. Despite a request by the Barclays branch manager, the clerk at the branch office allowed the documents to be signed apparently without explaining the effect of the security to Mrs O'Brien.

The House of Lords decided that the charge was only enforceable to the extent of £60,000 which the wife thought she was agreeing to secure. They held that a wife standing as surety for a husband's debt as a result of his legal wrong (undue influence or misrepresentation) had a right against him to set aside the transaction.

That right was enforceable against a lender if:

- The husband had acted as the lender's agent
- The lender had actual or constructive notice of the facts on which the right was based

Constructive notice is where knowledge of a fact is presumed or inferred by law.

The House of Lords expressed the view that, because of the nature of the business dealings between husband and wife, a lender would normally have constructive notice unless it took reasonable steps to satisfy itself that the surety's consent had been properly obtained.

A lender will have taken reasonable steps if:

- It draws attention of the wife to the nature of the risk she is taking
- It advises her to take independent legal advice

The House of Lords gave clear guidance on what lenders should do to meet the requirements on them. They should insist that the wife meets an employee of the lender, without the husband being present, and at the meeting:

- Tell her clearly of the potential liability
- Warn her of the risks, for example, failure to pay may result in sale of the house
- Urge her to seek independent legal advice

CASE STUDY

CIBC Mortgages v Pitt, 1993

In the other case, the result was different. The difference in the facts of that case with those of O'Brien was that the spouses in Pitt were joint borrowers. A joint loan case is different from a surety case because in the latter the possibility of undue influence by the husband was reinforced by the wife appearing to have no financial benefit from her guarantee.

The application of the O'Brien principles to Scots law must also be considered.

CASE STUDY

Smith v Bank of Scotland, 1997

In this case, the position was considered by the House of Lords on appeal by the pursuer, Mrs. Smith, to the decision of the Inner House of the Court of Session that the O'Brien decision was not the law in Scotland.

The House of Lords overruled the Inner House decision and decided that the O'Brien principles should be applied in Scotland in circumstances where a reasonable person would believe that owing to the personal relationship between the borrower and the proposed guarantor or grantor of third party security, the latter's consent may not be fully informed or freely given.

Where such a duty arises it is sufficient, in order to discharge it, to warn a potential guarantor, or grantor of third party security, of the consequences of entering into the arrangement and to advise him/her to take independent advice.

There have been further developments in England dealing with the issue of independent legal advice to wives, and the position of banks where there is an allegation that security granted by wives over the matrimonial home resulted from undue influence. In the Court of Appeal case, *The Royal Bank of*

Scotland v Etridge and associated cases, 1998, the court considered what constituted independent legal advice and the responsibilities of the solicitor giving the advice.

Lenders can rely on the matrimonial home security where they had requested the solicitor acting for the wife to explain the transaction to the wife and confirm that she appeared to understand it. The security could only be set aside if the lender was on notice that there was still a risk that the wife had entered into the transaction as a result of the husband's misrepresentation or undue influence. So the 'good faith' of the lender in dealing with the wife is still an essential element of taking the security, i.e. it would be unacceptable to ignore any evidence that the husband may be exercising misrepresentation or undue influence and attempt to rely on the provision of independent legal advice to obtain a good security.

8 The banker's right of set-off

QUICK QUESTION

What do you think we mean by the right of set-off?

Write your answer here before reading on.

Mr John Bland has two current accounts at your branch, a No 1 account and a No 2 account. The No 2 account is designated the 'Household' Account.

Mr Bland is a problem customer. He frequently overdraws on both accounts by anything up to £500. These overdrafts are not pre-arranged. You have arranged a number of appointments with him to discuss the situation, but he has always cancelled them at the last minute. There is no overdraft agreement on either account.

Today, there is a credit balance of £200 on the No 1 Account, but the No 2 Account is overdrawn by £450.

Would you be justified in combining the two balances and refusing to pay a cheque for £100 (drawn on the No 1 Account) which has just been presented for payment?

Mr. Albert Mason also has a No 1 Account and a No 2 Account. The No 1 Account is always in credit and the No 2 Account is always overdrawn; a net overdraft limit of £300 has been agreed.

Today, the No 1 Account has a credit balance of £150 and the No 2 Account a debit balance of £250. A cheque for £300, drawn on the No 2 Account, has just been presented for payment.

Would you be justified in returning the cheque?

Would you return the cheque if Mr. Mason was a valued customer who has never in the past exceeded his overdraft limit?

We will now look at this is more detail and see if we can answer the questions raised in the illustrations.

The right of set-off is the right of a person who finds himself both debtor and creditor of another person to set off one debt against the other with the result that there is total or partial extinction of the debt which is due.

So, if Andrews (debtor) owes Brown (creditor) £50, but, at the same time, Brown (debtor) owes Andrews (creditor) £30, the result of the operation of the principle of set-off means that Andrews owes Brown £20, i.e. his debt has been reduced by £30.

8.1 How can a banker use the principle of set-off?

Where you have two accounts in the name of the same customer, one in debit, and one in credit, you can, in the absence of express or implied agreement to the contrary, set off the debit balance on one account against the credit balance on the other by giving reasonable notice of your intention to do so.

Set-off can operate only if both debts are of known amount and are due by and to the parties concerned.

When calculating the balance available for drawing, you need not take any notice of any credit balance the customer may have at some other branch of the same bank. You would not be liable if you dishonoured a cheque because there were insufficient funds to pay the cheque at the branch on which it is drawn.

Unless there is agreement to the contrary, you may combine the two accounts, and dishonour a cheque drawn on the branch with the credit balance should the combined accounts show a debit or insufficient credit balance. Again, it is desirable for you to give reasonable notice to the customer.

As mentioned above, the banker is not bound to take notice of a customer's credit balance at another branch in deciding to dishonour a cheque at his own branch, but the banker can use the debit balance at another branch in deciding to dishonour a cheque drawn on his own branch in which there is a credit balance.

There may however be a risk associated with this action. If a customer had issued a cheque on the creditor account presuming it would be paid, you may run the risk of an action of damages if you dishonour the cheque without having given reasonable notice to the customer.

However, there are conflicting opinions on this:

One opinion is that if a customer is allowed to keep two or more accounts, there is a presumption that they will be kept distinct and separate. To save any problems regarding the operation of the banker's right of set-off, a letter authorising the banker to set-off should be obtained from the customer when more than one account is opened. Thus, a letter of set-off should be obtained if the banker foresees the need to combine accounts in this way.

8.2 Looking back

We will now return to our customers Mr John Bland and Mr Albert Mason, whose situations we examined earlier.

 QUICK QUESTION

What decisions did you reach?

Write your answer here before reading on.

In the case of Mr Bland, he has passed up several opportunities to call and negotiate the situation and you would be justified in combining the balances on her two accounts. There is no overdraft agreement on either of his accounts and your course of action would, at least, reduce his indebtedness to £250. In Albert Mason's case, you would again be justified in returning the cheque which would create an overdraft of £550 on his No. 2 Account – a net overdrawn position of £400. However, given that Mr. Mason is a valued customer, you might decide to pay the cheque and renegotiate the terms on which the account is to be operated.

CASE STUDY

United Rentals Ltd v Clydesdale & North of Scotland Bank Ltd, 1963

A customer of the bank who was a T.V. engineer was appointed as agent for the pursuers. He opened a No 2 Account but did not inform the bank that the sole purpose of this account was to keep the funds of United Rentals Ltd, which he was collecting on their behalf, separate from his own.

All the lodgements to the No 2 Account consisted of cheques or orders in favour of the customer.

He did not inform the bank of the true position even after receiving a written demand from the bank for repayment of the net overdraft at which time the operation of the set off was clearly shown.

Later, the bank proceeded to apply the sum at the credit of the No 2 Account to the overdraft on the No 1 Account, which was the larger amount.

United Rentals Ltd brought an action to have the funds restored to them.

QUICK QUESTION

What do you think was the decision in this case?

What do you think was the reasoning behind the decision?

Write your answer here before reading on.

The decision was that the bank was entitled to set off the credit balance on the No 2 A/C against the overdraft on the No 1 A/C.

The reasoning was that where the second account was opened by a customer newly appointed as an agent for the deposit of the principal's money, the banker may apply the principle of set-off if he is not informed of the reasons for the opening of the second account.

Accounts should only be set off after reasonable notice has been given to the customer unless:

- There is a definite agreement giving the banker the right to do so, such as a letter of set-off
- Such a right can be inferred from the course of business between the banker and the customer

9 The banker's lien

Lien is the right implied by law to retain some moveable property belonging to another until some debt due has been paid.

Special lien

This entitles the holder of an article to retain it until payment of the debt which relates to that property; for example, special lien of the carrier entitles the carrier to exercise a lien over every parcel carried for the carriage cost of that particular contract. A person who has possession of an article he has agreed to repair is entitled to retain possession of that article until the cost of the repair is met.

Compare this special lien with those who have a:

General lien

A general lien entitles the holder of an article to retain it until some general balance due arising from a series of transactions has been paid, not just the debt to which that property relates. A general lien is recognised by usage/custom and practice in certain trades and professions, and by statute.

For instance, an agent has a general lien over any property of the principal which comes into his hands in the normal course of the agency until payment of wages, commission or debts incurred while acting on the principal's behalf.

Lien of the banker

The banker has a general lien over negotiable instruments (e.g. bills, cheques, promissory notes) and securities (e.g. bearer bonds), which have come into their hands in the normal course of banking transactions. This would not cover property deposited with the banker for safe-keeping. If a customer, for instance, hands in bills for discount which are refused, the lien does not extend to them.

Thus, if a customer borrows £500 from the bank by depositing security worth £1,000, the bank secures a lien on that security to the extent of £500. Lien implies physical possession. The customer's property should actually be in the banker's possession and have been legitimately obtained. To part with the subject of the lien is to lose it. Even if possession is regained the lien is lost. For example, if a customer asks the banker to purchase bearer securities and pay for them to the debit of their account, the banker will have a lien on them. But, if for any reason the customer is allowed to take the securities away and later returns them requesting the banker to hold them in safe custody, the lien is lost.

Decisions on the banker's right of lien against articles lodged for safe custody are not consistent, but in general, a bank has no lien over such articles, whether negotiable instruments or not. There is, however, a general presumption that the custody of negotiable instruments belonging to a customer who is in debt to the bank, gives the banker a right of lien as long as there is no specific contract that they are held for safe custody only.

Generally, a person exercising a lien is only entitled to keep possession of the property, not realise it and convert it into money. To do this the court's authority would be necessary.

10 Appropriation of payments

What is meant by the question – How is a payment by a customer to be appropriated by the banker?

To answer this we examine how such a payment(s) by the customer is applied by the bank in the account(s) of his customer. The law regarding appropriation of payments was laid down in **Clayton's case** – *Devaynes v Noble, 1816,* which has huge significance for bankers.

Q U I C K   Q U E S T I O N

How do you think a payment by a customer is applied by the bank in a current account?

Write your answer here before reading on.

As far as a current account is concerned, the rule in Clayton's case states that the first in/first out principle should apply, in accordance with the dates of the transactions in the account.

In a current or running account, the sum first paid in is deemed to be the first drawn out, and, the earliest item on the debit side is extinguished or reduced by the first item on the credit side.

E X A M P L E   1

John Cavanagh Current Account

		Dr	Cr	Balance
		£	£	£
April 1				Dr 500
April 3	Cash		200 (A)	Dr 300
April 4	Cash		300 (B)	Nil
April 8	Cheque	400		Dr 400
April 10	Cheque	500		Dr 900
April 12	Cash		400 (C)	Dr 500
April 16	Cheque	600		Dr 1,100

The rule in Clayton's case will operate as follows:

1. Item A partly extinguishes the opening £500 debit balance (£500 to £300 Dr).
2. Item B totally extinguishes the opening £500 debit balance (£300 to Nil).
3. Item C extinguishes the debit entry of April 8th (i.e. £400).
4. The debit balance on the 12th is made up by the debit item on the 10th.
5. Similarly, the balance on 16th April is composed of the debit items on both 10th and 16th April.

CASE STUDY

CLAYTON'S CASE

Devaynes v Noble, 1816

Devaynes, one of the partners in a banking business, died, but the firm of Devaynes, Dawes, Noble, Croft and Barwick continued business under the same name. At the time of Devaynes's death the firm owed Nathaniel Clayton £1,713 – the credit balance on Clayton's account. Shortly afterwards the firm went bankrupt. Between the time of Devaynes's death and the firm's bankruptcy, Clayton continued to operate on his account, withdrawing and paying in funds. His total withdrawals (although offset by deposits) during this time amounted to more than £1,713. Clayton, on the bankruptcy of the firm, claimed against Devaynes's estate for the amount due to him at the date of Devaynes's death i.e. £1,713. But transactions had since taken place on the account. It was shown that the total drawings since Devaynes's death exceeded the balance of £1,713 and that the credit balance at the date of the firm's bankruptcy comprised fresh monies subsequently paid in.

Clayton's claim was not accepted. The estate of Devaynes, the deceased partner, should not be liable.

EXAMPLE 2

Betty Brown and Greg McPherson Joint Account

(Joint and Several liability agreed)

		Dr	Cr	Balance
		£	£	£
May 1	Balance			Dr 500
May 3	Cash		200 (A)	Dr 300
May 4	Cash		300 (B)	Nil
May 8	Cheque	400		Dr 400
May 10	Cheque	500		Dr 900
May 12	Cash		400 (C)	Dr 500
May 16	Cheque	600		Dr 1,100

In this example, if the bank receives notification of Brown's death on 11 May and stops operations on the account, then given the joint and several liability of the parties, the bank has recourse to the deceased's estate for the outstanding debit balance at that point, £900.

10.1 What if the bank does not stop the account but allows it to continue?

- The credit entry on the 12 May (£400) extinguishes part of the liability on Brown's estate (£900 down to £500).
- So although the debit balance on 16 May is £1,100, Brown's estate is only liable for £500.
- The debit on the 16 May constitutes new borrowing (£600) for which Brown's estate is not liable.

If further transactions took place before operations on the account were stopped, eventually the debit balance which existed at the date the bank received notice of death (£900) would be cleared fully by future credits.

If this happened the bank could claim nothing from the deceased's estate and would have to rely solely upon the survivor for repayment of any debt.

You can see the problems this might cause to the bank if the survivor, Greg McPherson, was unable to repay.

If the bank wishes to preserve rights against the deceased's estate for liability at the date of death, the account should be stopped on notice of death, otherwise that liability will be reduced or extinguished.

The rights of a banking customer can be found in the Banking Conduct of Business Sourcebook (BCOBS) which will be examined later on in this course.

11 Retail banking products and services

We are now ready to turn our attention to the wide range of products and services which are available from banks. Keep in mind that there may be some slight differences between the products outlined in this section and the specific features of products offered by your organisation. You should also be mindful that some of the products explained here may not be offered by all banks – for example, self build finance.

11.1 Current accounts

This is the most popular account available – it may also be called a '**Money Transmission Account**'. People in employment as well as those in receipt of pensions will have their salary paid directly into some form of current account by their employer and they can withdraw their money by a variety of methods, for example:

- By drawing a cheque against the account (although you will be aware that many retailers now no longer accept cheques)
- By setting up either Standing Orders and/or Direct Debits or using the Faster Payments System.
- By using a plastic card
- By withdrawing cash from an Automated Telling Machine (ATM)
- By using the internet and/or telephone banking services offered by their bank

The current account is used by many customers to finance their routine transactions. Money can be paid easily into the account, and as we have seen, there are a variety of ways for the customer to take money out of the account as well.

Sometimes banks will pay the customer interest for the credit balance on a current account – although any rate of interest paid will tend to be much lower than that paid on a designated savings account. At times of low interest rates, most banks will not pay credit interest on the account, however, it is normal for the customer to enjoy free banking services provided that the account always remains in credit.

There are a variety of different types of current account now available. For example a customer can have a basic current account as outlined above. However, some institutions also offer enhanced current accounts with additional features – in return for a fixed fee. Examples of additional features include free travel insurance, interest free overdrafts, etc.

To allow customers to keep track of their spending, institutions may send customers regular statements of account. However, the customer can keep track of the running of their account online, though the bank's contact centre, or by using the account and balance enquiry options available at an ATM.

11.2 Standing orders, direct debits and faster payments

Standing orders and direct debits are both automated payments and as such, act as a memory for the customer. Once set up, the payments are made automatically from the account – provided the customer has sufficient available funds to meet these payments.

With a standing order, the bank acts on behalf of the payee (the person making the payment) and will initiate the payment, remitting it direct to the beneficiary's bank account. On the other hand, with a direct debit, a similar process happens almost in reverse. Here, the beneficiary's bank initiates the payment and raises a claim against the payee's bank account. However, the same end result is achieved – a payment is made from the payee's account into the beneficiary's account – so for this to happen the original instruction must be signed by the payee, giving the authority for their account to be debited.

Standing orders are used for regular payments for fixed amounts – for example a subscription but are less popular than direct debits as the amount of the payment with a standing order is fixed. An important difference between standing orders and direct debits is that a direct debit can be set up for a variable amount on an unspecified date. This allows the beneficiary to decide on the amount of the payment and also on the date on which the payment will be made.

when first introduced, some customers were unsure of this type of payment, as they were relying upon the beneficiaries to claim the correct amount on the correct date. However an indemnity scheme exists, which allows customers the peace of mind in knowing that in the event of a dispute, they will receive a full refund. This increased confidence of consumers in the direct debit system has seen a growth in the number of direct debits in existence – with most direct debits now being set up for variable amounts on unspecified dates.

The main advantage of being able to set up an unspecified direct debit is that if the amount or payment date needs to change, this can still happen within the terms of the direct debit mandate – although the beneficiary is required to give the payee notice of any changes. Having a system like this means that the payment does not need to be amended. On the other hand, when using a standing order, if the amount changes, the standing order must be amended. This can be a time consuming process for both the customer and the bank.

Many banks now offer customers the **Faster Payments service**. Under this service, it is possible to make automated payments that are guaranteed to reach the beneficiaries account within two hours – although in reality receipt is almost instantaneous. Whilst banks have offered same-day payments services in the past (through the Clearing House Automated Payments System), these have been targeted at high-value transactions – for example, they are use in the settlement of house purchases and sales. Faster Payments on the other hand is targeted at smaller value transactions of up to £100,000 and can be used as a substitute for standing orders.

11.3 Basic accounts

As well as providing accounts that offer a range of features to cover a variety of possible needs that the customer may have, there is also the provision of a basic bank account.

This type of account will normally be operated by way of a plastic card allowing customers to lodge and withdraw funds from the account. There would be no overdraft facility involved. It is also possible that standing orders and direct debits could be set up on the account to facilitate regular payments from the account. As well as funds being lodged to the account by way of the plastic card, it is also possible to receive automated lodgements to the account – for example, wages, salary, pension or benefit payments.

11.4 Overdrafts

An overdraft is simply a negative balance on a current account.

An overdraft should be agreed in advance between the bank and the customer. An authorised overdraft is one that has been agreed in advance between the customer and the bank. An unauthorised (or unarranged) overdraft is one that the customer has created without the prior agreement of the bank, by drawing against the account when there are not sufficient funds in it.

An unarranged overdraft can come about in a variety of ways:

- The customer may issue cheques that overdraw the account which the bank chooses to honour.

- The bank may be willing to allow the account to become overdrawn as they know that the customer's monthly salary is about to come into the account, so remedying the situation.

- The bank may be willing to allow the account to become overdrawn as it is a customer of good standing. The bank will then contact the customer to obtain their proposals to remedy the situation.

11.5 Deposit/savings accounts

Whilst a current account is used for the customer to pay for their day to day expenses and perhaps to help manage any short term shortfall in funds, many customers will look to keep their savings in a different account – hence the need for a savings account.

Savings accounts are usually used to hold medium to long term surpluses of funds that the customer may have. Savings accounts are usually operated by way of a plastic card.

Interest is paid by the bank, usually based on the amount of money lodged in the account. The payment of this interest will vary from product to product. For example, some savings accounts will pay interest monthly to provide the customer with some form of monthly income, whilst other accounts will pay out interest say, quarterly, six monthly or even annually. Also, depending upon the individual account chosen by the customer, the account that the interest is paid into will also vary – some accounts will have the interest paid back into the savings account (where it will increase the balance of the account and so lead to the customer having the potential to earn even more interest in the future as the balance of the account has now been increased) or it may be paid into a separate account – perhaps with the intention of providing the customer with income that can be used immediately. In recent years with very low interest rates, the possibility of using monthly interest to provide a reasonable level of income has become unattainable for most.

The level of interest rate will vary on both the balance of the account and the terms of the account. Generally, the higher the balance of the account, then the higher the rate of interest that will be paid. This also holds true if there is a minimum balance on the account – an account that requires a minimum balance of, say, £10,000 will tend to pay a higher rate of interest than an account that only requires a minimum balance of £1.

The terms of the account will also affect the level of interest paid – for example, if there is a limited amount of withdrawals permitted each year, then that account will tend to pay a higher rate of interest than an account that allows the customer to make an unlimited amount of withdrawals.

Another condition that can affect the rate of interest paid is the notice required on withdrawals. An account that allows customers to withdraw funds without giving any notice at all will tend to pay a lower rate of interest than an account that requires the customer to give notice of withdrawals – this notice period could be seven, thirty or even ninety days. With some notice accounts it may be possible for the customer to obtain immediate access to their funds, but only upon payment of a penalty fee. This is normally linked to the notice period on the account – if the account has 30 days' notice of withdrawal required, the penalty could be that the customer has to pay the bank a sum similar to 30 days interest for the amount withdrawn.

11.6 Individual Savings Accounts (ISAs)

An **ISA** is a tax-free savings account. The basics of ISAs are:

- They can consist of cash or stocks and shares.

- There is no tax liability.

- There are maximum annual limits set for the amount that can be paid into an ISA. There are reviewed by the government annually.

- Stocks and shares ISAs can be taken out by anyone over 18 who is ordinarily resident in the UK for tax purposes. A cash ISA can be opened by anyone over 16years who is ordinarily resident in the UK for tax purposes.

QUICK QUESTION

What are the current limits for ISAs?

Write your answer here before reading on.

11.7 Personal loans

Personal loans are used by personal customers to finance the purchase of major assets. A range of assets can be financed by way of a personal loan. Here are some examples:

- Cars
- Caravans
- Holidays
- White goods – domestic appliances like fridges, freezers, tumble dryers, washing machines, etc.
- Home improvements
- Personal computers

To apply for a personal loan the customer must complete an application. This could be by completing a form, contacting a customer contact centre, or applying online. Once the application is received, the lender will complete a credit assessment process – usually using some form of credit scoring. If the application is agreed by the bank, an agreement form will be drawn up, and the customer and the lender will sign this. When this has happened, the funds can be released to the customer – usually by transferring the money from the Personal Loan account into the customers operating account.

At the same time, the customer will set up a standing order for the repayments to be made. These repayments are usually arranged to be monthly, but some customers may opt to make fortnightly or even weekly repayments. The rationale behind this decision usually depends on how often the customer is paid by their employers.

Interest is normally charged at a flat rate of interest over the life of the loan, with the total amount of interest being added to the capital sum at the start of the loan. The true rate of interest, the **Annual Percentage Rate** (APR) will also be advised to the customer.

11.8 House purchase loans

Traditionally, House Purchase Loans, frequently referred to as mortgages, were only offered by building societies, however, in recent years, banks have also offered this type of loan. This type of loan is granted for a long period of time – usually between 15 and 25 years and the loan is for a large sum of money. Security will be taken over the property being purchased.

The House Purchase Loan market is very competitive with a variety of products now available. However, there are only two ways in which a House Purchase Loan can be paid off – either by making regular payments covering capital and interest or by repaying only the interest, and then making a large one-off payment at the end of the loan to cover the capital sum.

Capital and interest mortgages

This type of House Purchase Loan requires the borrower to repay part of the capital borrowed along with an interest payment charged on the capital. Therefore, when we get to the end of the loan period, the balance of the account will be zero.

With this arrangement, the interest repayment element makes up a larger part of the repayment than the capital element in the early stages of the loan. It is only later on in the life of the loan – when these small reductions of capital begin to reduce the total amount of capital outstanding – that the amount of interest accrued reduces and so the capital amount of the repayment becomes more dominant.

The amount of the monthly repayment will only vary as the interest rate varies. You will probably have seen on the news that when Base (or Reference) Rate changes, there are illustrations of how this might affect the monthly repayments of a typical loan. As Base Rate increases, so will the loan repayments, conversely, as Base Rate falls, so too will the loan repayments.

Interest only mortgages

The main difference is that with an interest only loan, there are no repayments to the loan account of any capital at all during the life of the loan. Rather the loan is repaid in its entirety at the end. Therefore the monthly payments made by the customer to the lender only cover the accrued interest on the capital balance. Like a capital and interest loan, the only occurrence that will cause this amount to change is if there is a change in Base Rate.

It is up to the customer to ensure that they have the funds available at the end of the loan period to make a full repayment. They may have amassed savings over the period of the loan that would allow them to do this, but it is more common to have some form of **repayment vehicle** set up to allow these funds to be available. There are three commonly encountered repayment vehicles:

- An endowment policy
- A personal pension plan
- An ISA

The proceeds of any of these products would be used to provide the customer with a lump sum to make the capital repayment from. The main problem is that there is no guarantee that there will be sufficient funds to make the repayment in full. If there is a shortfall forecast, then the customer would be advised to do one of the following four things:

- Increase the level of premiums that they pay on their endowment policy

- Arrange to set aside additional funds to meet the shortfall

- Extend the term of the loan and/or the savings policy

- Convert all or part of their loan to capital and interest – by converting part of their loan to capital and interest the amount of the loan now outstanding could be reduced to the projected return from their repayment vehicle

Current account mortgages

These have been recently introduced to this country but have been available abroad for many years. Here, the customer's House Purchase Loan and current account are amalgamated into one account.

The main advantage is that as each month's salary is credited to the account, it will reduce the total amount outstanding. As a result, the interest that is accruing on the outstanding balance is slightly lower. The cumulative effect of this over the years of the Home Loan can produce savings for the customer – with the result that they can repay their loan earlier than if the Home Loan and current account were maintained separately.

Muslim mortgages

Mortgages are interest based and this is something that does not conform to the Islamic Shariah law. Therefore Muslims in the UK find themselves in a very difficult position as a mortgage contravenes their faith, but due to the mortgage products offered by the financial services industry, if they wish to own their home, they have no choice in many cases but to reluctantly take out a mortgage.

However, some providers do now provide a Sharia compliant mortgage that is based on Ijara and Murabha methods. These are:

Ijara:

- The financial institution purchases the property.

- Whilst the customer stays in the property, they make payments to the financial institution that total the purchase price of the property. These payments may be scheduled over a period of up to 25 years.

- During the loan repayment period, the customer is also charged rent on the property. This rental amount is reviewed annually and will decrease over the lifetime of the facility as the capital sum outstanding to the lender decreases.

- Once the customer has repaid the money that was spent on purchasing the property, then the property is sold to them.

- It can be possible to borrow up to 90% of the value of the property in this way.

- The precise details and operation of this arrangement can vary from lender to lender.

By following this arrangement, the financial institution makes its money from the rent that the customer pays to them. As rent is not another name for interest, it is seen to be a fair payment for living in a property that is owned by the financial institution, rather than being a charge for borrowing money.

Murabha:

- The financial services organisation purchases the property from the seller at the original price. They then sell it to the customer at a higher price.

- The amount of the higher price can be paid back to the lender over a period of up to 15 years.

The financial services company will make their profit through the higher price that they sell the property to their customer at.

A major disadvantage to both of these arrangements is that stamp duty must be paid twice in each transaction.

This type of mortgage is not, at present, available from all lenders.

11.9 Equity release loans

Equity release is a way of getting cash from the value of your home. These schemes can be helpful in certain circumstances but are not suitable for everyone. For example, they can be expensive and inflexible if your circumstances change in the future and may affect your current or future entitlement to State or local authority benefits.

An equity release loan may be used for almost any purpose, and once the facility is agreed between the lender and the borrower, the customer does not need to go back to the lender if they wish to fund the purchase of another asset through the equity release, as they would need to do were they financing through a personal loan.

With this product, you take out a loan secured on your home. You can choose to borrow a lump sum or to opt for a drawdown facility. This is suitable if the customer wishes to borrow smaller sums from time to time (say as instalments for the purchase of an asset falls due) rather than one lump sum, as it means they only pay interest on the outstanding balance.

These loans are based on the notion of rising property values and they give certain borrowers the opportunity to borrow on the strength of the equity that they have in their home. By equity we mean the difference between the market value of a property and the amount of borrowing (if any) on that property.

For example: if a house has a market value of £250,000 and a mortgage of £150,000, then the equity is £100,000 – i.e. £250,000, less £150,000 = £100,000.

There are a number of ways in which a bank may be willing to lend against this asset:

Conventional mortgage or remortgage

Here, the borrower makes an application to the bank (who have provided the original mortgage) to lend against the equity in their home. Using the figures above, we will assume that the bank is willing to lend up to 60% of the equity in the property.

In this example, what is the maximum amount that the customer could borrow?

It would be £60,000 – in other words, 60% of the equity, which is £100,000. This assumes that the borrower's financial circumstances confirm that they could afford to repay such a loan.

Second mortgage

In this case, the borrower seeks to borrow against the equity in their home – but with a different lender. This may not always be the best way forward for the borrower, as the lender would wish to take security over the property, by way of a second bond (or mortgage), and the borrower would need to pay the fees associated with this.

What other drawback can you see with this proposal?

From the lender's point of view, they may feel that it would have made more sense for the borrower to approach the mortgage lender first. It may be assumed that the borrower did, in fact, do this and for some reason the mortgage lender has declined the deal. This would make the second potential lender cautious about proceeding.

Lifetime mortgage

This is a facility that is generally looked at by people aged 55 years and over. They are mostly taken out by people who have no borrowing on their property, but wish to raise some cash on the basis of the equity on their home. With such an arrangement, the amount that can be borrowed rarely exceeds 25% of the market value of the property. Normally, such a loan will not have a fixed repayment date – rather it will be repaid either on the death of the borrowers, or when the house is sold.

Home reversion plan

This final arrangement is not a loan at all – rather it is where all or part of the property is sold to a finance provider and the occupant then becomes a tenant for life, or until the property is sold. Such an arrangement could mean that the property owner is able to raise a larger cash sum than they could have under a lifetime mortgage, but the amount would still be expected to be significantly less than the market value of the property.

In the UK, these products are regulated under the Mortgage Conduct of Business (MCOB) rules and most second mortgages fall under the Consumer Credit Acts 1974 and 2006.

11.10   Bridging loans

A bridging loan is a short term loan used to cover the situation where a customer has to pay for a major purchase before receiving the proceeds of a major sale. The most frequently encountered example of a bridging loan is when a customer is involved in the purchase and sale of property.

Imagine the situation where a customer has agreed to purchase a house on 1st July. They intend to finance this purchase from the sale of their present home as well as taking out a House Purchase Loan. However, it is extremely difficult for the customer to arrange to buy and sell the two homes on the same date. Therefore, if they have agreed with the purchaser of their old home that settlement of this transaction will take place on 7th July, then they will be substantially out of pocket for the period 1st – 7th July. This is where they would use a bridging loan.

The bridging loan is used to cover the period when the customer has paid for the new house, but is still waiting to receive the sale proceeds of the old house. Interest is charged on a daily basis and is applied to the bridging loan account.

The lender will also require that the customer provides an **irrevocable mandate**. This is a letter addressed to the customer's solicitor informing him/her to remit the free sale proceeds to the bank. It is called an irrevocable mandate as part of this letter will state that the customer cannot revoke, or cancel, this instruction. In England and Wales a similar type of security is taken, but is called a Letter of Undertaking.

Once these proceeds are received, they are credited to the bridging loan account, which then has the interest applied to it before being closed off.

Normally a bridging loan is only required for a matter of days.

Whilst these loans were popular for a number of years, fewer and fewer banks are now willing to offer them, so the customer may need to finance this arrangement through their mortgage.

11.11   Electronic funds transfer

This is the now familiar system whereby consumers can pay for goods and services at the point of sale by way of a plastic card.

The card is swiped through or inserted into a card reader at the point of sale by the retailer and the customer is required input their Personal Identification Number (PIN) into a keypad. The transaction will then be debited from the customers account, credit card or **electronic purse** to complete the transaction. It is also possible in some retailers to simply present the card at the reader and a contactless payment may be made.

There is also a cash-back facility available with this form of payment. Here, when the customer is paying with their debit card, they may also obtain cash from their account from the retailer. This facility is mainly available from supermarkets.

There are two main advantages for the retailer:

- Firstly, as they make cash-back payments to customers, they are reducing the cash held in their tills which is an added security measure.

- As the retailers cash holdings are reduced, they will have less cash to pay in to their bank, thus reducing the cash handling aspect of service charge that their bank will charge them.

The most popular way for the customer to pay via electronic funds transfer is by debit card. These are cards that will automatically debit the customers account when used to pay for a transaction. However, an additional feature of these cards is that they can be used to withdraw cash from an ATM. There the card is used in conjunction with a PIN to withdraw cash from ATM machines. There are a number of additional services now available from many ATM machines, including:

- Balance enquiries
- Make a deposit
- Mini statements
- Cheque book requests
- Alteration of PIN number
- Top up a mobile phone
- Make a donation to specified charities

There is another form of card that we have not discussed yet – the electronic purse. This is a plastic card that is topped up with money – rather like a pay as you go mobile phone. As the card is used, this sum of money is reduced, until it comes to zero, when it needs to be topped up again. The main benefits of an electronic purse are:

- Customers can only spend what is on the card – they cannot create overdrafts on their account. The electronic purse is particularly attractive for those customers who do not want to get into debt.

- If the card is lost or stolen, the maximum exposure to loss is the balance on the card at that time.

- There is no need for a live link to the customer's bank account at the time that the card is used – the amount spent is simply deducted from the card.

The Transport for London Oyster Card is probably the most popular example of an electronic purse.

11.12 Credit cards

A credit card is another form of plastic card. It allows the customer to buy goods and services and pay for them at a later date. The two providers of credit cards are MasterCard and Visa. In the UK, financial services organisations will offer their own version of one or other of these providers' cards.

To obtain a credit card, the customer must complete an application form which will be credit scored by the bank as part of their credit assessment process. If the application is successful, the customer will be issued with a credit card and advised of their credit limit. This is the maximum balance that the customer may have on their credit card account.

The customer will receive a statement from the credit card company monthly, or manage their account online and has the option of either paying the entire balance or making a payment towards the balance. The minimum payment that the customer may make is 5% of the outstanding balance or £5, whichever is the greater. The period of time that the customer has to make this payment varies from card to card between 15 days and 25 days.

By using a credit card, the customer can get up to 56 days of interest free credit on purchases. However, should the customer choose not to repay the entire balance of the account, they will be charged interest by the credit card company and the rates of interest can tend to be high. Should the customer choose to withdraw cash using their credit card, then interest starts to accrue immediately. Credit cards are therefore looked upon as an expensive form of consumer credit.

11.13 Term loans

Due to the specialist nature of term loans, they tend not to be credit scored – rather they require to be **manually underwritten**. By this we mean that the application is scrutinised and credit assessed by a lending official of the bank and a decision is then made whether or not to agree to the loan application. As a result of this manual intervention, the underwriter has the opportunity to mould the features of a loan to meet the specific requirements of the customer unlike a credit scored product, such as a personal loan, where the customer has to fit in with the set features of the product.

As the name would imply, term loans are agreed for a fixed period of time – normally up to 20 years. There are normally no maximum or minimum amounts for a term loan facility.

The rate of interest is negotiated according to each case and the inherent risk involved to the bank. Generally this rate fluctuates with base/reference rate but can at times be fixed for the whole or part duration of the loan.

Ongoing repayments may include both the capital and interest elements of the borrowing – alternatively the accrued interest may be applied to another account on either a monthly or quarterly basis. It is also possible for a Term Loan to be an interest only loan which means that during the life of the loan the customer need only pay interest on the loan and not make any reductions in the capital amount. However, in this type of case the banker must be satisfied that the customer has some form of repayment vehicle in place that will allow them to repay the entire capital sum outstanding at the end of the loan term. This repayment vehicle should be reviewed periodically during the life of the loan to ensure that it will still provides a sufficient sum at the end of the term to allow a full repayment to be effected. If for some reason a shortfall is forecast, then the earlier this is identified the better as it allows the customer the maximum amount of time to make suitable arrangements to make up any potential shortfall or alternatively reschedule to capital and interest repayments.

The term loan may be either secured or unsecured depending on the individual customer's circumstances. However, if the loan is of a long-term nature, then it is to be expected that suitable security would be taken.

When agreeing the repayment schedule, attention should be given to the future earnings potential of the customer, with the repayments geared to tie in with their income. For example, if the customer is due to receive the maturity proceeds of a life policy during the term of the loan; it may be that a bullet payment (or additional one-off payment) at that point is built into the repayment schedule. This one off payment may also be referred to as a balloon payment.

Unlike an overdraft, the term loan is not repayable on demand. Rather, the loan should be allowed to run for its agreed term – provided that any conditions that were agreed at the outset have been kept and scheduled repayments are being fully met. It is quite normal for either lending conditions or covenants to be set for a term loan. These are conditions that the borrower must fulfil before drawdown and/or throughout the tenor of the loan.

Term loans tend to be used by customers for purposes such as the purchase of an asset. Here the term of the loan would be tied into the useful life of the asset – after all, you would not want still to be making repayments on a loan for an asset that you no longer have the use of.

You should also bear in mind that if a term loan to a personal customer is agreed then this will normally be deemed to be a regulated agreement under the terms of the Consumer Credit Act. However, we will look at this statute and some exceptions in more detail later in this book.

The interest rate on a term loan may also be linked to LIBOR.

QUICK QUESTION

What do you understand by LIBOR?

Write your answer here before reading on.

LIBOR stands for London Inter Bank Offered Rate. This is the rate of interest that banks borrow funds from other banks on the London interbank market. Unlike base rate, LIBOR fluctuates daily. In times when LIBOR and Base Rate are out of line with one another, with LIBOR being higher, then it may be that some term loans are charged at a rate of interest aligned to LIBOR. If this is not the case, then there is a risk that if the bank has borrowed funds on the interbank market to finance the term loan, then they may be paying more in interest than they are charging to the customer and so are making a loss on the deal.

11.14 Self build and property investment finance

In this section we are going to look at the situation where a bank will lend to a customer who is building their own home, primarily for their own occupation or at times as part of their overall investment strategy. This is a complex undertaking, which requires the involvement of a number of external parties – for example, builders, solicitors, architects, bankers, quantity surveyors, etc.

QUICK QUESTION

What do you think constitutes a self build?

Write your answer here before reading on.

A self build is an advance that will finance the building, converting and renovating of a property as the customer's principal/secondary residence or alternatively for investment purposes.

It is important to be aware that the self-build facility is not a 'mortgage' in the traditional sense of the word – rather it is structured as an overdraft that is secured over the plot of land upon which the house is being built.

You should bear in mind that as self-build facilities require a standard security/legal charge to be granted in support of the borrowing, this kind of facility may fall under the auspices of current mortgage regulation. Transactions captured are therefore know as Regulated Mortgage Contracts.

By the nature of the project, the funding for this type of borrowing must be flexible. Either of these potential options could be used:

- Funding of the project in arrears being granted on confirmation of stage completion. This is the most common funding arrangement.

- Funding of the project in advance may be considered dependent upon individual proposition.

QUICK QUESTION

In light of the above, where do you think the repayment of a self build loan will normally come from?

Write your answer here before reading on.

In most instances, the repayment of the self build will come from the drawdown of a mortgage.

11.15 The system for clearing cheques

Whilst cheques are used far less frequently than they once were, they are still in existence and are commonly used by business customers. We will therefore look at the way in which cheques are processed – or cleared. When a cheque is issued it can take some time to reach the bank account on which it was drawn. We shall now take a look at how a cheque finds its way from the customer's cheque book to their bank account.

The method of clearing cheques may vary from bank to bank but the basic principles remain constant. When a cheque is issued, the payee of the cheque will take it and any other cheques payable to them (and any cash) to their bank and have their account credited with the total sum. The cash paid in does not need to clear or be confirmed by anyone. The cheques paid in will fall into two categories:

1. Those that have been drawn on the same branch of the bank as the one where the payee is making the lodgement – sometimes called 'house cheques'.

2. Those that have been drawn on other branches of the bank and other banks.

The cheques that have been drawn on the branch of the bank where the payee is paying in should not be too difficult to deal with – the banker will look at the cheques and decide whether they will be paid or dishonoured; if they are to be paid they will be debited to the drawers' accounts. If any cheque is to be dishonoured, it will be returned to the person making the lodgement. As soon as a house cheque has been paid, the payee can have full credit for its proceeds.

The cheques that have been drawn on other banks and branches are not quite as straightforward. These cheques must find their way to the account-holding banks and branches in order that the relative bankers can make a decision on whether or not the cheques are to be paid. We shall look at how this is done shortly, but you can see that there is a potential problem for both the payee and the payee's banker:

- The payee has provided goods or services but even when the cheques received from customers are lodged to their account, it is still not certain that they have been paid.

- The banker has permitted funds to be credited to the account in the name of the payee, but has no guarantee that the bank will not have to debit the account at a later date should the cheques not be honoured when they are presented to the relative account-holding bankers.

QUICK QUESTION

What do you think would happen if the payee were to issue cheques on the strength of the funds lodged to their account and shortly after all or some of the cheques lodged were returned unpaid?

Write your answer here before reading on.

The proceeds of cheques that have not yet been paid by the drawee bank are known as 'uncleared funds' or 'uncleared effects'. Banks will accept uncleared funds for lodgement into an account and the amount will immediately be added to the balance of the customer's account. If a bank statement were produced for the customer the following day, or if the customer were to check their account online, the full amount of the lodgement would be shown as being credited to their account, but the customer would not be entitled to draw against uncleared funds until they have been cleared. The banker accepting the lodgement would 'defer' full credit for the amount of uncleared cheques for a number of days.

If cheques were presented prior to the funds being cleared, the banker would be entitled to return the cheques unpaid. If the banker permitted the cheques to be paid then, whilst technically the account of the customer would remain in credit, if the banker looks at cleared funds only, then an overdraft has emerged and the customer will be charged interest – sometimes called 'deferment interest'.

The cheques that have still to be cleared will be remitted to the bank's head office. These cheques will fall into two categories:

1. Those that have been drawn on branches of the bank
2. Those that have been drawn on other banks

Cheques that have been drawn on branches of the bank can be passed to them by head office. Cheques that have been drawn on other banks will be passed to the banks concerned. The bank should receive payment for the cheques from the head office of the drawee banks, but it is more than likely that the other banks will hold cheques which will require to be passed over to the bank. The banks will therefore exchange cheques and settle for only the net sum due. Once received, the head office of the bank will pass the relative cheques either to the branches concerned or, more commonly, to a centralised location.

You will probably be aware of discontent expressed by customers regarding the amount of time it takes for a cheque to clear in the United Kingdom. This has been expressed not only by individual customers but also by consumer groups and has featured on a number of consumer affairs items in the media. As a result of this, changes were implemented to standardise the treatment of these items by members of the Cheque and Credit Clearing Company and the Belfast Bankers Clearing Committee. These changes are now summarised.

The information regarding when a deposited cheque will start to earn interest, when funds may be withdrawn against a deposited cheque and when a cheque may be reclaimed from a beneficiary's account is expressed in terms of, for example, T + 2 (days). The precise definition of T will need to be made clear in the terms and conditions of each account. This will need to take account of branch cut off times, and it may also vary according to the way in which the cheque is lodged – for example, at an ATM, at a post office, or by post. Normally, for a counter deposit, T will be the day of deposit if it is made before the advertised cut-off time at the bank counter. If the deposit is made after this cut-off time, then T would be the following business day. For a postal deposit, T would be deemed to be the day that the cheque is received by the bank.

Assuming that a cheque has been deposited in an interest bearing account, then it will start to either earn interest, or reduce the amount of overdraft interest charged by no later than T + 2.

QUICK QUESTION

If a cheque was paid into such an account on a Monday at 10am, when should interest start to accrue on it?

Write your answer here before reading on.

In this case, interest should start to accrue no later than Wednesday.

When a cheque is deposited to a current or basic bank account, it will be available for withdrawal no later than the start of business on T + 4.

QUICK QUESTION

If a cheque is paid into a current on Monday at 10am, when should these funds be available for withdrawal?

Write your answer here before reading on.

In this case, the funds should be available for withdrawal no later than start of business on Friday.

For a savings account from which withdrawals are allowed, funds will be available no later than start of business on T + 6.

QUICK QUESTION

Again, thinking of a cheque paid in at 10am on Monday of this week to a savings account...when will the funds be available for withdrawal?

Write your answer here before reading on.

In this scenario, the funds will be available for withdrawal no later than start of business on the Tuesday of the following week.

Regarding the fate of cheques, no cheque will be reclaimed from a beneficiary customer's account any later than T+6 – without the agreement of the beneficiary customer, or unless the beneficiary was a knowing party to a fraud. This proposition applies to all types of account. The practical implication of this is that if a cheque is deposited on a Monday, it will be deemed to be irrevocably paid if it has not been dishonoured or reversed by the close of business on the Tuesday of the following week.

12 Regulated products

We have now looked at a wide range of products that are offered by most banks. Later on in the course, we will look at the work of the regulators of the UK financial services industry However, whilst looking at products, it is germane to consider what are referred to as **regulated products**. Whilst financial services firms in the UK need to be authorised by the Financial Conduct Authority (FCA), there are also a number of products which are subject to regulated requirements – mainly that those members of staff giving advice in respect of these products must be qualified to an appropriate level.

These regulated products include:

Investments, including:

- Life assurance
- Endowments
- Personal pensions
- Open ended investment companies and unit trusts
- Shares
- Debentures
- ISAs
- Futures, options and spread betting
- High-income products

12.1 Most types of insurance

Most types of general insurance, including:

- Motor insurance
- Travel insurance
- Home contents and buildings cover
- Private medical insurance
- Extended warranties
- Payment protection insurance including mortgage protection insurance

Most types of pure protection insurance, including:

- Credit and mortgage protection insurance
- Accident, sickness and unemployment insurance
- Critical illness insurance
- Term assurance

13 Establishing and meeting customer needs

As discussed at the start of this chapter, the client-centred approach requires the customer to be at the heart of the organisation. This is never more important that when we are in conversation with the customer, seeking to determine what their financial services needs are and how best we can satisfy these needs.

13.1 The client-centred approach to meeting customer needs

The complete client centred approach to meeting customer needs is:

- Pre-meeting preparation
- Introduction
- Explore and listen
- Identify and agree the customer's needs
- Introduce the product(s) to meet these needs
- Overcome objections (objections can occur at any stage in the process)
- Closing
- Ask for referrals
- After care

13.2 Pre-meeting preparation

When meeting with a customer who has an appointment to see you, the preparation should be looked upon as an integral part of the process – not something that you can do if you have 5 minutes to spare before the appointment.

Your success in the interview will be determined to a great extent by how well you carry out this preparation and by how well you use the information that you have gained during the preparation.

We all have a natural fear of the unknown – the unknown breeds uncertainty. Preparation allows us to remove the unknown. You cannot know too much about a customer or a potential customer, so it helps if we start to gather this information before we meet up with the customer.

It is important not only carry out this preparation; but to let the customer know that this has been done. This should be done in a subtle way of 'leaking' information that lets the customer know that you have done your homework. When you do this, the customer will then know that you have prepared thoroughly for the meeting and that winning their business is important to you – therefore they feel valued.

QUICK QUESTION

You have an appointment tomorrow morning with Ms West to discuss a new loan facility. What preparation could you do for this meeting?

Write your answer here before reading on.

You could look to find out the following information about Ms West:

- Address

- Occupation

- Family details – e.g. married, single, in a civil partnership, divorced, number of dependent children

- What other family connections are there with your organisation – what additional information can you glean from this source?

- What products does Ms West currently have with your organisation?

- Why does Ms West want a loan?

- Has Ms West mentioned whether or not she wants to use part of the new loan to repay any existing loans?

- Has Ms West declined any of your previous offers – if so, why, and what did you learn from this?

- What potential cross selling opportunities do you think that you may have at this meeting?

- What information can your colleagues tell you about Ms West?

You will have seen from the above that there is lots of information that you can find out about a customer before you sit down with them. You will also have seen that all of this information is available from within your company – so you don't need to go far to look for it and collating this information will only take a matter of minutes.

QUICK QUESTION

Why should we carry out this preparation?

Write your answer here before reading on.

As mentioned earlier, most people have a fear of the unknown and preparation will help remove the unknown from a meeting. As a result, you will approach the meeting in a confident frame of mind. Also, customers are more amenable to suggestions and advice if the person giving the advice comes over in a professional manner – by letting the customer know that you have done your homework, you are displaying professionalism.

Preparation will allow you to have an idea of the likely support material that you will need during the meeting – for example, application forms, leaflets, brochures, illustrations, etc.

Preparation also gives you some of the background information about the customer that will allow you to start to build rapport with the customer once you come face to face – we will talk more about rapport building in the next stage of the process.

Finally, by preparing, you are beginning to build up a picture about the customer and gain an impression of the types of product that they are *likely* to need. However, a word of warning – don't make your mind up at this stage as to what the customers needs are – it is only when you meet up with the customer and by using the questioning and listening techniques that we will discuss later that you will be able to determine what their real need are.

So, you have now carried out the preparation that you need. You are now ready to sit down with the customer and move onto the next stage of the selling process – the introduction.

13.3 The introduction

The aim of the introduction is to build rapport with the customer.

QUICK QUESTION

What should we do during the introductory phase of the meeting?

Write your answer here before reading on.

During the introduction, you should:

- Greet the customer by name, giving them eye contact

- Smile

- Shake hands with the customer and tell them your name. Remember the point earlier that you may want to give them you name twice – for example, Good morning, Mr Customer, my name is Peter, Peter Adams...

- Guide the customer over to the interview room/area.

- Maintain an open body posture. In our overall communication – 55% is made up of how you look and 38% is made up of how you sound, and only 7% is made up of what you say. So it is important that you come across in a genuine manner to the customer.

- Chat to the customer to build rapport with them. This is where you can start to use some of the information you gathered during your preparation. You may want to chat about their journey to your office, one of their hobbies or even the weather. It is best to avoid politics at all times, or sport unless you know the customer well.

- If your preparation has told you that the customer doesn't like to spend time chatting, you must remember that at this stage.

- You could ask if the customer would like a cup of tea or coffee if you think that this has the potential to be a longer meeting.

It is important that before you start to promote any specific product, you promote the organisation first. Some of this will have been done even before you meet the customer – for example, by brand advertising carried out by your organisation, and also by the location and image of your premises.

To promote the company you should mention factors such as:

- The types of market your company operates in.

- The organisation itself – is it part of a global financial services group, or is it a small company that is proud of the personal service it can give customers?

- The structure of the company and your place in it – for example, does your role reflect the fact that your company gives a specialised service? If so, you should mention this to the customer so that they know that you and the company are experts in the field.

- Your company's local representation – how many offices do you have in the area and what type of services do they provide?

By this stage the customer should be feeling comfortable and you have started the interview on a positive footing. You will now be able to move from the introduction to the next stage of the process – explore and listen.

13.4 Explore and listen

This is a vital stage in the process – it is only when we ask the customer questions and listen to what they say to us, that we can firstly, identify what their financial needs are and secondly decide what products we have that could help the customer to satisfy these needs.

It is important to emphasise that we cannot make assumptions about what the customers needs are likely to be, rather we must allow them to tell us. For this approach to be successful we must listen to what the customer is really saying – not what we think they are going to say.

When we explore and listen we are communicating with the customer. Communication can be described as:

The interchange of thoughts, opinions, or information by speech, writing, or signs (Anderson, 1992).

QUICK QUESTION

Look at the above definition – what do you think is the most important word in it?

Write your answer here before reading on.

The key word is interchange. For communication to work it must be a two-way process – in other words, there must be feedback. When you consult with the customer, to communicate effectively there should be a dialogue between you and your customer.

QUICK QUESTION

What methods do we use to communicate?

Write your answer here before reading on.

We communicate in two ways:

- Verbally
- Non-verbally

The more common of these forms of communication is the non-verbal. **Non-verbal communication** accounts for two thirds of our communication.

To be successful at identifying customer needs, you must be an excellent listener.

QUICK QUESTION

What is the first thing an excellent listener must do?

Write your answer here before reading on.

The first thing you must do to be an excellent listener is to ask the right questions.

QUICK QUESTION

What is an open question?

Write your answer here before reading on.

An **open question** is one that cannot be answered with a simple yes or no. Open questions always begin with one of the following words:

- Who
- What
- Where
- When
- Why
- How

Open questions are used to gather information from the customer. Therefore they are the predominantly used questions during the explore and listen phase of the process.

Open questions allow the customer to tell you what their current situation is, what their aspirations are, what financial products they currently have, what their financial and lifestyle goals are, etc. This is all vital information for you to use in the next stage of the process, when you identify and agree needs with the customer.

There are two further points to keep in mind about open questions:

- Once you have asked the question, you must then be quiet. There is often a temptation to answer the question for the customer, especially if they seem a little reticent. If you listen to people talking, you will be amazed at how often an open question is asked and then the person asking the question goes on to answer it. For example, 'what kind of car are you going to buy with your car loan – the same make as your last one?'

- Silence can be an effective open question. Most people find silence in any conversation unpleasant, unless they know the other person really well. This is especially true if they feel that they are in a tense situation. So if you want the customer to expand on what they have just said, the best policy is to say nothing. In a very short space of time, the customer will start talking again to break the silence.

QUICK QUESTION

Write down five open questions that you could use during the explore and listen phase of the process.

Write your answer here before reading on.

There are obviously lots of questions that you could have. Here are five:

- What are your financial goals for the next 10 years?
- What are your plans for retirement?
- When will your children go to university?
- What improvement plans do you have for your home?
- How do you plan to repay your mortgage?

The opposite question to an open question is a **closed question**. This is a question that the other person can answer fully with a simple yes or no.

Closed questions have their place in the process when looking for the customer to confirm information. They can be put to particularly good effect when overcoming objections or closing, which will be discussed later.

Closed questions are not so effective during the explore and listen phase as they will restrict the amount of information that you are gathering in from the customer.

A lot of people fall into the trap of asking too many closed questions. However, with a little thought, you can change these into open questions.

QUESTION TIME 3

Consider the following closed questions and re-draft them as open questions.

- Are you here for the Festival?

- Have you booked a holiday this year?

- Are you working in the theatre?

- Are you happy with our product range?

- Do you work locally?

- Did you hear about us though a colleague?

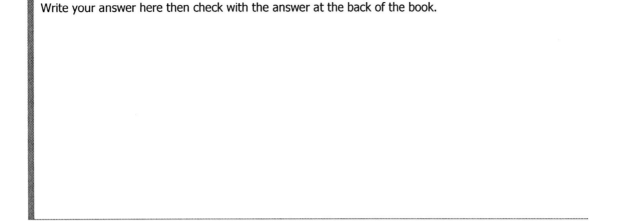

Write your answer here then check with the answer at the back of the book.

Having asked the right questions, you now need to listen to what the customer has to say. A technique to help you listen better is called 'active listening'.

QUICK QUESTION

What do you think is meant by active listening?

Write your answer here before reading on.

Active listening is a way of communicating to another person that you are listening carefully to them. As the other person feels that they are being listened to, they are likely to give more information. Active listening comprises of:

- Taking notes of what the other person is saying. In a consultative situation as a matter of courtesy to the customer, you should always ask for their permission for you to take notes.

- Maintain strong, genuine eye contact with the other person.

- Nod as the other person is talking to you. Also, putting your head slightly to one side will also encourage the other person.

- Make 'encouraging noises', for example, I see, yes, uh-huh, etc.

- Summarise or paraphrase what the other person has said.

By summarising, you are demonstrating that you have heard and understood what the customer has said. Summarising will also improve your recall as you are imprinting the information in your mind. Also, if you have mis-interpreted what the customer has said, when you summarise, they will be able to put you right.

As mentioned earlier, our non-verbal communication is felt to be around two thirds of our total communication.

QUICK QUESTION

What do you think non-verbal communication is?

Write your answer here before reading on.

We all communicate non-verbally and we have done it since we were born. Most babies cry from the moment they were born – at this point they are communicating hunger, fear, cold, etc.

We communicate non-verbally in the following ways.

- By body movement – if you move around in a clumsy way, you can communicate nerves to the customer, which may make them doubt your ability. On the other hand, leaning slightly forward can create interest. Crossing your arms and legs whilst also turning your shoulder towards the customer is a very defensive position to adopt and is unlikely to build rapport with the customer.

- Facial expression – you should match your facial expression to the message you are communicating. Therefore, if you have to turn a customer down for a loan, you shouldn't smile as you tell them. Frowning can make a customer feel uneasy and form the opinion that you do not trust or believe them..

- Eyes – by maintaining eye contact with a customer you are maintaining the positive relationship you built with them during the introduction phase. If the customer is talking and you give them no eye contact, it is very difficult for them to continue talking.

- Gestures – if you continually repeat a gesture in front of a customer, the gesture becomes a mannerism which will only serve to distract the customer. Aim to have open hand gestures to demonstrate confidence and trustworthiness.

- Voice – remember earlier when we discussed how important tone of voice is to impact. Similarly, as the conversation develops, you should match your tone of voice to the words that you are saying.

Be aware that whilst we all communicate non-verbally, we can send out messages that the customer doesn't always pick up on, or may misinterpret. If someone folds their arms, that may be interpreted as adopting a defensive stance – but the person may have folded their arms as they are feeling cold.

The important point to bear in mind about non-verbal communication is to think how you can use your non-verbal communication to back up the message you are sending to the customer. Also if you are picking up non-verbal signals from the customer, don't rely on only one piece of information, rather test this information to see if you can validate it.

Throughout the explore and listen stage you are working to find out what the customers needs are – these needs may be apparent to the customer or you may, during the conversation, discover needs that the customer is not, as yet, aware of – these are called 'hidden needs'.

During this stage you are discovering what the customers needs are and taking notes, you have not, as yet, spoken about your product(s). This is because you need as much information as you can get about the customer so that once you do start to talk about products, then they are the right ones for this customer.

You are now able to move to the next stage, where you can identify the customer's needs and agree these with the customer.

13.5 Identify and agree needs with the customer

This stage is important as it provides the link between the information gathering stage of the process and the point where the banker will introduce to the customer the products that their organisation can provide that will satisfy these needs.

By this stage in the process, a lot of information about the customer has been gathered – indeed the customer should have done most of the talking by this stage.

There is now enough information to be able to select what the most important financial needs of the customer are and you should explain to the customer what you perceive these needs to be. You should also ask the customer to confirm that they agree that these indeed are their financial needs.

QUICK QUESTION

Why do you think that it is important to have the customer agree what their financial needs are?

Write your answer here before reading on.

Once the customer can see clearly what their financial needs are, it is more likely that in the next stage of the process they will be able to see how the products recommended to them will meet these needs and be of benefit to them. As a result, it will be easier to gain their commitment when closing.

QUICK QUESTION

What could you say to the customer to outline their needs and gain their commitment?

Write your answer here before reading on.

You will say something along the lines of:

'So Ms West, from what we have discussed so far, it seems to me that you need to make provision for your pension if you wish to retire at 65 and you also need a savings plan to help support your son through university in seven years time. Is this an accurate reflection of our discussions?'

The customer will either agree or disagree. If they agree at this stage, the banker is now able to move straight into the next stage of the process – introducing products to meet these needs.

On the other hand, if the customer disagrees, it is necessary to find out why. Is it because the banker did not listen carefully enough to the customer, or perhaps the use of questions was not good enough to unearth a need that the customer thinks is pressing, but they have not yet told you about? Whatever the reason, the dialogue needs to continue until you feel that you now know the customers needs and you get the customer to agree these new needs. When this happens, you are in a position to move into the next stage.

13.6   Introduce product(s) to meet needs

You are now able to talk about the product(s) we discussed earlier in the chapter.

A lot of people fall at this hurdle as they do not take the time to look at their product from the customer's point of view. As a result, they talk about their product in terms of features rather than benefits. As a result, they tell every customer the same things about the product.

Rather than tell the customer everything there is to tell about the product, the successful salesperson will only discuss those aspects of the product that are of interest to the customer. By doing this, they will not bombard the customer with a lot of information that is of no interest to them.

Another disadvantage to this approach is that if you are saying the same things to every customer, you will quickly become bored with what you are saying and this will come across in the way that we communicate with the customer. For example, your tone of voice may become flat and you give the perception that you are not interested in what you are saying. Remember that the way you look and sound have a far greater impact with the customer than the words that you use.

To be successful, you must let the customer see what the product can do for them – so you are making a connection between the product and the specific needs that the customer has told you about earlier in the conversation. When you do this, you will talk to the customer in terms of product benefits, rather than product features.

QUICK QUESTION

What is a product feature?

Write your answer here before reading on.

A feature is something that the product has. Every product will have a huge amount of features and the features for the same product will not vary from customer to customer. For example, here are some product features of a car:

- Five doors
- Power assisted steering
- Airbags
- 50 litre fuel tank
- 1400 engine
- Metallic silver colour
- Tinted glass
- Windscreen washers front and rear
- Third rear brake light

The list goes on and one – however, every model of the same car has exactly the same features.

QUICK QUESTION

List some of the features of a product that you have recently promoted to a customer?

Write your answer here before reading on.

The list will vary depending on the organisation you work for and the product that you have chosen. However, here are some generic features associated with financial services products:

- Fixed monthly repayments
- Rate of interest
- Unlimited withdrawals
- Able to use the card to pay for goods and services at the point of sale or online
- Monthly statements

QUICK QUESTION

What is a benefit?

Write your answer here before reading on.

A benefit is what a feature can do for an individual customer that will meet the needs of that particular customer.

For example, fixed monthly repayments means that a customer is able to budget more easily and so their account won't go overdrawn – as a result they won't have to pay service charge. However what is the benefit to the customer? The benefit is that they save money by not paying service charge. In this example, every customer who takes this product will have fixed monthly repayments, but you would only talk to a customer about this feature being able to save them money if you knew that this was of interest to them. It is important that you explain to them how the fixed monthly repayment can save them money rather than just state that there are fixed monthly repayments. If you only mention fixed monthly repayments, the customer may not make the connection and so a sales winning benefit can be lost.

QUICK QUESTION

If a car has a high level brake light, what would a potential benefit of this feature be?

Write your answer here before reading on.

If a car has this feature, it is statistically less likely that the car will suffer a rear-end collision. However the benefit of this for a customer is increased safety. Again, a car salesperson would only mention this if during the conversation, the potential customer had agreed that safety was an important need of theirs.

If you only talk in terms of features, as you mention each feature, the customer could say 'so what?' For example, if you rhyme off that the savings plan you are recommending to this customer has a rate of interest that will be credited to the plan monthly, the customer can legitimately say 'so what?'. This is because they do not necessarily know what this means to them. Rather you could say that monthly interest means that the capital value of the plan will grow more quickly and so they should be able to retire at 65 – which they told you during the explore and listen part of the process.

Customers must be able to see what the product can do for them. This is often referred to as WIFFM, which means:

What's
In
It
For
Me?

If a customer cannot see what's in it for them, then they are very unlikely to take the product. You cannot assume that the customer will see what's in it for them and so you must take the responsibility of explaining this to them.

Promoting benefits allows you to personalise the product to each customer. This means that each conversation you have with customers about the same product will be different as each customers needs are different. This allows you to explain the product differently to each customer and so you avoid appearing stale to the customer.

When you are talking in terms of benefits you personalise the product in front of the customer and let them know what the product can do for them.

To do this, you must be able to look at things from the customer's perspective.

Consider - does a customer have any desire to have a mortgage? No, what they want is to buy their new home – therefore, that's what you should focus in on when talking benefits.

Similarly, do customers' really want to put their hard earned cash into a savings plan every month? No, what they really want to do is to provide for their children's' education – so the focus of your benefit statements should be on that.

However, to get to benefits, you will still need to mention the relevant product features to the customer. The phrases you should use to link to the benefits are:

'...which means that.... and`...so...'

If we look at the example of the car earlier, the salesperson could say something like:

'You mentioned earlier that safety for you and your family is one of your prime needs. You will see that this car has a third rear brake light, **which means that** you are statistically less likely to have a rear end collision, **so** it is a safer car than the one you are presently driving.'

Had the salesperson merely pointed out the third rear brake light, the customer should have said to themselves 'so what?' as they may not have made the connection between this and increased safety.

QUICK QUESTION

Write a benefit statement for a customer who has stated that they like to keep a tight control on their finances and are interested in a product of yours that provides online banking.

Write your answer here before reading on.

Your statement should be along the following lines:

'You mentioned earlier that you like to keep on top of your financial affairs. This account allows you to have access to internet banking, which means that you can check on your accounts every day and, if necessary switch funds from your savings account to your current account, so you have peace of mind that your accounts are in order.'

It is often said that promoting a service is more difficult than promoting a tangible product. Once way to overcome this is by painting pictures in the customer's mind of what your service can do for them. There are also some visual aids that you could use, for example:

- Leaflets
- Quote illustrations

You should always have a good stock of current leaflets wherever you are seeing customers. Once you have identified the product to meet the customer's needs, you can use the appropriate leaflet to back up what you are saying to the customer. It is also useful to personalise the leaflet to the customer – for example by circling or highlighting those parts of the leaflet or brochure that directly meet the needs that you have agreed with the customer. Then when the customer takes the leaflet away, they can see clearly those areas that are of interest to them. This is particularly important if they need to talk to a spouse or partner about the product.

Another type of visual aid you can use is a product quote. The technology systems used in financial services will now allow you to print out a quote to illustrate, for example, the repayment schedule on a personal loan or a mortgage. Often you will also have the opportunity to show this illustration in the form of a graph, whereby the customer can see clearly how their monthly payments reduce the capital and interest elements of the loan to end up with a zero balance.

Until now, things have been going really well – you have carried out your preparation, you have met the customer and built rapport with them before asking them questions and listening to the replies to determine what the customers needs are. You have also agreed these needs with the customer and explained to the customer what products you have that could meet these needs and explained the customer the benefits. You could almost look to close at this point – but life doesn't always run as smoothly as this. At any time after you have met the customer you could meet with resistance – in other words, you will have to deal with objections. That is what we will move on to look at next in the process.

13.7   Overcoming objections

We are now moving on to the part of the process that many people fear most...overcoming objections. An objection can occur at any stage in the process – it is when the potential customer makes some negative comment about the product, which on the face of it, appears to be a reason for them not to take the product. If you don't deal with the objection properly, then it may become a strong reason for them not to take the product. We will look in this section at ways to deal with objections professionally and so make the customer even more likely to take you up on a product that will be of use to them.

QUICK QUESTION

Should objections be viewed as something positive or something negative?

Write your answer here before reading on.

You should always view an objection positively.

There are a number of reasons for this:

- An objection is a signal of interest form the customer. If they had no interest in what you are talking about, they could simply tell you so. However, if they are objecting about some aspect of the product, they must be thinking seriously about taking it.

- When you answer an objection, you are dealing with an area of specific interest to the customer. In stating the objection, the customer highlights what they are concerned about – if you can allay their fears, then you are likely to have a customer who is keen to sign up for the product.

- Objections can often allow you to move swiftly to the close. As stated on the last two points, when you get objections, you are dealing with the areas of particular concern to the customer – however, if you can resolve these concerns, the likelihood is that the customer will now want to take the product and so you may move straight to the close.

Look on objections positively – they are stepping stones on the way to the close. Even if you get a number of objections, as you resolve each one, you are one step closer to winning the business.

You should never take objections personally – always remember that the customer is objecting to some aspect of the product; they are not objecting to you, so do not take it as such. By keeping this in mind, you will avoid becoming embroiled in an argument with the customer.

QUICK QUESTION

Why do you think that we get objections?

Write your answer here before reading on.

Objections can arise for a number of reasons:

- You may already have told the customer the information that they are asking you for – but they were not listening. When you respond to the objection, you should avoid saying things like 'I've told you this already!' Rather take the time to explain this patiently to them again.

- The customer may have misunderstood you. Although you gave them this information, they may have picked you up wrongly – for example, the customer may be looking for a product that pays interest monthly. You may well have told them this, but they have picked up wrongly that you said interest is paid six monthly – so their objection could be that the account doesn't meet their needs as they don't get monthly interest. In this situation, all you have to do to is tactfully correct the misunderstanding and you have resolved the objection.

- The objection may be what is called a 'true objection' in that there is a **limiting factor** in the product that the customer is not happy about. For example, they may feel that the fixed charge on a current account is too high, or that the interest rate you are quoting for a personal loan is not as competitive as that charged by one of your competitors. When faced with a true objection, you should:

    – Use the information gained during explore and listen to show the customer that whilst there is a limitation to the product, it is more than compensated for by the agreed benefits of the account.

    – Choose another product that better meets this customer's needs.

Before moving on to look at the process you should follow to resolve an objection, there are a few points to think about before you answer the objection.

QUICK QUESTION

What should you think about before answering an objection?

Write your answer here before reading on.

No one looks forward to hearing an objection, and the thought of receiving an objection can make many people feel nervous. However, you should keep the following points in mind.

- Let the customer finish talking – if the objection makes you feel nervous, it is tempting to jump in with a response before the customer has finished talking. However, the customer may feel nervous about objecting and being interrupted won't help their state of mind. It can irritate them and make the eventual sale less likely.

- Show that you are interested in the objection – even if the customer is objecting to something you have already told them, don't show any impatience – after all, the objection is real to the customer.

- Don't rush your response – use a short pause before dealing with the objection to convey to the customer's subconscious that you are considering the response. Even if this is an objection that you have heard and deal with 100 times before, it is the first time for the customer, so deal with the objection courteously.

Objections are classified under the term real objections and hidden objections.

QUICK QUESTION

What do we mean by hidden objection?

Write your answer here before reading on.

A real objection is a genuine objection about the product that the customer has and once answered will clear the matter up in the mind of the customer.

On the other hand, a hidden objection is one that hides behind a smokescreen. The customer may feel uneasy about voicing their real objection so they make up another objection in the hope that this will get them out of having to state what their real objection is. Consider the following example:

You are going to go to a night out and decide to buy a new pair of shoes. You see a pair that you really like and would go well with what you are planning to wear to the night out. You go into the shop and ask of they have the shoe in your size – they do and you try the shoes on. You are really happy with the shoes, and then the fateful moment – you look at the shoebox and see that the price of the shoes is double the amount you are willing to pay?

QUICK QUESTION

What do many people do in this situation?

Write your answer here before reading on.

Most people are embarrassed about saying that the price is too high, so they start to make other objections to get them out of the shop. The types of thing they could say are:

- I don't like the colour
- They aren't comfortable
- They won't go with what I'm planning to wear

If the salesperson is able to overcome these objections, you will eventually have to state what the real objection is...probably much to your embarrassment.

This can happen in any situation – the customer may not be happy saying what they really object to and so put up a smokescreen. You must get through the smokescreen as quickly as possible to give you the opportunity of dealing with the true objection. You will then be able to either overcome the objection; or if the objection is insurmountable, you won't waste any more time on business that you are not going to win.

So, how should we deal with objections?

We are going to look at a model which should help overcome objections. To help your understanding of this material, think about an objection that you could hear from a customer and write it down in the space below. You will use this as we work through the model.

An objection I could hear from a customer is...

The model is:

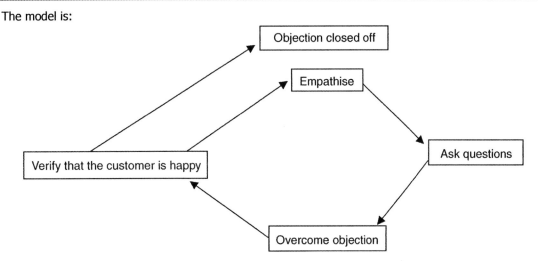

Let's work through this model, focussing on how we can use it to overcome objections. The starting point is empathise':

Empathise

Empathy is being able to show another person that you understand how they feel, but without necessarily agreeing with what they are saying. It is vital to display empathy with the customer to avoid the possibility of ending up in an argument with the customer.

Also, as the customer may feel nervous about voicing an objection, showing empathy will help calm the customer.

QUICK QUESTION

Using the objection you have noted above, write down what you could say to empathise with the customer.

Write your answer here before reading on.

The terminology you will use will vary depending upon what the customer is objecting about and what your relationship is with the customer.

Phrases that show empathy include:

- I can understand that you think this...
- It does appear that way on the surface...
- A number of other customers feel that way...
- When this product was introduced I thought this too...

By showing this empathy you are demonstrating to the customer that you can see things from their point of view.

It is important to note that at this stage you are showing that you understand the **sentiment** behind what they are saying, but you are not agreeing with the **content** of the comment. This is an important differentiation to make – if you are seen to agree with the content of the objection, when you try to overcome the objection later on, then you will be contradicting yourself! So, you must avoid phrases like:

- I agree...
- You are right...
- That's a valid point...

Displaying empathy will let the customer see that you are not going to move into a confrontational situation with them – it also displays that you are confident in the product and will be able to overcome the objection.

Empathy helps to take the sting out of the objection. Although it may be tempting to jump straight in to answer the objection, you are not ready to do that yet. To have a successful outcome, you need to spend the time at the start showing the customer that you can see things from their perspective – displaying empathy helps you to do that.

Even after empathising, you are still not in a position to answer the objection – you need to move to stage two in the process – ask questions.

QUICK QUESTION

Why do we need to ask questions at this stage?

Write your answer here before reading on.

It is easy to assume that we know what it is that the customer is objecting to, only to find that after we have answered the objection that the customers says '…that's not what I meant!' To avoid this happening, you should ask open questions to the customer to make sure that you are absolutely clear what the customer's objection is.

Either once you have had the customer answer your questions, or if the objection is so stated clearly at the start, you should summarise what the objection is.

QUICK QUESTION

Why do you want to summarise the objection at this stage?

Write your answer here before reading on.

By summarising, you are doing a number of things.

- Firstly, you show the customer that you have been listening to them – remember in the Explore and Listen section, we saw that a component of active listening was summarising.

- You are giving yourself some time to think of how you are going to overcome the objection.

- You are again taking any potential heat out of the situation by acting in a non-confrontational way.

If you feel that this objection is all that stands between you and the customer signing up for the product, you can test this by saying something like:

- 'If I am able to show you that for your circumstances, our savings plan will give you a greater return that the plan you currently have, then would you like to go ahead?'

When you say this, the customer will either agree or disagree. If they agree, then all you need to do is overcome the objection, then you can move to the close. On the other hand, if the customer says no, you can now find out what the other hidden objections are, so at least you now know what you are dealing with.

QUICK QUESTION

Again, using your sample objection from earlier, show how you would summarise the customer's objection.

Write your answer here before reading on.

What you have written down will vary depending upon what the objection is. However, here are some suggestions:

- So, you are unsure of how this account will pay you a greater annual return than the account that you currently have with National Bank?

- Am I right in thinking that you feel that the arrangement fee quoted is excessive?

If you wanted to test that either of these were the only objections between you and the close, you could say:

- If I can show to you that this account will give you a greater annual return than the account you currently have with National Bank, then would you be willing to transfer the account today?

- If I can show you that our arrangement fees are reasonable for the work involved in setting up this account, would you be willing to open the account today?

You can see the use of closed questions in both of these examples. In this situation, we are not looking for the customer to expand on what they have already said – rather we are looking for confirmation – hence the use of closed questions. However, you should not take this approach with every objection you receive, as you run the risk of wishing to push the customer into taking the product. This approach is useful if you are confident that this is the only objection that lies between you and a successful sale.

At last – you are now in a situation to actually answer the objection that the customer has given you. By using the first two steps in the process you are in a much better position to be able to be successful actually answering the objection. This is because:

- You have preserved your relationship with the customer, by using empathy.

- You are quite clear about what exactly the customer is objecting about.

- You are calmer when overcoming the objection than you would have been had you jumped straight into an attempt to overcome the objection.

If the objection arises from a misunderstanding on the customer's part, you should clarify the misunderstanding at this stage.

It could also be that the customer sees one limitation of the product but you can overcome this by restating the benefits that you have agreed with the customer earlier. For example, if the customer objects that the monthly fee for a packaged current account is too high, but they have been greatly attracted by the benefits of the extras they would receive with this product, then you should remind them of the benefits of the product to overcome the fee objection.

By talking to the customer again in terms of benefits, you are looking at the situation from their perspective.

There are also different general tactics you can use when dealing with objections. For example:

The cautionary tale	This is used when a customer makes an objection and you paint a picture of what could happen if they didn't take the product you are suggesting.
	▪ If you have suggested to a self-employed customer that they take level term assurance and they object to the premiums. You could point out what would be the consequences for their family if something were to happen to them.
The lowest common denominator	When a customer is objecting to the annual fee for a product you should break the cost down to what the cost is per month, per week, or even per day.
	This is particularly effective if you then relate the cost to the price of an everyday item. For example, if a customer is objecting to the cost of a premium, you may break the cost down to be 50p per day – you can then link this to the cost of their daily newspaper, or a chocolate bar..

If you have worked through the entire process, then it will be easier to overcome any objection as you will have lots of information about the customer that you can use to your advantage.

QUICK QUESTION

Again, using the objection example you noted down earlier, write down how you would actually overcome this objection.

Write your answer here before reading on.

As with the previous examples, the text you have written will vary according to your objection. Here are some examples of the types of phrase you may have:

▪ You receive interest on this account monthly, as this interest is added to the capital sum, your next interest payment will be even higher and so by the end of the period, you can see that your total return is greater than under your current plan – so you make more money.

▪ This account does have an arrangement fee which covers the administration costs in settling up the loan account. However, you only need to pay this when the account is opened. On the other hand, if you chose an overdraft, then you would need to pay an annual arrangement fee to renew the overdraft – so you can see that choosing this account will save you money in the longer term.

It would be tempting at this stage to feel that we have dealt with the objection and either move on, or attempt to close the sale.

 QUICK QUESTION

What do you not know at this stage?

Write your answer here before reading on.

What you do not know at the moment is whether the customer thinks that you have dealt with the objection to their satisfaction. If you have not, you are highly unlikely to close – but you won't know this until you attempt to close...then you will need to go back to the overcoming objections stage.

You need to get the customer's agreement to move on. This is done by simply asking the customer if they are happy with your response.

If the customer is happy, you are getting their confirmation of this and so you are more likely to win the business. On the other hand if the customer is not happy with your answer, by asking them you can find out what aspect they are not happy with and you can move through the objection resolution model again. The advantage of this approach is that if you find out what the customer is not happy about, you are still in control and in a position to do something about it.

A further advantage of verifying with the customer that they are happy with your response is that you display confidence in your ability and, as was mentioned earlier, a prospective customer is far more likely to do business with a confident person.

Having dealt successfully with any objections that the customer may have, you are now able to ask the customer for their business – you can close.

13.8 Closing

Again a lot of inexperienced staff do not like this stage of the process – probably because they do not want to appear to be pushy. As a result, they do not close and allow the prospective customer to walk out of the door. This is a pity as, if they have used the process we have been working through, the customer is now aware of what their unsatisfied financial needs are – indeed this awareness could have been heightened by the person successfully overcoming any objections that they have. However, the conversation will have petered out as the individual felt uncomfortable about asking for the business, so it was probably left that the customer would take a leaflet or brochure with them and call the person at some point in the future.

Another reason for some people not wanting to close is that there is a fear of rejection – what if the customer says no? It is important to bear in mind that no one ever has a 100% success level with customers, so you will experience customers saying no from time to time – so it is important to acknowledge this and build up some resistance to it.

However even if the customer does say that they don't want the product, you can still find out why they feel this way. It may then be that you are given an objection to deal with and if you can overcome this objection, then you are on your way to getting the business. On the other hand, if the customer is still

BPP
LEARNING MEDIA

adamant that they don't want the product, then you can accept this and concentrate on those customers who do have a need for your bank's products.

You will remember the point made earlier that customers are far more likely to buy from a professional and confident person – if you have not asked for the business, then you appear to be lacking in both of these qualities.

Also keep in mind that by using the process we are working through, by the time you get to closing, it is likely that the customer will want the product as you have agreed with them that they have a need for it and will have overcome any objections that they may have had. So the chances are that all you need to do at this stage is to close.

You should also keep in mind that closing does not always mean getting the customer to take a product. Depending on your role, your 'business' may be getting the customer to agree to have an appointment with another member of staff – say a financial advisor to discuss some of the bank's regulated products, or perhaps someone from a specialised head office department, perhaps to discuss your organisation drafting a will for the customer and agreeing to act as their executor.

QUICK QUESTION

If you don't close, what do you think the customer is likely to do?

Write your answer here before reading on.

As the customer now has an unsatisfied need, they are motivated to take steps to satisfy the need – unfortunately, they are most likely to go to a competitor organisation. So, by not asking for the business, you have done all of the hard work – for your competitor.

Asking for the business is crucial, so let's look at how we know when the time is right to attempt to close the sale and also what the different types of close are.

The right time to close is when the customer is at the top of the buying plateau. This can be expressed diagrammatically:

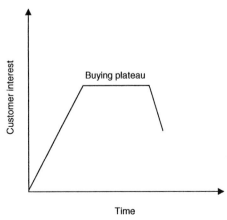

As the conversation between you and the customer develops, you are increasing the customer's interest in the product – this is done through a combination of the steps we have discussed in this process. Eventually, the customer's interest will reach a peak – this is called the 'buying plateau'. When the customer is on the buying plateau, you should close.

If you do not close at this point, the customer's interest will eventually wane – they will be come bored and lose interest in the product. When this happens, it will become very difficult for you to get the business.

You will see from the above, that if you attempt to close too early, the situation is not lost – you can always keep the process going, and then have another go at closing later. However, if you leave the close until too late and the customer has moved off the buying plateau, then you will probably have lost the business altogether.

 QUICK QUESTION

How do you know that a customer is on the buying plateau?

Write your answer here before reading on.

The customer will let you know that they are ready to buy by displaying '**buying signal**s'. However, often these buying signals are discrete and so you must be able to detect them and act upon them when seen.

Buying signals may be either involuntary buying signals or voluntary buying signals.

 QUICK QUESTION

What is an involuntary buying signal?

Write your answer here before reading on.

An involuntary buying signal is one where the customer displays that they are interested in the product through their non-verbal communication. They could show this interest by:

- Looking more interested than they were earlier – for example, by sitting further forward, nodding their head more or giving stronger eye contact.

- Looking more specifically at any leaflets or illustrations you may have been using.

QUICK QUESTION

What is a voluntary buying signal?

Write your answer here before reading on.

A voluntary buying signal is one that is usually more apparent and less open to misinterpretation. Voluntary buying signals include:

- Asking very pointed questions about the product. For example, asking how long it will take for the plastic card to be produced, how long before the loan proceeds are credited to the account, how soon an appointment could be made with a financial advisor, etc.

- If there are two customers they may talk to one another about how well the product will meet their needs.

When you see these signals then the time is right to move in to close.

QUICK QUESTION

How do you close in on a deal?

Write your answer here before reading on.

There are a variety of ways to close a sale – you should seek to use a range of them depending on circumstances.

The closing techniques we will look at are:

- Ask for the business
- The either/or close
- The assumptive close
- The cautionary tale
- Closing on an objection
- The 'yes' close
- The narrowing the options close

Ask for the business

This is the simplest close of all to use. Here you will have worked through the process with the customer and in doing so will have answered any questions and objections that they may have. Once you have done this there is nothing else to do but close the deal.

The danger at this point is that the customer will often be waiting for you to take the lead and ask for the business. If you don't, then you run the risk of losing out as we discussed at the start of this section – the customer may lose interest and move off the buying plateau. Therefore it is imperative that you simply ask the customer if they would now like to go ahead and order the product.

QUICK QUESTION

What is it vital to do once you have asked for the business?

Write your answer here before reading on.

Once you have asked for the business, you must maintain eye contact with the customer and maintain silence until they speak.

If you are nervous at this point, then the pause before the customer speaks to you may seem long...but you **must** allow the customer to speak next. They will either say to you that they are happy to proceed, or they may give you another objection. If they do give you an objection, answer that as discussed earlier, then ask for the business once more.

If you do talk before the customer has replied to you, then you are simply going to start talking about the product again and could even end up losing the business if the customer has moved off the buying plateau.

The either/or close

This is where you give the customer a choice – but the choice includes closing. Therefore, once the customer has made the choice, they have also agreed to close on the sale.

QUICK QUESTION

What options could you give the customer with an either/or close?

Write your answer here before reading on.

There are a host of options here. Some include:

- Based on the figures we have discussed, would taking the loan over 24 or 36 months best fit your budget?
- Would you like the appointment with the financial advisor to be on Wednesday afternoon, or some time next week?

Once the customer has chosen the option they would prefer, they have also told you that they would like to take the product.

The assumptive close

This close assumes that the customer will go ahead and take the product without being asked formally.

This can be an effective technique to use if you are completing some form of documentation with the customer. Once the form is complete, all you have to do is print it off and ask the customer to sign. Again, by signing, the customer is agreeing to take the product and so the close is completed in a subtle manner.

You can also use a variation of this technique when dealing with the customer over the phone. Say, the customer has phoned to discuss a personal loan. Once you have gathered enough information to make a decision and have given the customer repayment figures, you can explain to the customer that you will print the form off and post it to them for signature.

The cautionary tale

You will remember that we discussed the cautionary tale when dealing with objections.

This technique can also be used when closing – for example, when the customer does not want some additional aspect of the product, or even the whole of the product. To use the cautionary tale you paint the downside of not taking this product to let the customer see that signing up for the product will better meet the customer's needs. Once the customer has made this decision, then matters are concluded.

Close on an objection

Again, in the objections section we discussed how you can test if a customer only has one objection to your product by saying something like… 'If I can show to you that this account will give you a greater annual return than the account you currently have with National Bank, then would you be willing to transfer the account today?'

In this scenario, provided that you can overcome the objection to the customer's satisfaction, then you have closed the deal. When the customer has confirmed that they are happy that the objection has been overcome, then you can simply ask the customer for the business at that stage.

The 'yes' close

This technique involves the use of closed questions.

Here we use closed questions to have the customer agreeing on:

- What their needs are
- How the product meets their needs
- That the price of the product is one that the customer is happy with

Then by asking for the customer's authority to proceed, the customer will again agree and the sale is closed.

Narrowing the options close

This final technique is used where the customer has been presented with a variety of products, or options within products to meet their needs. By removing those that the customer is less interested in, we can reduce the customer's choice to more manageable proportions, thus making the buying decision easier for the customer. Again, once the customer has made this choice, then we have closed, as the inference all along has been that the customer will take the product, we are just discussing how to best tailor the product to meet their needs.

An example of this type of close would be where a customer is looking for some form of money transmission account. Your organisation has a number of products that offer this. However there are a number of varying features on these products, which results in different terms and conditions for each product (for example, there may be a minimum level of balance on once account, a monthly fee on another account, a preferential overdraft interest rate on a third, a better credit interest rate on a fourth, and so on)

Faced with a wide number of choices, the final buying decision may be too much for the customer to take in and there is a risk that they become overwhelmed by all of this and decide to ...go away to think about it....

We can make this decision easier for the customer by removing from the decision-making process those products that do not offer the best benefits to meet the customer's needs. For example, if the customer has told you earlier in the conversation that they do not envisage having an overdraft on the account, then you can, with the customer's agreement, withdraw that particular product from the equation. Thus you have made the customer's buying decision easier.

Before leaving the subject of closing, we will look at the situation mentioned above where the customer says that they '...want to go away to think about it....'

QUICK QUESTION

How would you deal with a customer who says this?

Write your answer here before reading on.

There are a couple of issues to consider here:

- Firstly, this may be a genuine point made by the customer, in that they want to mull over what you have explained to them; compare your product with that of a competitor; or discuss the product with someone else.

- On the other hand, it may be that they are not sure if the product actually meets their needs as you have not done your job as well as you could have.

QUICK QUESTION

If the customer genuinely wants to mull the situation over, or talk to someone else, what could you do to stay in control of the situation?

Write your answer here before reading on.

In this scenario, it is easy to lose control of the situation and things are left in limbo as there is no agreement between you and the customer as to what will happen next. To overcome this, you should agree with the customer that they should take some time to consider the product – you should also agree a timescale with the customer and you can retain control by advising the customer that you will contact them at the end of this period.

By doing this, even in the worst scenario – namely if the customer says that they no longer want the product, you can find out what the underlying reasons are. Then you may be able to:

- Use the objection resolution model to overcome this resistance
- Advise the customer that there is another product that may better meet their needs
- Accept the customer's decision

If you need to accept the customer's decision – perhaps there is a limitation with your product that cannot be overcome – then you are still maintaining a relationship with the customer and may still be able to do business with them at some point in the future.

By this stage in the process you have been successful in promoting a product to your customer. However, if this product meets the needs of this customer, then it is likely that it will meet the needs of similar customers. A quick and easy way to find this out is to ask the customer for a referral – i.e. someone else that they know who could also benefit from the product.

13.9 Asking for referrals

A referral occurs when we ask one customer if they know of anyone whom they feel could also benefit from our products and services. Then when we contact this person, we already have some connection with them, which can make it easier to build the relationship with them and so ultimately, to sell to them.

However, before we get to this point, we need to think about the best time to ask a customer to give us a referral.

QUICK QUESTION

When do you think is the best time to ask a customer for a referral?

Write your answer here before reading on.

You certainly don't want to ask for referrals when the customer is in to make a complaint.

To have the best chance of getting a referral, you need to choose a time when the customer is happy with the service they are receiving from your organisation. This could be when:

- You have just sold them a product that they need.

- They have expressed satisfaction to you about the levels of service you have given them.

- You have gone the extra mile for the customer in some way and again they express their satisfaction.

It is best not to think of referral seeking as an extra part of your job – rather, it is something that you should always be looking out for and as soon as you spot the opportunity, ask for the referral. After all, the worst thing the customer can say is that they don't want to give you anyone's name.

QUICK QUESTION

What should you agree with the customer once you have obtained a referral from them?

Write your answer here before reading on.

You should always agree how the referral is going to be contacted. It may be that:

- The customer would like to position your approach with the referral before you contact them. If this is the case, you need to agree with the customer how you will know when this has been done. In this situation, you may want to give the customer a business card with your details on it for them to pass on to the referral.

- The customer is happy for you to contact the referral directly, merely stating that you have been given their name from the referral source.

QUICK QUESTION

If the customer cannot think of a referral name whilst they are with you, what could you do to still have a chance of obtaining a referral from them?

Write your answer here before reading on.

You could still give the customer your details on a business card and ask them to think about this for a couple of days. You should also agree with the customer that you will call them at the end of this period to see if they now have a referral for you.

If you were involved with a profession that was only interested in one off promotions, then this would mark the end of the process. However, in financial services, we are focussed on the client-centred approach. So, there is still something we can do to complete the process – after care.

13.10 After care

Think about a time when you have made a major purchase. You probably spent a lot of time researching the right product and talking to different organisations that could supply you with this product. Then you had to choose which organisation you were going to buy the product from. After all of that, you placed your order and waited for delivery.

How did you feel once you had placed the order? Were you happy or did you still have a few lingering doubts about how well you had made your decision?

If you felt the latter way, then you were experiencing something that most people feel once they have made a major purchase – this is called '**buyers' remorse**'.

Buyers' remorse is when you being to have some negative thoughts about what you have just bought. You may start to think:

- Did I make the right choice?
- Should I have considered more suppliers?
- Can I really afford this product?
- Do I really need this product?

The list can go on and on.

Customers who buy financial services products can feel the same way too. Therefore, it is important that we reassure them that they have indeed made the right decision, by providing them with after care.

QUICK QUESTION

What could you do to give your customer after care?

Write your answer here before reading on.

One of the simplest things you could do is diarise to call the customer to ask them if everything went according to plan. For example, did they receive the plastic cards on time, did the financial planner call them to arrange an appointment, how did the meeting with the financial planner go, were the loan proceeds credited to their current account at the right time, etc.

In this conversation, you could also enquire about the underlying transaction. For example, if the customer was obtaining a personal loan to book a holiday, then did they manage to make the booking; if the loan was to buy a car, then what type of car did they choose, etc.

The advantages of making this type of call are:

- You are demonstrating excellent service to the customer.

- If there has been a problem, you are now given an opportunity to resolve it. This will be easier to do if you have initiated the call rather than if the customer has had to make a complaint.

- You are more likely to be able to do more business with this customer at some future date as the customer can see that you are interested in them and their needs.

You could also diarise to contact the customer some time later to ensure that the product is operating in the way that they envisaged. Again, this is demonstrating excellent customer service, with the added advantage that you would be able to ascertain at this point if the customer has any new financial needs that your organisation would be able to help them with.

As you can see, these forms of after care are conducted over the phone. If you work in an organisation that operates a branch network, you can easily carry out this after care the next time you see the customer in the branch.

14 Customer complaints

In the last section we looked at the process that should be used when identifying customer needs, and identifying how your organisation can best meet these needs. However, the client-centred approach also requires that we have the customer at the heart of the business even when they are not happy. To this end, we will conclude this chapter by considering how best to deal with customers who make complaints.

14.1   What is a complaint?

QUICK QUESTION

Write down a short definition of a complaint.

Write your answer here before reading on.

That task may have proved more difficult than you first thought.

The dictionary definition of a complaint is:

> An expression of pain, dissatisfaction or resentment. A cause or reason for complaining: a grievance.

For simplicity's sake, it is fair to say that when a customer complains, it is because some aspect of what the organisation does has not met with their expectations.

Working in a service industry, it can be easy to feel that customers complain about the least thing on a regular basis....but does this match with your experience when the boot is on the other foot and you are the customer? Probably not. Most of us have to be very upset before we go to the length of complaining to the organisation that has let us down. What we are far more likely to do is to talk to other people about the poor experience that we have had and possibly to move our business away to another organisation. We will return to this theme shortly when we consider the positive aspect of complaints.

14.2   Why do customers make complaints?

QUICK QUESTION

Write a list of all of the complaints that you have had to deal with over the past four weeks.

Write your answer here before reading on.

The type of complaint that you have received will vary depending upon where you work and the type of role you carry out. Having said that, the typical complaints that we receive in financial services are around the following areas:

- Lack of satisfaction with the features of products – for example, the rate of interest paid or received by the customer, the level and frequency of charges levied on a particular product, or the frequency of interest applications for a savings product.

- Lack of satisfaction with the level of service provided – this would include the length of time the customer has had to wait in a queue (either a physical queue, or a queuing system in a contact centre), the level of difficulty regarding accessing online information or service.

- Lack of satisfaction with the person that the customer is dealing with. What we are considering here is when there is possibly a communications breakdown between the member of staff and the customer, with the result being that the customer wants to complain about the person they have been dealing with, rather than a specific aspect of a product.

- Lack of satisfaction with the organisation – this was a frequent complaint heard during the banking crisis, when many customers lost faith and trust in their financial services provider and could be quite vocal in making these concerns heard.

- Lack of satisfaction with the organisation's decisions – this can happen when a customer has applied for a credit facility and their request has been declined. Often when a customer approaches a bank for credit it is to finance some aspiration that they have, for example to finance a new car, pay for a holiday or even to consolidate debt and as a result have a lower monthly payment. Understandably, if the bank says 'no' the customer is unhappy and this can manifest itself in the form of a complaint.

From the discussion above, you can see that complaints may be about hard or soft factors. Hard factors are things like the features of a product or the service provided by the organisation. Soft factors are more emotive. These are things like personal issues between a customer and a member of staff. However, this simplifies things a bit too much. When you look at the list above, it tends to pigeon hole complaints into one category or another, whereas in reality, customers can complain about a number of these issues simultaneously. It may be that they are unhappy with having to wait for service from their bank but this sparks off the thought in their mind of an advert that they saw on television last night about a competitor's launch of a new savings product with a higher rate of interest than that which they get from you and when they mention this to the advisor they are dealing with they do not like the way in which this person deals with them, so we now have a complaint about the poor level of customer service, the rate of interest on their savings account and the attitude of the person with whom they are dealing.

14.3 The positive aspect of complaints

Most people who deal with customers would say that they dread dealing with complaints. This can be for a wide range of reasons – for example, we may feel that there is just not enough time in the day to deal with the complaint and attend to the hundred other things that we need to do before we go home, it can be stressful and upsetting to deal with a customer who is making a complaint, we may feel that we are being victimised by this particular customer for whom we do not seem to be able to do anything right, and we may also feel anxious that the result of the complaint of that the customer is going to take their business elsewhere. There can also be a fear that we will not be able to resolve the complaint. Every product and every service offered by every organisation in the world has 'limiting factors'. These are features of the product or service which, when compared to that offered by rival organisations do not compare well. When you work in the one organisation, it is easy to concentrate on these, rather than looking at what your organisation offers which is better than the competition – but human nature tends to make us look at the negative aspects of our organisation more readily than the positive ones.

Whilst all of the above is true, we should look at complaints in a more positive light.

QUICK QUESTION

Why do you think it is important to view complaints positively?

Write your answer here before reading on.

There are a number of reasons why complaints should be looked at in a more favourable light. Firstly, by making the complaint, the customer is giving us the opportunity to put things right. If a compliant is handled well, then there is the possibility that we can turn an unhappy customer into a happy one. By complaining, the customer is giving you the opportunity to put things right – this is satisfying for both you and your organisation. Secondly, most unhappy customers do not complaint – they just take their business away to a rival organisation. Across all industries, it has been found that less than half of an organisation's unhappy customers actually complain. This statistic can lead many organisations into a false sense of security – they may incorrectly assume that if they are not receiving complaints, then their customers are happy – yet they cannot understand why their market share is falling.

QUICK QUESTION

Why do you think that many unhappy customers choose not to complain?

Write your answer here before reading on.

In order of frequency, the three main reasons why customers choose not to complain are:

- They did not think that making the complaint was worth the time or effort.
- They felt that no one in the organisation was concerned about their problem or about resolving it.
- They did not know where to go or what to do about making the complaint.

Had you been studying a course like this before the turn of the century, at this point we would have discussed statistics about the scenario when a customer is unhappy with the service that they provide, then they will tell a further (say) 9 people, whereas if they are satisfied with the service that they get, then they only share this with another 4 people. However the arrival of social networking websites has made these sorts of statistics irrelevant. Unhappy customers now have the opportunity to broadcast this news to a much wider audience – and many of them do.

You may find the following statistics interesting:

According to a study by the Society for New Communications Research, 59% of consumers use social media to vent their frustrations about customer service experience, and research other companies' customer service before dealing with them.

- 74% choose companies/brands based on others' customer-care experiences shared online.

- 72% research companies' customer care online prior to purchasing products and services at least sometimes.

- 84% consider the quality of customer care at least sometimes in their decision to do business with a company.

- 81% say blogs, online rating systems and discussion forums can give consumers a greater voice regarding customer care, but less than 33% say they believe that businesses take customers' opinions seriously.

As well as blogs and social networking sites there can also be websites set up exclusively for unhappy customers of just the one organisation to share their experiences with the global virtual community.

Progressive organisations (and their people) do not fear the arrival of complaints – rather they welcome them as an opportunity to improve their service. Complaints do not necessarily lead to lost business – provided the organisation offers a satisfactory response to the person making the complaint, then it is likely that the customer will remain loyal. On the other hand, those who are unhappy, but do not make complaints are the least likely to repurchase.

14.4 An introduction to the legislation and regulation of complaint handling in the financial services industry

As you know, we will look at this area in detail later in this book. However, it is worth introducing the topic at this stage to allow you to put it into context.

Most financial services firms have a two-tier approach to complaints. The first tier is the original contact with the customer – where a complaint is made and is resolved immediately to the customer's satisfaction. The vast majority of complaints are dealt with this way – the customer contacts the firm, expresses their concerns, which the person they deal with addresses and that is an end to the matter. The second tier is what happens when these complaints remain unresolved by close of business on the day following that on which the complaint is made. This can be due to the firm either having to investigate the complaint, or where the complaint has to be referred to a centralised complaint handling department in the organisation. Such complaints are logged and are reported to the Financial Conduct Authority. The three most complained about areas reported to the FCA in the second half of 2013 were:

- Payment protection insurance

- General insurance

- Current accounts

The procedures that the FCA look for firms to follow is:

- The firm should aim to resolve the complaint at the earliest opportunity.

- If a firm has not been able to resolve the complaint by close of business the next business day, the firm should send the complainant a written acknowledgement promptly. This acknowledgement should give the name or the job title of the individual who is handling the complaint for the firm, together with details of the firm's internal complaint handling procedure – often this is in the form of a leaflet.

- When the firm is able to issue a final response to the complainant, it must issue details of its complaints handling procedure along with information about the Financial Ombudsman Service.

- Within eight weeks of receiving a complaint, the firm must have issued a final response to the complainant.

Complaint handling procedures will be subject to review by the FCA.

You may have come across the terms reportable and non-reportable complaints. A non-reportable complaint is the first type of complaint discussed above, where the customer makes a complaint and it is resolved to their satisfaction by close of business on the next business day. A reportable complaint is the latter type where it is subject to the reporting requirements of the FCA.

14.5 The business impact of complaints

Whilst there can be a financial cost of reimbursing and compensating customers, there are other costs to think about too.

QUICK QUESTION

What other factors do we need to think about under this heading?

Write your answer here before reading on.

The other things that we need to consider are:

- Opportunity cost
- Financial loss
- Reputational damage

We will now look at each of these in turn.

14.6 Opportunity cost

QUICK QUESTION

How would you describe opportunity cost?

Write your answer here before reading on.

Opportunity cost can be defined as the cost of following one course of action at the expense of another. Most people employed in financial services are required to generate a certain level of income for their employers – either through the pricing of services or even the provision of these services, for example by promoting a credit card to a customer, an advisor is generating future income for their employer. However, when we are dealing with a complaint, we are not actually adding any value to the revenue stream of the organisation. That is not to say that dealing with complaints is a pointless activity, far from it. However, in the most basic terms, it is a 'damage limitation' exercise...if we deal well with the complaint, then the customer will not take their business elsewhere. However, had the complaint event not happened in the first instance, then the advisor's time could have been employed in a more profitable way for the organisation.

The opportunity cost here is what income-generating activities have been foregone by the advisor by having to handle the complaint.

14.7 Financial loss

There is also a financial cost involved in complaint handling. Large organisations will normally set up specialised departments to deal with unresolved complaints centrally. Again, there is the financial cost associated with this – the salaries of the people who work in these departments and the overheads (office rent, heat and light, computers, etc) incurred to run these areas.

There can also be a financial loss if we are not able to resolve the complaint to the customer's satisfaction and they choose to take their business elsewhere. The organisation is then losing future income and revenue that they would otherwise have earned from this customer.

Also, as mentioned at the start of this section, there can be the financial cost in making reparation to the customer or even having to compensate them in some way. These costs are increased should the customer be so unhappy as to take their case to the Financial Ombudsman Service.

14.8 Reputational damage

QUICK QUESTION

You may have encountered the term reputational risk before. What does this mean?

Write your answer here before reading on.

Reputational risk is the risk of damage to the image and/or trustworthiness of an organisation. If you think about the fallout of the banking crisis, many organisations in the sector were damaged reputationally as customers did not trust them in the same way as they had before.

Similarly, if there are a number of complaints received about an organisation, then its reputation both with existing and potential customers will suffer. Existing customers have less faith in the organisation, and may well be more inclined to complain in the future, as well as be more inclined to take their business elsewhere. Potential future customers are now far less likely to engage with the organisation.

14.9   Positive language

Earlier on in this chapter when we looked at the impact of the three elements of communication, we saw that the impact of the words that we use is only 7%. However, that is not to say that you should not be careful about what you say to a customer. It is important that you portray a professional image of both yourself and the organisation and one of the ways in which you can do this is through the use of positive language.

Language is a very important tool and the words that you choose to use can have a great effect on how your communication is received. Even when conveying unpleasant or unwelcome news to the customer, the language that you use can have quite an effect on the impact of your message. Most of us will have experience of working with some people who have a negative outlook on life and have felt the fatiguing effects of having these people around us. When dealing with a customer complaint, it is easy to fall into the trap of using negative language – for example, 'I'm really sorry to have to tell you.......'

Negative phrasing and language has the following characteristics:

- It tells the customer what cannot be done

- It has the hint of blame attached to it

- It often includes words such as can't, won't, unable to, etc

- It does not stress the positive actions that can be taken to remedy the situation for the customer

- It sounds impersonal and focusses around the organisation rather than the person who is dealing with the customer.

Positive language has the following qualities:

- It tells the customer what can and what will be done to resolve the situation

- It suggests the choices that may be available to the customer

- It sounds helpful and encouraging, rather than bureaucratic

- It sounds personal – talking about what the person is going to do to remedy the situation

- It stresses the positive actions and positive consequences that can be anticipated by the customer.

Expressions that infer carelessness on the part of the customer

- You failed to tell us...
- You did not confirm your request in writing...
- You did not enclose...

Expressions that infer that the customer is lying

- You claim that...
- You state that...
- According to your account...

Expressions that infer that the customer is lacking in intelligence

- I can't see how you....
- I am at a loss to know why you...
- I don't follow you on this point...

Expressions that infer that you are putting the customer under pressure

- You should...
- You ought to...
- I must ask that you...

14.10   Positive phrasing

As we have discussed, you need to be vigilant in your choice of words when dealing with an unhappy customer – although careful thought must also be given to the other two aspects of communication impact when talking to these customers. The more positive you can make these conversations, then the easier it will be for the customer to see that you are doing your utmost to remedy matters for them. Here are some examples of positive phrasing that you might want to use:

- If you can send me the missing document, then I can complete processing the transaction for you.

- The options open to you are...

- It seems that we both have a different perspective on this matter. Perhaps the best way to move forward is for us to meet up to consider solution options?

14.11   The complaints resolution model

You should be familiar with this model as it follows the same structure as the objections resolution model we discussed earlier.

The model is best described as following the following steps:

1.   Empathise with the customer
2.   Get all of the relevant facts
3.   Work to a solution
4.   Verify that the customer is happy with the outcome

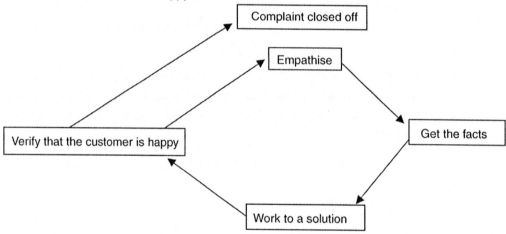

1. Empathise with the customer

Remember that empathy is the ability to show another person that you understand how they feel, but when empathising you are not necessarily agreeing with the customer. Therefore empathy is quite different – although often confused with – sympathy. Sympathy is where we feel sorry for another person, whereas empathy is an understanding of their feelings.

It is also important that you avoid any unnecessary small talk – this will only serve to escalate the situation. Think about a time when you have had to make a complaint – often you feel quite stressed you go to make the complaint. So, someone talking to you at this stage about the weather would hardly help your state of mind. This is another demonstration of empathy – by our actions we are showing the customer that we are in tune with their feelings. It would be foolish to think that this display of empathy makes a connection with the customer's conscious mind – they are unlikely to think ...this is great, the advisor is showing concern for my situation by empathising... – rather the power in this situation is that it makes a connection with the customer's subconscious. Also, by not doing this, we would be fanning the flames of a confrontation.

QUICK QUESTION

If the customer is making a complaint about a charge that has been levied on their account, what phrases could you use to demonstrate empathy?

Write your answer here before reading on.

There are a number of phrases you could use, for example:

I can understand that you don't want to pay charges...

I appreciate that you feel angry about this....

I see that this has upset you...

By empathising, you are showing the customer that you understand how they are feeling, but in none of the suggestions above are you necessarily agreeing with what the customer is saying. Indeed, you are not yet in a position to either agree or disagree with them, as you have not, as yet, gathered in all of the facts.

As you know, a further benefit of displaying empathy is that you are attempting to remove the aggression from the situation. Using empathy with a complaining customer is often called 'cushioning' in that you are absorbing the conflict in the situation.

2. Get all the relevant facts

QUICK QUESTION

What do you need at this point to allow you to understand the problem that the customer has?

Write your answer here before reading on.

You need to allow the customer to talk, to get things off their chest and also to let you know what their complaint is. At this point, we need to get all the relevant information – so the customer has to be allowed to talk and we need to listen without pre-judging the situation. This is the time to use the questioning and active listening techniques we looked at earlier in this chapter. You should make sure that you summarise what the customer has said so that the customer confirms your understanding of the situation.

These behaviours will also help the customer as they now feel that someone is listening to their concerns and want to help them.

3. Work to a solution

You have now taken the heat out of the situation by using empathy and you have gathered in the facts from the customer.

It may be that you need to get more information from colleagues or another part of the organisation to allow you to progress the complaint. If this is the case, you should explain to the customer what it is that you have to do and why. You should also make a firm commitment to the customer of when you will be able to get back in touch with them. If events conspire against you and you are not able to get all of the information that you require in this timescale, then you should still go back to the customer to explain the up to date position and to let them know what the revised timescales are going to be.

However, once you have ingathered all of the information that you need, you are in a position to work to a solution.

QUICK QUESTION

What actions could you take to work to a solution?

Write your answer here before reading on.

The particular actions you would take will depend upon the specific complaint that you are dealing with. However here are some suggestions:

- Ask the customer what they would like to happen. This may seem a very obvious action to take, but not many people offer it. If you know what the customer wants then it is much easier for you to give them what they want. For example, they may want an apology or a refund/compensation, etc. Alternatively the customer may want us to contact some third party. Say an automated payment to the customer's mortgage provider has been set up incorrectly and the mortgage provider has advised the customer that they are now in arrears – the customer may want us to contact the mortgage provider to explain that we have made an error and to let them know when they are likely to receive the funds.

- Explain your firm's position. It may be that you need to explain what your organisations complaints procedure is. If the customer is looking for a refund of charges, it may be that you are not authorised to make such a refund and the matter has to be referred on – again you should explain this to the customer and give them timescales of when you will be back in touch.

- Give alternative solutions if you can. If this is an option, then the customer can choose which solution they prefer.

You will find that your own organisation will have a policy surrounding the redress that it will offer to customers as a result of a valid complaint being made. This may focus on monetary as well as non-monetary compensation. Monetary awards may be along the lines of a refund of interest and charges arising as a result of an error on the part of the organisation. It may also be that the organisation is

willing in certain circumstances to make financial awards to customers as a remedy for upset caused by errors by the firm. To be successful, these awards need to have some structure around them as the organisation must be seen to be treating customers both fairly and consistently.

However, redress need not be limited to financial awards. It may be that your organisation has a policy of making small gifts to customers who have been the victims of service failure. It is important that these types of redress are tailored to both the severity of the error and the customer involved. If a large corporate customer has had a series of errors posted on their account, then the delivery of flowers or a tin of Quality Street are only likely to exacerbate the situation. Yet there will be other customers who could be delighted with such an approach.

It may also be that your firm operates a policy of redress on a goodwill basis, even if there is no fault pertaining to the organisation. An example of this is those firms who would be willing to refund service charge on a money transmission account on one occasion if the reason for levying the charge was a genuine oversight on the customer's part. To be successful, such refunds must be recorded to ensure that each customer does, indeed, only receive the refund once.

4. Verify that the customer is happy with the outcome

As you come to the end of the solution stage, you should ensure that the customer is clear about what is going to happen next – for example, you are going to make a refund to their account; or they will get a letter of apology; or you are having to refer the matter to your team leader who will contact the customer by close of business the next day.

You should also make sure that the customer is happy with your proposals.

If the customer is happy with the situation, then you have come to the end of the process. If, however, they are not happy, you simply have to move into the empathy stage again and work round the cycle a second time. It may also be that the customer is happy with the way that you have dealt with this complaint, but there is something else they want to draw to your attention.

This stage is often missed from the complaints resolution process as the member of staff is worried by what the customer might say at this point – they have worked through the complaints process and want to get away from the customer. By asking the customer if they are happy, you are demonstrating confidence and belief.

5. How customers respond to service failure

The first thing to bear in mind that many victims of service failure simply choose to do nothing. At some point, these customers will decide whether to keep their business with the organisation or switch to a rival provider. Those who fail to complain, but switch are the least likely to return to the original organisation.

Customers can be grouped under four headings depending upon how they respond to service failure, namely:

- Passives
- Voicers
- Irates
- Activists

While the proportion of the types of complainers is likely to vary from industry to industry, it is likely that these four categories of complainer types will be relatively consistent and that each type should be found in all organisations and industries.

14.12   Passives

This is the group who are least likely to take any action when faced with a service failure. They are unlikely to say anything to the firm and are less likely than the other groups to complain to a third party. They see little point in complaining, thinking that the time, effort and stress involved are not worth it.

14.13 Voicers

As can be inferred by the name, voicers are those who will actively complain to the service provider, but they are less likely to spread negative word of mouth, to switch patronage or to go to third parties with their complaints. These customers are very valuable to service providers as they are willing to give them a second chance. This not only gives the firm a chance with this customer, but also provides them with valuable feedback of how their processes and procedures can be tightened up in order to avoid a repetition of the service failure with other customers.

Voicers have a belief in the social benefits of complaining, so they have no concerns about voicing their complaint in the first instance. They are more comfortable about making a complaint to the organisation, rather than spreading negative word of mouth to third parties.

14.14 Irates

These are people who are likely to engage in negative word of mouth to friends and relatives and also to switch providers. They are about average in their propensity to complain to the organisation. They are less likely to give the service provider a second chance and will switch to a competitor, spreading negative word of mouth on the way.

14.15 Activists

These consumers have an above average propensity to complain to the provider on all aspects of service. They will also discuss their concerns with third parties and are willing to complain publicly about the service failures they have encountered.

This categorisation suggests that there are some customers who are more likely to complain than others. Customers who complain often believe that their actions will result in social benefits and expect to receive compensation. They have the belief that fair treatment and good service are their right. They can feel a social obligation to complain in order to help others avoid a similar failure and to punish the service provider. Only a very small number of consumers have complaining personalities.

Others fail to complain as they feel that the process is pointless and they simply do not know how to complain. In some cases people fail to complain as they feel that they are the ones to blame for the service failure.

The personal relevance of the service failure can also affect the propensity of customers to complain. If the service failure is of a relatively minor matter, that does not have critical consequences for the consumer, then the customer is less likely to make a complaint. For example, we are more likely to complain about high risk services such as holidays then less expensive products such as fast food.

14.16 Are all customers good customers?

We often hear the expression that the customer is king – or consumer sovereignty. However, are all customers good customers? It is worthwhile to give some thought to those customers who behave in abusive or other unacceptable ways. As with complaining customers, it is possible to categorise awkward customers under a number of headings:

- The thief
- The rule breaker
- The belligerent
- The vandal

14.17 The thief

These are customers who set out to obtain products and services without paying for them. Whilst it is easy to think of these types of customer only being a problem for organisations that sell tangible goods, which the thief can abscond with, they apply just as much within the financial services sector.

QUICK QUESTION

What examples can you list of thief's within financial services?

Write your answer here before reading on.

The main area which comes to mind here is that of fraud. As you will be aware, fraud within the sector manifests itself in a number of ways – for example, card fraud, identity fraud, forgery, money laundering and so on.

14.18 The rule breaker

Organisations need to put in place a number of rules for both staff and customers to follow. Much of this focuses around a need to provide consistent decision making across the organisation. This is particularly true when the organisation is geographically dispersed – such as a retail bank. An example of rules that the organisation may communicate to customers is around their charging policy. Financial services firms publish tariffs around the levels of fees which they charge for items returned unpaid, unarranged overdraft letters, loan arrangement fees and so on. It is common to encounter a number of customers who will seek to exempt themselves from these rules by challenging their imposition, and looking to be dealt with as a special case. The challenge for any organisation in this situation is to deliver consistent service whilst having a concern for the needs of the individual customer.

14.19 The belligerent

Working with the public, you no doubt have personal experience of particular customers for whom your organisation can seem to do no right. They appear to wish to complain about the slightest thing – down to the fact that the sun shines in the ATM screen making it difficult to read. Dealing with large numbers of customers can make it impossible for the organisation to eliminate this type of customer from the books. Rather, the approach taken by most is to invest in the training and development of their staff in effective ways in which to deal with this type of customer. The establishment of customer service standards can also help, as this type of customer can be directed to these standards to let them know what the organisation has committed to provide and what it has not.

14.20 The vandal

As most financial services firms have a presence on the high street, they can be subject to wanton acts of vandalism, which although these acts may not be caused by customers, they do affect the public perception of the organisation. After all, if you were thinking of moving your money transmission account, would you be tempted to move to one whose ATM is covered in mess?

An effective way to deal with vandalism is to try to prevent it from happening in the first place. Improved security, better lighting and the use of vandal resistant materials can help here.

14.21 Relationships with customers

Of course, the vast majority of customers do not fall into any of these categories, but organisations need to have a clear view of the type of customer that they need to attract to deliver their strategic vision.

Given that financial services firms look to engage in long-term relationships with customers, it would then appear foolish for firms to refuse to engage with new customers, or to terminate relationships with existing customers – although from time to time these events will happen. The assumption that all customers are good customers belongs to a past age. Indeed, in those days, many of the customers who were deemed in a branch to be a good customer were possibly those customers who were very effective in negotiating terms with their local manager which were more in favour of the customer than the bank. It was only in the 1980's that firms seemed willing to tell staff that good customers were profitable customers. Up till then, many bank staff were of the opinion that good customers were those who were affluent and had negotiated very good deals (for themselves) with the bank. The reality of the situation was that very little, if any, profit was made from these customers.

Therefore firms will seek to avoid long-term relationships with unprofitable customers. At the individual level, it may be that there is little point in a firm engaging in a relationship with a customer who has a poor repayment history, or whose credit history is, in some other way, unreliable. This extends beyond the provision of banking services – many insurance companies will decline to quote for business if they feel that the customer does not match with their target market segment, or simply present too high a level of risk. For example, many elderly motorists can find it difficult to obtain a quote for car insurance.

QUICK QUESTION

What do you think would be the effects of attracting the wrong type of customer?

Write your answer here before reading on.

In addition to the likely financial costs associated with attracting the wrong type of customer, there is also likely to be a substantial amount of time spent dealing with these types of customer, which can make them unprofitable for the organisation. The wrong type of customer is likely to demand a considerable amount of time from the organisation, the cost of which may not be recouped by the amount of profit, if any, made from this customer. Also, dealing with this type of customer may place unacceptable levels of stress on the employees of the firm, and this may manifest itself in a declining level of service quality provided by these employees to other customers.

14.22 Typical complaints

QUICK QUESTION

List the most common types of complaint you have to deal with in your current role.

Write your answer here before reading on.

The types of complaint that you need to deal with can vary depending to the role that you are currently engaged in. For many of us, customers will complain about the imposition of charges, or the level of them, the level of service provided by the organisation – for example, the incorrect setting up of an automated payment, the decline of a credit request or the features of a product. Other complaints may come from a more public arena – examples here include the mis-selling of endowment insurance or, more recently, PPI cover.

In today's highly competitive financial services market, many firms aim to attract new business by making introductory offers whereby new customers are offered preferential terms and conditions when they transfer business to the firm. Whilst this tactic can be successful in obtaining new business, it can lead to dissatisfaction amongst existing customers whose accounts are subject to the same terms and conditions as before and they may feel that their loyalty to the organisation is not being recognised. Their response to this may be to transfer their business to a competitor firm which is offering similar lucrative deals, or they may choose to raise a complaint with their existing provider.
We will now look at an example of a customer complaint and how it can be dealt with.

CASE STUDY

Andy Coyle

Your bank has recently launched an integrated current account which combines savings, money transmission, personal lending and mortgage facilities into the one account. As a result of customers effectively being able to off-set their savings against their borrowing, the amount of interest payable on their borrowing is substantially reduced. As a result of this, the reduction of the capital balance on a mortgage is accelerated, which means that the customer's mortgage can last for a substantially shorter period of time and the amount of total repayments is reduced. From the firm's perspective, this type of account needs to be offered to the market in order for the firm to remain competitive and an account such as this ties customers into a long term relationship with the firm and allows the firm to offer a wider range of financial products and services to the customer.

To support the launch of the product, the firm has invested in a promotional campaign, and a number of existing customers have been approached with an offer of access to this new type of account.

A couple of months after the launch, you are approached by Andy Coyle who has maintained his business and personal accounts (including a mortgage) with your branch for a number of years. He is a well-respected local businessman and his business has been a profitable connection for the bank. Andy is irate that the existence of this account has only come to his attention thorough a conversation he had with a business associate at a Rotary Club lunch. His associate had been offered the new account and was singing its praises at the lunch. Andy's associate also expressed surprise that a customer of Andy's standing in the community had not been made aware of the account by the bank. During the initial telephone conversation with Andy, he not only expressed his anger and disappointment at not being offered the account, but he also said that the bank must now owe him '....thousands of pounds in interest...' which he has paid on his mortgage over the years. The basis of his argument is that he has always maintained a sizable balance in his money transmission account and had this been offset against his mortgage, then he would have paid much less mortgage interest over the years.

How should we respond to Andy?

Before starting on this task, it would be useful to recall the complaint resolution model which was introduced earlier.

The four phases of the model are:

- Empathise
- Get the facts
- Work to a solution
- Check that the customer is happy with the outcome

Obviously, we need to empathise with the customer. When communicating our impact is:

- How you look: 55%
- How you sound: 38%
- What you say: 7%

The words that you use with this customer will be vitally important, but it is important to show him that you are empathising through both your non-verbal communication and your tone of voice. You must appear sincere and adopt an assertive solution-focussed mode of communication. As well as empathising in a non-verbal manner, it is important that you use some words of empathy. The words each person uses can vary – and you would certainly want to avoid this customer feeling that you are dealing with a routine matter. Therefore you would want to say something along the lines of:

- I can see that you are unhappy about this error....

It may well be that you would want to find out why Mr Coyle had not been offered the account – although for the purposes of illustration, we can assume that this was simply an oversight on the bank's part. This oversight must be communicated to the customer and it would be appropriate at this stage to offer an apology. Remember that what you are doing here is apologising on behalf of the firm – even if you were not personally responsible for the oversight. It is important that you do not waste this customer's time by going into a long explanation as to why you were not the culprit. That would only make the situation worse.

We are now at the stage were you work towards a solution for the customer. If we assume that it was an oversight which meant that the customer was not informed about the account, then you would be able to offer to open the account and do the necessary work to get the account set up. If this is the case, great care must be taken to ensure that this process is carried out without any further errors compounding matters. It would also be important to ensure that any timescales communicated to the customer are adhered to. It may also be useful to keep in touch with the customer during this transition phase to ensure that they are happy with the way that things are progressing.

QUICK QUESTION

How would you deal with the customer's insistence that they are refunded '...thousands of pounds of overpaid interest over the years?'

Write your answer here before reading on.

When dealing with the complaint, it may well be expected that the bank would make a payment to the customer for the amount of overpaid interest that the customer has paid since the introduction of the integrated current account. However, no matter how good a connection this customer is, it would not be practicable for them to have this payment backdated to the opening of the mortgage many years before. However, this needs to be explained to the customer in a tactful manner. The explanation could be along the lines that in common with all banks, your firm regularly reviews the products and services that it offers and it was as the outcome of such a review that this new integrated account was developed. However, as with any business, it would not be possible to backdate the benefits of a new product to a time when the product was not in existence. Therefore the offer that is being made is to compensate the customer for the extra interest they have paid as a result of the bank's error.

Hopefully, this tactic will resolve the matter. If not, then there may be other compensation that the firm is able to offer in line with its own policies and procedures. However, were you to accede to this customer's request, then you are leaving the door open to a host of other customers looking for compensation for 'additional' interest paid over the years, which would not be a sustainable position for the bank to be in.

Again, depending upon the structure of your organisation, it may be that other members of staff would need to be involved in this solution and the communication of it to the customer – for example, a colleague who is Mr Coyle's business relationship manager.

At the end of this process, it is important that you check with the customer that he is happy with the solution which you have provided. There is no point investing time and effort into this process, only to find that you have not given the customer what he feels he is entitled to and as a result, his business is transferred anyway.

Finally, keep in mind that you must communicate to the customer in an assertive manner throughout this interaction.

14.23 The customer lifecycle

The customer lifecycle is a way of forecasting and mapping likely customer behaviour. This is done by mapping out the life cycle of a customer's interaction with the organisation and the services that it provides. Quite often the lifecycle is looked at as being akin to a corridor – the customer enters the corridor at one end and each door along the corridor represents an interaction with the organisation. For a bank, possible doors would be:

- Opening the account
- Registering for direct banking provision

- Opening an ISA
- Buying foreign currency and arranging travel insurance.

The customer travels along the corridor until they reach the end when their relationship with the organisation ceases.

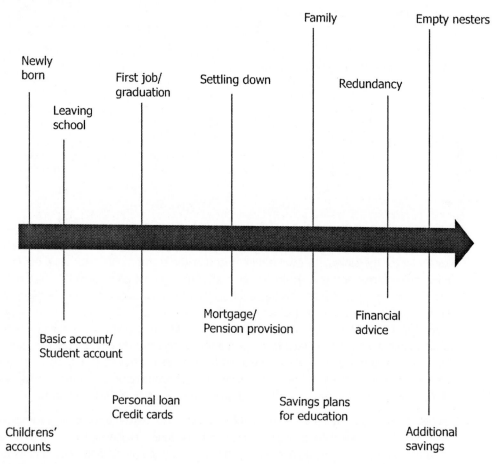

KEY WORDS

Key words in this chapter are given below. There is space to write your own revision notes and to add any other words or phrases you want to remember.

- Queue management
- Distribution channels
- Undue influence
- Set off
- Lien
- Clayton's case
- Money transmission account
- Faster payments service
- Individual Savings Account (ISA)
- Annual percentage rate (APR)
- Irrevocable mandate
- Electronic purse
- Manual underwriting
- Repayment vehicle
- Regulated products
- Open question
- Closed question
- Active listening
- Non-verbal communication
- Empathy
- Buying signals
- Buyers remorse
- Limiting factors

REVIEW

Now consider the main learning points that were introduced in the chapter.

Go through them and check that you are happy that you fully understand each point.

- The client centred organisation puts the customer at the heart of its operations.

- Effective customer service is the bedrock of the client centred organisation.

- The banker-customer relationship is based on the relationship of debtor and creditor.

- There are a number of rights and duties incumbent on both banker and customer.

- If a customer has more than one account with a bank – one in credit and the other overdrawn – then the banker may be able to combine these balances when determining whether or not to pay an item presented.

- Clayton's Case established the first in/first out principle with regard to the appropriation of payments on a customer's running account.

- The products and services offered by a retail bank include: current accounts, automated payments, savings accounts, personal loans, house purchase loans, equity release loans, bridging loans, electronic funds transfer, credit cards, term loans, and self-build and property investment finance.

- Cheques are processed through the clearing system.

- Advice on many investment, mortgage and protection products can only be given by members of staff who are appropriately qualified.

- The process of establishing and meeting customer needs is: pre-meeting preparation, introduction, explore and listen, identify and agree the customer's needs, introduce products to meet these needs, overcome objections, close, ask for referrals, and after care.

- Complaints that are not resolved by close of business on the day following receipt are reported to the FCA.

- The business impacts of complaints can be categorised as opportunity cost, financial loss and reputational damage.

- The model for dealing with complaints is similar to that used for overcoming objections.

- Customers who respond to service failure can be classified as passives, voicers, irates and activists.

chapter 3

DISTRIBUTION CHANNELS AND THE IMPACT OF TECHNOLOGY

Contents

Learning outcomes

In this chapter we are going to examine the different ways in which retail bank customers are able to access the services of their bank. To do this, we will consider not only the various ways in which these services can be accessed, but we will also examine the different ways in which money can be transmitted in our economy.

On completion of the chapter you should be able to:

- Identify and explain the demands of managing delivery through diverse distribution channels in a retail banking environment

- Compare and contrast a range of distribution channels used by retail banks to reach customers

- Assess the impact of technology on a retail banking operation and its customers

- Distinguish between different methods of money transmission and examine the processes that apply to each method

- Evaluate the significance of systems and processes in creating and implementing an effective customer retention strategy

1 Distribution channels

Distribution channels is the name given to the different ways in which the customer can avail themselves of the services offered by their banks. In this section we will consider:

- Automated telling machines
- Automated pay in machines
- Direct banking – telephone and internet banking

1.1 Automated Telling Machines (ATMs)

The ATM has been one of the most notable developments in the financial services industry in recent decades. These machines are located on the exterior walls of branches, inside branches and at other locations – for example, in supermarkets, petrol stations, sites of recently closed bank branches, etc.

A distinct advantage of ATMs is that they give the customer access to cash 24 hours a day, 7 days a week. The LINK network, which was originally set up by the leading building societies, has now been joined by the big UK retail banks, which makes it possible for customers of virtually every UK bank to use over 50,000 cash machines throughout the country. However, this access does not necessarily mean free withdrawals – some machine providers levy a charge to customers for using their dispensers.

It is also possible to use ATMs in many parts of world. This means that rather than buying travellers' cheques before going abroad many customers now opt simply to access local currency through the ATMs in operation at their destination. As a security measure, it is normally incumbent upon the customer to advise their bank of their destination and the duration of their trip to allow the card to be activated for use abroad.

The ATM works on the basis that the user inserts their ATM card into the dispenser and keys in their PIN. Instructions are then given by the customer via screen guidance and by pressing appropriate keys on the dispenser – thus information is conveyed electronically to the main computer.

Financial services organisations realised that the ATM had become an accepted way for customers to access their accounts and so they capitalised on this new delivery channel by adding to the number of functions that it could perform.

QUICK QUESTION

What functionality does your organisation's ATMs have?

Write your answer here before reading on.

ATM's originally had only one purpose – to allow the customer to withdraw cash. Now many ATMs can:

- Accept deposits
- Send out marketing information
- Print the customer's balance
- Print a statement of the customer's most recent transactions
- Pay bills
- Change the customer's PIN
- Transfer funds between different accounts
- Top up a mobile phone
- Make donations to charities

Ironically, the ATM is perpetuating the use of cash in that access to cash is now very simple and speedy.

1.2 Automated pay in machines

This facility is becoming more prominent in banking halls. Rather than the customer having to queue to make a lodgement to a teller, they can carry out this transaction at a machine. To do this, the customer will insert their lodgement slip into a slot in the machine where it will be scanned. The cash and/or cheques that make up the lodgement are then inserted into the machine and this will be reconciled with the amount recorded on the pay-in slip. Assuming all is balanced; the machine will accept the lodgement and credit the customer's account. The customer will also have the option of receiving a copy of the pay-in slip and any cheques in the lodgement. The cash element of the lodgement can be notes, coin or a combination of both.

A less high-tech approach but producing a similar end is the 'Quick Deposit' envelope. Here the customer will put the pay-in slip and lodgement – notes or cheques, but no coin. On the outsider of the envelope, the customer also records details of the transaction along with contact details should the bank need to get in touch with them as a result of the transaction. The sealed envelope is then placed in a secured letter box within the branch and processed by the bank in the normal manner.

1.3 Direct banking

Banks offer customers a direct banking facility – indeed some of the newer players in the market operate solely as direct banks.

With direct banking, the customer has access to their account 24 hours a day, 7 days a week – either by providing them with telephone or internet access to their accounts. The customer needs to identify themselves by way of security protocols to be able to access the system.

QUICK QUESTION

What are the advantages to a financial services provider of offering direct banking?

Write your answer here before reading on.

There are two main advantages of offering direct banking:

- Routine enquires can be dealt with directly, thus removing the need for branch staff to have to deal with these enquiries and so allowing them to concentrate on those tasks that can only be dealt with in the branch.

- It allows the organisation to provide a better service to customers through the use of specialist staff and software.

We will look at the **money transmission** aspects of both telephone and internet banking now.

1.4 Telephone banking

As you may be aware, there are some organisations that operate solely as telephone banks, whilst other financial services organisations offer telephone banking as part of a wider range of options available to their customers.

When using a telephone banking service the customer will usually have the option of using either an **Automated Telephone Service** or of speaking to an advisor.

QUICK QUESTION

What do you understand by the phrase Automated Telephone Service?

Write your answer here before reading on.

If a customer uses an automated telephone service, when they telephone the organisation they are greeted by a recorded message that will offer them some service options – for example, press 1 for balance enquiries, press 2 for recent transactions, etc. Then the call will be dealt with automatically – for example, under option 1, the system will advise the customer of the relevant balance without the need for an advisor to intervene.

Alternatively, the customer may prefer to speak to an advisor – perhaps as their call is of a more complex nature.

QUICK QUESTION

What money transmission could a customer make when using telephone banking?

Write your answer here before reading on.

When using telephone banking, a customer could carry out the following money transmission transactions:

- Transferring funds between accounts
- Paying a bill
- Standing orders
- Amending/cancelling a direct debit
- Arranging a Faster Payment
- Share dealing
- Arranging an overdraft
- Third party payments

We have already looked at some of these transactions elsewhere in the course, but we will now examine the following in a bit more detail – transferring funds, paying a bill, share dealing and third party payments.

Transferring funds

If a customer wishes to transfer the same amount of funds between two of their accounts on the same date each month, then they could set up a monthly standing order. However, if the amount and date of transfer is varied, then they can have the option of giving this instruction to the call centre. There will also be the option for the customer to have the transfer carried out immediately, or diarised for some future date.

Paying a bill

Most call centres will give customers the facility where they can give instructions for bills to be paid over the phone. All that the customer needs to do is give the bank information about the bill payment and the transaction will then be processed.

QUICK QUESTION

What information would the bank need about the payee to carry out this instruction?

Write your answer here before reading on.

To make a bill payment over the phone, the bank would need to know the following information:

- The payee
- The payee's bank sorting code number
- The account number that should be credited
- The customer's reference number with the payee

Once these details have been logged into the system, all that the customer need do in future is to telephone the call centre with the amount that they wish to pay.

This is a far more convenient way for the customer to make the payment as opposed to having to call in at the branch to make the payment with the giro credit that will be attached to the bottom of the bill. A further downside to visiting the branch is that the customer could only go on the day that they wished to pay the bill – they would not be able to give the branch instructions to pay the bill at some date in the future.

Share dealing

Another service that the call centre allows banks to offer is the telephone instructions from customers to buy and sell stocks and shares. Customers can also transact via Internet banking with appropriate registration.

In the past, only written instructions could be taken from customers who wished to buy or sell on the stockmarket. Now, provided that the customer has completed the appropriate level of security, the call will normally be passed through to a stockbroker, who will attend to the sale or purchase on behalf of the customer.

Once the deal has been concluded, the customer will receive a contract note detailing the transaction and if the instruction is to sell shares, and then the customer must complete the appropriate transfer from and return this to the stockbroker. The proceeds of the sale or the cost of the purchase will be sent through to the customer's account at the relevant time.

1.5 Third party payments

QUICK QUESTION

What do you understand by a third party payment?

Write your answer here before reading on.

A third party payment is a payment made by a customer, through their financial services provider to another person.

It has been possible to make this type of payment for many years by using a bank giro credit at a bank branch.

Normally the funds will be debited from the customer's account on the date requested and sent through the clearing system to reach the beneficiaries account in two – three working days.

In addition to these services, many banks can offer the customer a facility whereby they will receive a text message at a pre-agreed trigger point – perhaps when the balance of the account reaches a certain level.

Internet banking

Banks have their own brochure websites that allow customers to obtain information on the products and services offered.

There are two types of internet banks.

QUICK QUESTION

What do you think are these two types of internet banks?

Write your answer here before reading on.

The two types of internet banks are:

- Stand alone internet banks that offer competitive interest rates and service charges due to them having lower overheads than their High Street competitors. The cheapest type of bank transaction is one carried out online, those processed through a telephone centre are more expensive, but still cheaper than those made in branch.

- Traditional banks that provide branch, telephone and internet banking facilities.

Once a person has opened an account with the bank, they can then register for the bank's internet banking service. This will allow the customer to:

- Transfer funds between their accounts
- View past transactions and statements
- Make third party payments
- View and amend automated payments
- Find out about other products and services that may be of use to them.
- Apply for other products or services

With both telephone and internet banking, it is possible for the customer to request credit facilities. Once the application is made, the bank will credit score this request – but how does this system work?

QUICK QUESTION

How would you describe credit scoring?

Write your answer here before reading on.

At its simplest, **credit scoring** would take the form of a credit scorecard. This would be a set of rules that create a numeric score for the various elements that are in a credit application. Examples would include how long the customer has lived at their current address, whether or not they have a land telephone line, and so on. Each score is added up to produce an overall figure that represents the risk for the application and so determines whether or not the facility should be approved. The minimum score that an application must obtain is called the cut off level.

The premise behind credit scoring is that by looking at past performance, the bank is able to predict the future repayment patterns of customers who share similar characteristics. So by looking at similar customers to the one making the application and how they have repaid in the past, we have a good indication of what their repayment record will be in the future. Credit scoring is therefore a measure of risk – the risk in this case being the non-repayment, or default of the customer. In its simplest terms, if a customer passes the cut off score set by the organisation, then the bank is saying that this person represents an acceptable risk for the proposal. On the other hand, if the person does not pass the cut off score, then the bank is taking the view that they do not represent a reasonable risk.

QUICK QUESTION

Credit scoring can use either a bottom up, or a top down approach. What do you think is the difference?

Write your answer here before reading on.

With the bottom up approach, a high score is good and a low score is bad. With the top down approach, the opposite holds true – a high score is bad and a low score is good. With the bottom up approach, the customer starts with zero points and points are awarded depending upon the details in their application – the more positive the application, then the more points the customer receives. With a top down approach, each customer is given the same number of points at the start of the process and points are deducted depending upon the detail of the application. The more positive the application then the more points are deducted from the original number of points.

When we refer to a scorecard in the context of credit scoring, we are looking at the points used in assessing the application. These points are allocated to the customer based on the characteristics drawn from their application. This score is them compared to a number of previous applicants who either:

1   Repaid fully on time
2   Were slow to repay
3   Did not repay the loan in full.

Points are allocated to a range of characteristics in the application to determine this end score.

Credit scoring has been developed further to give us behavioural scoring. This determines the credit risk associated with an existing account, as opposed to an application for new credit. Factors that would be considered include turnover through the account, regularity of credit payments, unpaid items and so on. Information on previous and current credit facilities may also be taken into account. Behavioural scoring is further enhanced by live feeds of information from Credit Reference Agencies which can verify the behaviour of the account.

Fraud detection tools can also be built into the credit scoring process to highlight potentially fraudulent applications. Typically this will be internal to the Bank and is where verification checks are carried out for specific products or credit applications. This can produce significant savings for banks as they help to prevent advances being made where the loan would eventually be written off due to fraud.

Originally credit scoring was used in generating credit card limits or approving fixed rate personal loans. Its use has now been extended to include current accounts of personal customers in setting overdraft limits and determining whether or not items presented to the account should be paid of their payment will result in an irregular position on the account.

Credit and behavioural scoring has been further extended to small business customers when considering their borrowing requests.

QUICK QUESTION

What do you think are the benefits of internet banking?

Write your answer here before reading on.

The advantages of internet banking are:

- Services are available 24 hours a day, seven days a week.

- The time and effort it takes for customers to visit branches are removed and customers can transact their banking from home, office or any site where they have access to a personal computer or suitably enabled mobile phone.

- Fees are often lower than traditional banking fees.

- Despite concerns about security, the technology used ensures the privacy and safety of the customers' financial information.

- Customers can check the balances of their accounts, transfer funds between accounts, and make electronic bill payments.

These services are available either through a traditional a personal computer, lap top or through apps available for the customer's mobile phone.

QUICK QUESTION

Whilst the provision of a range of different distribution channels may be attractive to both the bank and the customer, from the bank's point of view there could be a number of potential disadvantages. What do you think these are?

Write your answer here before reading on.

First and foremost, the bank is in danger of losing its personal contact with the customer. Many customers have expressed disappointment that their bank does not know them or their needs, when compared to years gone by when the bank manager was seen as a professional member of the community along with doctors, lawyers and accountants.

With the development of technology, we have seen a fragmentation of delivery amongst banks, with some parts of the organisation being run almost as autonomous units with little contact with other parts of their banking group. As a result, the customer may be approached by different business units, albeit from the one organisation, perhaps carrying out sales campaigns for products that the customer may have told another part of the bank that they have no desire for. Alternatively, one part of the organisation may be asking the customer for information that is already held in another part of the firm, but not accessible throughout the business.

In the Client Centred Approach chapter, there was much discussion around the need for the client to be at the centre of everything that the bank does. However, with the availability of direct banking, it is now possible for the customer to manage their accounts without the need for much intervention from the bank, with the exception of the bank providing the platform to allow the customer to carry out their own financial management. Were there more face to face discussions between the bank and the customer, then it is possible that more of the customer's financial needs would be highlighted with the bank having the opportunity to meet these needs.

The complexity in the structure of banks brought about by these differing distribution channels has presented the challenge of cohesion in approach from differing parts of the organisation. For example, there is the danger that different parts of the bank start to compete with one another for the same business – should the customer finance their car purchase through a traditional personal loan from their local branch, or through a similar loan from the internet banking arm of the same firm? It can be quite possible that the terms and conditions of these loans can be different, which presents a confusing – not to mention unprofessional - picture to the customer. From the bank's point of view, if two parts of the same firm end up undercutting one another, the result is a reduction in the profitability of the bank.

2 Money transmission

QUICK QUESTION

What do you understand by the term money transmission?

Write your answer here before reading on.

Money transmission is the transfer of money from the receiver of goods and services – the debtor – to the provider of goods and services – the creditor. Therefore, when we talk about money transmission we are talking about how we pay for goods and services with money. We all need to buy things and we need funds to pay for them which comes from your income, savings or wherever else.

People have income and expenditure, businesses have income and expenditure and financial services organisations help with the process of money transmission by providing products and services to make it as easy as possible for buyer and seller, debtor and creditor to settle their transactions.

QUICK QUESTION

What methods of money transmission are you aware of?

Write your answer here before reading on.

There are lots of different methods of money transmission and the various common methods are all facilitated by financial institutions. The different methods are:

- Cash
- Cheques
- Bank Giro Credits
- Standing orders
- Direct debits
- Faster Payments
- Credit cards
- Debit cards
- ATMs
- Direct banking – telephone and internet banking

We have already considered a number of these when examining the client centred approach, but those not already covered will now be looked at.

3 Cash

This is the most liquid form of asset and banks deal in large amounts of cash.

Cash is still very popular with private individuals, particularly when it comes to making small, everyday payments – for example, buying a newspaper, or a bar of chocolate. The heavy usage that we see of Automated Telling Machines (ATMs) backs this up. However, financial services organisations, and the traditional banks in particular, would prefer to see a continuing reduction in the level of cash transactions with their customers using other forms of money transmission services which are more profitable and much more efficient.

QUICK QUESTION

If consumers use cash, what costs do you think this will impose on banks?

Write your answer here before reading on.

There are heavy costs for banks in handling cash. These costs are incurred for the collection, issue, storage, security, insurance, distribution and loss of interest. Therefore, banks are keen to encourage customers to use the other forms of money transmission that we will look at in this chapter. Ideally, the banks would like us to move towards a cashless society.

QUICK QUESTION

How close do you think we are to achieving a cashless society?

Write your answer here before reading on.

We are probably further from a cashless society than you think. Around 58% of all transactions in the UK were made in cash in 2011 according to a British Research Council survey. Therefore, it is likely that cash will remain the dominant means of money transmission for the foreseeable future.

4   Cheques

Cheques are another popular form of money transmission, although you should be aware that there use is much diminished in recent years.

QUICK QUESTION

How would you define a cheque?

Write your answer here before reading on.

A cheque may be fully defined as:

> An unconditional order in writing addressed by one person to a bank or other financial institution signed by the person giving it requiring the bank/financial institution to pay on demand a sum certain in money to, or to the order of, a specified person or to bearer.

Cheques have been around in some shape or form since the 18th century, and were really the first step on the road to reducing the amount of physical cash in the economy.

QUICK QUESTION

What recent developments in money transmission have reduced the usage of cheques?

Write your answer here before reading on.

The introduction of debit cards, telephone banking and internet banking has resulted in a significant reduction in the use of the cheque as a means of payment or money transmission.

Using a standard form (blank cheque), the person writing out the cheque (or Drawer) provides particular instructions – by filling in the name of the Payee (the person to whom payment is to be made), along with the amount and date. The drawer will grant the authority (by signing the cheque) and gives the cheque to the payee. To obtain payment, the payee either encashes it or pays it into their bank account.

The cheque then begins the process of passing from the payee's bank/branch to the drawer's bank/branch (or Drawee) and settlement is effected between banks/branches. This process of cheque clearing was described earlier.

QUICK QUESTION

List what you think are the advantages of cheques.

Write your answer here before reading on.

The convenience and safety of the system is evidenced by its popularity and history:

- Cheques may be made out for any amount, thus avoiding the need to carry large sums of money and, unlike cash they are convenient to send through the postal system.

- The requirement of signed authority makes it a safer method of money transmission than cash.

4.1 The cheque clearing process

The process for the clearing of cheques has already been discussed (Chapter 2, section 11.5), but you may want to refresh your memory of this process now

4.2 The banker's viewpoint of cheques

Although preferring cheques to cash, the volume of paperwork associated with this form of money transmission service involves considerable handling and processing costs.

The solution lies with encouraging the greater use of electronic transfers (such as the plastic chip and PIN cards), the use of online payment methods, mobile technology and cheque truncation.

Cheque truncation simply involves trying to halt or restrict the flow of cheques through the clearing process. Banks now exclude the service of returning paid cheques to customers and are examining other ways in which the process can be shortened. You will no doubt be aware of discussions in the press and consumer affairs programmes, where customers express dissatisfaction with the clearing system in the UK compared to some other countries. The dissatisfaction also led to the standardisation of clearing timescales.

5 Bank giro credits

Giro payments are credit transfers because they allow anyone to transfer funds to another party via the latter's bank account. They are initiated by the payer making a request to a bank or their own bank asking that a credit be made to another individual's account. Giro credits are used for the payment of bills, such as mail order, utility bills, etc. Giro forms are pre-printed with details of the account that is to be credited, including a reference number. Paper based credit transfers pass through the credit clearing system.

6 Customer retention strategies

There are a range of strategies that can be implemented to retain customers and they can be summarised based on a customer's position in the 'customer lifecycle'.

The lifecycle is shown below along with the value that different types of customers contribute to the business at different parts of the cycle.

Time to y-axis

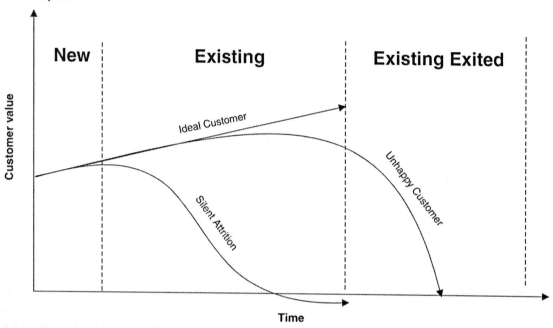

6.1 New customers

The single largest group of customer retention strategies that can be implemented in the New section of the customer lifecycle can be described as Customer Onboarding. This is the process of bedding a customer into the organisation and includes ensuring that their personal data is correct, that they understand the products they have purchased and how to quickly contact the organisation. When this process happens smoothly and efficiently, then customers will be more likely to stay with the bank longer and spend more money than other customers.

The process should aim to introduce new customers to a company in an organized and effective manner. It generally commences at the time of initial contact and may continue for up to three months, depending on the complexity of the product or service.

6.2 Existing customers

The best bank customer retention strategy for existing customers is to classify each type of customer (silent attrition, ideal and unhappy) and create appropriate initiatives to change their behaviour. You should recall that a number of classifications were explained when we discussed complaining customers in Chapter 2.

You should also keep in mind that many customers choose not to complain at all. In this instance the relationship ends in silent attrition where they reduce or stop using a product but where the account is still open. Examples for instance are credit card accounts with little or no spending. For these customers the bank must determine why they are no longer using your product and create initiatives and incentives to change their behaviour.

Examples of existing customer management programs include:

- Product design evolution
- Payment automation optimisation
- Active customer complaints management
- Cross-sell leads management
- Product activation
- Usage stimulation
- Preapproved products
- IVR messaging offers
- Leveraging sponsorships
- Leveraging affinity marketing
- High value relationship programs
- Low value relationship programs
- Local area marketing

6.3 Exiting customers

Customers that are exiting are those customers that have started the process of moving their business to another bank or are in the process of considering that move.

Whilst in the past many unhappy customers were unwilling to do this as it could be a difficult process, banks now offer a dedicated **switching service** that streamlines this process. Previously, as the bank that was losing business had little motivation to prioritise this work, it meant that the process of moving banks was drawn out and often strewn with errors on the bank's part. As a result, many customers carried out the process themselves, by arranging to have new standing orders and direct debits set up on the new account, before cancelling these instructions on the old account.

The process now is that the new bank will set up the automated payments and advise the customer of a transfer date when the switch can take place. At this point, the new bank will also advise the customer of the details of all of these automated payments – this allows the customer to confirm that these details are correct and that they are happy for the transfer to go ahead. Regarding regular credits that are received to the account – for example, salary, pension, etc, the customer still has to contact the crediting organisations to let them know the new account details – however, there is a standard form that can be used for this purpose.

The first step in creating bank customer retention strategies for exiting customers is to identify which customers are in each camp and devise appropriate strategies and rewards to keep them on-board.

QUESTION TIME 4

Compare and contrast cash and cheques from the viewpoint of money transmission.

Write you answers here then check with the answers at the back of the book.

QUESTION TIME 5

Your customer, Mr Bruno, is somewhat confused as to whether he should use debit cards or credit cards for money transfer. Assist your customer by briefly:

(a)   Clarifying the main purposes for which these cards may be used

(b)   Describing the benefits of debit cards over credit cards and vice versa

(c)   Reminding him of the main advantages of plastic cards over cheques and cash

Write your answer here then check with the answer at the back of the book.

KEY WORDS

Key words in this chapter are given below. There is space to write your own revision notes and to add any other words or phrases you want to remember.

- Distribution channels
- Automated telephone service
- Third party payments
- Share dealing
- Credit scoring
- Money transmission
- Switching service

REVIEW

Now consider the main learning points that were introduced in this chapter.

Go through them and check that you fully understand each point.

- Customers are able to access banking services through ATMs, automated pay-in machines, telephone banking and internet banking.

- Money transmission can take a variety of forms – for example cash, plastic cards, giro credits, direct banking, etc.

- As with all organisations, banks have strategies in place to retain profitable customers.

chapter 4

PEOPLE, PROCESSES AND RISK

Contents

Learning outcomes

On completion of this chapter you should be able to:

- Identify the key drivers of outsourcing decisions and discuss the advantages and disadvantages of outsourcing elements of a retail banking operation

- Examine the operational factors that contribute to the effective delivery and maintenance of service quality

- Identify sources of risk in a retail banking operation that could impact on both service delivery and profitability

Introduction

In this chapter we will consider the significance of the processes and relationships between customer facing and support roles in a retail banking operation and explain how this impacts on the delivery of service to the customer. The chapter starts by discussing how jobs in retail banking have changed over recent years and how these changes had led to the development of the concept of the internal and external customer, Service Level Agreements and an increase in outsourcing.

We move on to define what is meant by risk and risk management, before explaining how risk is managed in organisations. The management of data is covered next, before the chapter concludes with a description of a range of business process re-engineering techniques.

1 Jobs in retail banking

QUICK QUESTION

Reflect upon your current role and write down how wide your range of responsibilities is.

Write your answer here before reading on.

Assuming that you are working in a retail bank environment, it is quite likely that, unless you are in a managerial role, your range of responsibilities is quite narrow. It may be that you carry out cash handling and transaction processing duties – either for personal or business customers, but probably not both – or carry out customer service duties – for example, talking to customers about opening or closing accounts and/or making amendments to the arrangements that exist on these accounts, or perhaps you have conversations with customers about the best type of products and/or services that would meet their financial needs. You may even carry out duties behind the scenes – although the majority of these will no doubt be carried out in a centralised processing centre. What is quite likely though is that you will carry out tasks only in one of these areas.

If you compare this situation with what prevailed 20 – 30 years ago, the range of tasks carried out is quite different. For example, it used to be that once new entrants were recruited into a bank, they would go through a training period that would last in the range of 18 – 24 months, which, if successfully

completed would result in them being designated a 'Multi Skilled Bank Officer'. This would mean that the individual would be capable of working either on the counter as a bank teller, in addition to this, they could also work as a Ledgers Clerk, where they would open and close accounts, set up, amend or cancel standing orders and direct debits (there were no Faster Payments in those days), and they could also carry out a range of other back office tasks, such as filing customer's cheques and credit slips (as these would return to the account holding branch through the clearing system), preparing and sending out statements to customers and processing vouchers presented over the counter.

If an individual had ambition, they could possibly progress to the role of 'Senior Bank Officer', either through internal promotion or by the successful completion of the examinations set by the Institute of Bankers. Holders of this type of post would be given a greater degree of responsibility by the bank, for example working as a Foreign Clerk, liaising with the Bank's Overseas Department processing Documentary Credits and Documentary Collections for those customers who took part in international trade. Another role for a Senior Bank Officer would be as a Securities Clerk where they would deal with customers who wished to deposit items with the bank's safe custody service, or they would deal with items that borrowing customers would pledge as security for loans as well as instructing the bank's stockbrokers to buy and sell shares on behalf of customers.

The next level of promotion would have some members of the team appointed as 'Bank Supervisors' – these people would either assist the Office Manager in ensuring the smooth running of the branch, or could act as a Manager's Clerk where they would work with the Branch Manager completing the necessary paperwork for those customers who were borrowing funds, arranging the renewal of annual overdraft facilities and even interviewing some customers for small loans and overdrafts.

It is also important to note that these roles and arrangements applied to all of the major banks – so no matter where you worked, the structure of jobs within a branch were similar. However, and rather surprisingly, there was very little movement of staff from one organisation to another and it was not uncommon for individuals to join a bank when leaving school (there was very little graduate recruitment, if any) and staying with the same employer until retirement.

Returning to the Multi Skilled Bank Officer, whilst the Office Manager would allocate roles within the branch, normally on either a weekly or monthly rotation, due to the multi skilling of staff, it was possible to move staff around roles to match the peak and flow of demand during the day. Therefore, a member of the team may have been allocated Ledger Clerk duties this week, but if the queue of customers at the counter built up – for example, close to closing time – then it was possible for this individual to be deployed as a Teller/Cashier until the queue was served.

As you will be aware, this is in marked contrast to the current situation where staff are trained in a narrow range of skills so this ability to move staff around to meet dynamic customer demand is not an option in many organisations.

Returning to staffing levels, we have looked at the situation that prevailed amongst clerical staff. As you can imagine, as more tasks were carried out in branches at this time, the number of staff employed in branches was much higher than is the case now. If you work in an older bank branch, you may be aware of this either from the amount of vacant space in your office, or from comments made from time to time by some of your older customers.

Managerial posts in branches were also quite different then. It was commonplace for each branch to have at least two members of staff who were in managerial roles. The more senior of these roles was that of the 'Branch Manager'. Whilst this person was responsible for the branch overall, their main focus was in the management of the branch's lending book. They would either interview customers who were looking to borrow funds, or they would visit the premises of business customers. Depending upon the amount that the customer wished to borrow, the Branch Manager could either sanction the request personally or would have to refer it to the bank's centralised lending department. The more junior manager would have responsibility for the smooth running of the branch, although the job title was 'Branch Accountant'.

2 The internal customer

QUICK QUESTION

There were two main developments in UK banking in the 1980s and 1990s that changed the structure of branch banking.

What were these?

Write your answer here before reading on.

The first thing that changed was the advent of credit scoring in the mid-1980s.

QUICK QUESTION

How did credit scoring change the structure of bank branches?

Write your answer here before reading on.

As a result of credit scoring techniques, it was no longer necessary to have Branch Managers in each branch as many of the decisions that had been made by these individuals were now the subject of an automated procedure. This not only increased the consistency of credit decision making within organisations, it made the need to employ the number of branch managers unnecessary. Different banks responded in different ways, with some going for a clustering approach whereby the one manager would have responsibility for a number of branches, whilst others choose to centralise much of routine credit decision making.

As well as streamlining credit decision making, a substantial cost saving was made as these Branch Managers received by far the highest reward package in the branch.

The second factor that changed the structure of branches was the decision to open a number of centralised back office processing centres. This meant that much of the routine back office functions were removed from branches and moved – generally to purpose built facilities in out of town business parks. The tasks that exited from branches included:

- Dispatch of customer statements
- Opening and closing accounts
- Setting up, cancelling and amending automated payments
- Clearing suspense accounts

Again, this move streamlined the ways in which customers' accounts were managed, but also reduced the number of staff employed in each branch. An added incentive to the banks was the economies of scale which came from this move and so resulted in an overall reduction in staff employed in this type of work. For example, if an individual worked all day clearing the suspense accounts for a number of branches, they would become more proficient with this type of work and so the time it would take them to clear a suspense account would reduce.

Those staff remaining in the branch network had to adapt to further changes in their working lives – not only were the traditional tasks that they completed on a daily basis disappearing, they also had to cope with being asked to carry out some different duties – including the promotion and selling of products and services to customers, which met with a high level of hostility and resistance from many staff – especially those who had been employed by the bank for a long time in what had been quite a stable operating environment.

As a result of the introduction of these processing centres, customer facing staff no longer had the responsibility for carrying out most of the work on their customers' accounts – this was being done by colleagues in the processing centre, therefore a new player entered the equation – the **internal customer**.

QUICK QUESTION

What is the difference between an internal and external customer?

Write your answer here before reading on.

The **external customer** is the end user of the bank's products and services – the person who holds their account with the bank. The internal customer is someone who relies on a colleague in another part of the organisation to input to the service which the original colleague provides to the customer. Therefore in the scenario just described, the external customer is the account holder, with the member of staff in the branch being the internal customer – as they are dependent upon their colleagues in the processing centre delivering a service to them and in turn this service is delivered to the customer.

The internal customer concept is much wider than the example just described. You are the internal customer of your colleagues in the HR department for the services that they provide to you by way of processing your salary, maintaining your staff records in an appropriate and confidential manner, their liaising with your pension provider and so on.

If you reflect upon matters, you will have a large number of colleagues within your organisation to whom you are the internal customer and no doubt you have a number of internal customers of your own.

QUICK QUESTION

What problems can you see with this internal customer concept?

Write your answer here before reading on.

Whilst in the past, were there a problem with a customer's account – for example, some error in the setting up of a standing order, it would normally be a fairly quick and simple job to remedy matters as all of the relevant information would be held in the branch and it would be simple for the person who had carried out this piece of work to be identified and for matter to be sorted. Once the work moved away from the branch, the time taken to investigate and remedy an error was increased due to the physical distance between the branch and the location where the work actually took place.

There was also an argument that as the person completing the work would never actually face the customer, then the motivation to complete work without error was reduced. An added difficulty was that either delays or errors in work could now be blamed on the processing centre, rather than on an individual – none of which would serve to enhance the customer experience. As far as most customers are concerned, it is the bank that has made an error and they want this to be remedied immediately rather than having to listen to a disaffected member of staff complaining about the lack of professionalism in the processing centre.

One of the methods that was used to clearly outline what tasks were to be covered and the timescales within which this would happen was the introduction of **Service Level Agreements**.

QUICK QUESTION

What do you understand by a Service Level Agreement?

Write your answer here before reading on.

A service level agreement (SLA) is a negotiated agreement between two parties, in this case the branch network of the bank and the processing centre.

The SLA will record a common understanding about the services to be provided, priorities, responsibilities, guarantees, and warranties. Each area of service scope should have the level of service defined. The SLA may specify the levels of availability, serviceability, performance, operation, or other attributes of the service. The level of service can also be specified as target and minimum, which allows the branch network to be informed what to expect (the minimum), while providing a measurable (average) target value that shows the level of organisational performance. In some contracts, penalties may be agreed upon in the case of non-compliance of the SLA – however in this case we are simply talking about internal penalties within the bank which will not add any value to what the bank is doing, or the profits it is making. It is important to note that the agreement relates to the services that the branch network receives, and not how the service provider delivers that service.

Therefore, the SLA will set out in advance the roles and responsibilities of each party along with a description of what in included (and possibly what is excluded) from the services provided. If this is done at the start of the relationship, factors can be negotiated in, hopefully, a calm and professional manner – rather than under the stress of a situation which has arisen once the service has started to be provided.

At this point we have looked at the situation where the service has been provided within the organisation, but you will also be aware that there are some scenarios where the services provided to the customer is not actually provided by the bank, but by a third party – in other words, **outsourcing**.

3 Outsourcing

Banks in line with many other businesses globally now use third parties to assist with their business activities far more so than they did in the past. Previously medium and large organisations would carry out most of their activities in-house – however this has changed dramatically over the past 20 or so years and the use of third parities to provide services to a business is now the norm.

QUICK QUESTION

How would you describe a third party?

Write your answer here before reading on.

A third party is a person or organisation that provides a service to a company, but it is not permanently employed by the company.

As mentioned above, previously most of a businesses specialist services were provided in-house by employees. As discussed, over recent years, retail banks have changed shape. As a result, many banks have concentrated on their core business. Due to this, many specialist and support functions have been removed from the organisation and firms have entered into contractual agreements with external suppliers of specialist services. An example of this include the maintenance of ATMs by security firms.

QUICK QUESTION

What other potential benefits can you see from using third parties?

Write your answer here before reading on.

Using third parties can provide businesses with cost and productivity savings. Whilst it can be that they require specialist services from time to time it may not be cost effective to employ people full time to provide these services – so the service only needs to be bought in as and when required. In the example above, were the bank to service it's own ATMs there would be the need to employ staff to carry out this function, buy or lease specialist vehicles to transport the cash around the country, liaise with the organisations that have ATMs (for example supermarkets) to arrange suitable times to service the machines as well as pay the heavy insurance premiums for holding and transporting this cash around. It can make commercial sense for a bank to pay a security services company to provide these services.

Whilst the focus thus far has been on the provision of outsourcing to meet direct customer needs, in line with many other organisations, banks will often choose to outsource services that are intended to benefit staff. For example, if an organisation has identified the need for a Leadership Development Programme for senior executives. To employ leadership development specialists on a full time basis would prove to be very costly – so it is more cost effective to engage a third party to provide this service as and when required.

A further benefit from using third parties is that the organisation becomes more flexible and able to use the right specialist services at the right time. The outcome of this will be a better service to the customer and a better return to the organisation's stakeholders.

On a note of caution – it may seem attractive and cost effective to constantly look to bring third party expertise into the business – especially when developing a new initiative. However, an organisation should only look on third party provision as one possible source of services. It may well be that the expertise the initiative is looking for can be found in-house, so this avenue should always be explored thoroughly before utilising a third party. The business should always keep in mind that there are areas of expert knowledge and skills available internally – often it is just a case of looking wider in the organisation to identify this talent.

Using internal expertise can prove more cost effective as well as providing motivational and developmental opportunities for the organisation's own people. Using a third party may be a higher risk than providing the service in house – therefore when using an Outsource model, best practice would dictate that the bank will develop and follow a 'Third Party Policy' to mitigate the risks involved in this strategy.

3.1 The need for a third party policy

As a result of this trend to concentrate on core business, many business units within organisations are now contracting with third parties for the provision of specialist services. It is therefore important that the organisation takes a consistent and standard approach is taken when engaging third parties.

Often the initiatives in an organisation that leads them to engage a third party can be complex. As a result, there are a number of specialist areas that should be involved in this process from an early stage – this not only makes good business sense, but it will probably also mean that the requirements of the organisation's third party policy are being adhered to.

The overall objective to having a Third Party Policy is to ensure that the firm is consistent in its dealings with third parties – both when looking to hire them and also in the way that they manage the performance of the third parties once they have been engaged.

QUICK QUESTION

What do you think the objectives of a Third Party Policy would be?

Write your answer here before reading on.

In general terms, the objectives of an organisation's Third Party Policy would be:

- To ensure that Business Units, Project Sponsors and Project Managers are aware of their obligations and requirements when considering entering into an arrangement or initiative with a third party

- To ensure all staff and business units involved in dealing with third parties adopt a fair and consistent approach

- To provide details of the roles and responsibilities of those areas of the business who will become involved when considering entering into an arrangement or initiative with a third party

- To provide a clearly stated approval process for the risks associated with third party initiatives and appropriate approval authorities through completion of the agreed documentation

- To ensure that an appropriate risk assessment is undertaken on the suitability of the third party, both for the financial strength and ability to service the businesses clients and meet the organisation's long term requirements

- To ensure that the organisation complies with, and adheres to, all regional legal/regulatory requirements of the regulator of the country in which they intend to enter into a third party initiative

- To ensure that accountabilities and responsibilities are clearly defined and documented, together with an agreed supplier management strategy

4 Managing risk

QUICK QUESTION

How would you define risk?

Write your answer here before reading on.

In its simplest terms, risk can be defined as 'the possibility of loss, injury, disadvantage or destruction.' **Operational risk** can be thought of as 'the risk of loss resulting from inadequate or failed internal processes, people, systems or from external events' – we will return to this theme shortly.

However, knowing what risk is will not, in itself, prevent either an individual or an organisation from suffering loss or injury as a result of risk. What we must do is to think of ways to manage risk. If you think about it, risk is not just something that we could potentially encounter at work – we are exposed to risk all of the time. Therefore we all need to take steps to manage and minimise risk.

QUICK QUESTION

What actions do you take to manage risk?

Write your answer here before reading on.

BPP
LEARNING MEDIA

If you ask ten people this question, you will get ten different answers. Here are some of the steps that you may have taken to minimise risk:

- Buy a car with safety features, such as air bags
- Buy breakdown cover for your car
- Purchase an extended warranty when buying a major and expensive item
- Take out life assurance
- Warm up before working out at the gym
- Have a computer keypad with wrist rests
- Look both ways before crossing the road

If individuals take steps to manage risk, it follows that it is sensible for organisations to do the same.

QUICK QUESTION

How would you define risk management?

Write your answer here before reading on.

Risk management is 'the sum of all the actions taken by an individual or organisation to acceptably mitigate risks that could occur.' Look back to the list of the steps above. Remember that one of the steps was to buy a car with airbags. This will reduce the risk to what most people consider to be an acceptable level. Having a car with airbags does not guarantee motoring immortality. What they do is to reduce the level of risk were a motorist to be in an accident to a level that most people would be happy to accept. Also, by taking out breakdown cover, a driver does not guarantee that their car will never break down. What they are doing is putting something in place to deal with a potential breakdown and to minimise its consequences.

Similarly, organisational risk management does not *remove* risk completely, rather it seeks to identify potential risks, then put steps in place to minimise these risks and to put measures in place to deal with any potential loss, injury, disadvantage or destruction arising.

QUICK QUESTION

How doers your organisation interact with its customers?

Write your answer here before reading on.

Your response to this question will be driven partly by where you work, but it could include:

- Direct banking through the internet and a contact centre
- ATMs
- The use of independent financial advisers
- Dedicated centres for high net worth customers

All of these factors present risks that did not exist 30 years ago. If you reflect on these channels, many have been introduced by the traditional banks in response to the new players who have entered the market in recent years – for example, building societies and internet-only banks. This change in the structure of the industry has also contributed to the range of risks that need to be managed by banks.

There have been other factors contributing to the heightened profile of risk – for example, mergers and acquisitions, regulation and the changing demands of the consumer.

5 What is operational risk?

Mention was made earlier of operational risk – but what exactly do we mean by this term?

There are a number of risks that can be faced by banks and these can be grouped under a number of headings.

QUICK QUESTION

How would you classify these headings?

Write your answer here before reading on.

The headings used are:

- Credit risk
- Market risk
- Liquidity risk
- Regulatory risk
- Operational risk

5.1 Credit risk

At its most basic level, banks take deposits from some customers and lend funds to other customers. When anyone lends money to another party, there is always a risk that the loan will not be repaid – either in full or in part. Remember that when credit is assessed, the banker will give very careful consideration as to how the customer will repay the loan – maybe from future income, or from the sale of an asset. However, repayment by definition comes at some point in the future, and as the future is uncertain, there is the possibility that circumstances can change and as a result the borrower is not able to make repayment. For example, the borrower's future income could fall, or the asset they intend to sell may sell for less than anticipated at the time that the loan is agreed. This is what we mean by credit risk, although the risk can be a bit wider than this simple explanation – for example, if we take shares as security from a customer and they default on their repayments, there can still be a credit risk if the value of the shares falls and the bank does not obtain full repayment of the loan. This possibility of default by borrowing customers is a risk quite specific to banking. You may have heard discussion in your banks about risk and reward – but what do we mean by this?

Basically, the higher risk that we take then the greater the potential reward we are looking to get as a result of our actions. For example on Grand National Day, if you decide to place a £5 bet on a horse quoted by the bookmaker at 100 – 1, then the probability of that horse winning the race is deemed to be less than a horse running at 4 – 1. therefore if you bet on the 100 – 1 horse, there is a greater risk of it not winning, however should the horse win, then the potential reward you are going to enjoy is much higher than if you had bet on the 4 – 1 horse. Similarly when lending money, the higher the risk that the bank is taking, then the greater the reward it will look for. This is reflected in the rate of interest charged on the loan. If the loan is deemed to be of a higher risk, then the rate of interest charged to the customer by the bank will be higher. This is why the rate of interest charged on a secured loan will be lower than the rate for a similar loan that is unsecured. When the bank holds security, then should the customer default, the bank still has a repayment source through realising the security – as the risk is lower, this is reflected in a lower reward – i.e. a lower rate of interest.

You can also see this principle manifested with credit scored loans. Should the score reflect a higher risk to the bank, then, whilst the loan may still be sanctioned, it will be at a higher interest rate payable by the customer. This is why your bank may have a policy that states credit scores below 40 are declined, those scoring 41 – 70 are charged interest at 10% and those scoring 71+ pay interest at 7.5% - the higher the score then the lower the risk of not getting repayment, hence the lower interest rate charged.

Whilst credit risk is of huge significance to banks due to their core business of lending money, it also applies to other businesses – apart from those that deal exclusively in cash. For example, a joinery business could carry out some work for one of their customers and then they submit an invoice to the customer. There is always a risk that the customer will not pay the bill – this risk is also deemed credit risk. By carrying out the work before they receive payment, the joiner is offering a level of credit to the customer and there is always a risk that the customer will not make payment.

5.2 Market risk

This is the risk of suffering a loss due to changes in the market – for example, movements in interest rates, the foreign exchange market or the stock market. again, it is not just banks that are exposed to market risk, but due to the nature of a bank's work, they have a greater degree of exposure here than many other organisations.

5.3 Liquidity risk

A bank will always need to have sufficient funds available to meet the withdrawal demands of its depositors – any failure here results in a loss of confidence in both the individual organisation and the industry as a whole, as was seen in the funding crisis of 2008. Liquidity risk is the risk that a business or indeed an individual, will not have sufficient funds available to meet their debts when they fall due. Whilst a business may make profits, it must also ensure that it can meet its financial obligations on time, otherwise it runs the risk of failure.

Again, this is a significant risk area for banks, as their stock-in-trade is money. Just as a pub must make sure that it does not run out of beer, so a bank must make sure that it does not run out of cash. However, there is a cost to the bank in holding cash, so it will always seek to keep its cash holdings as low as possible, but bearing in mind that they must always have enough to meet the withdrawal demands of depositors.

This was discussed at the end of Chapter 1.

5.4 Regulatory risk

This is the risk of material loss, reputational damage or liability arising from the failure to comply properly with the requirements of regulators or with the various Codes of Practice (for example, the Lending Code) that oversee the way in which banks conduct their regulated business.

Regulatory risk can link with reputational risk as any reported breach of regulation can damage the reputation of the organisation.

5.5 Operational risk

The Basel Committee has produced a definition of operational risk. The definition is:

The risk of direct or indirect loss resulting from inadequate or failed internal processes, people and systems or from external events.

QUICK QUESTION

Look at the definition of operational risk. There are a number of distinct risk areas that are mentioned there. What are they?

Write your answer here before reading on.

The areas of operational risk are:

- Process risk
- People risk
- Systems risk
- External risk

5.6 Process risk

This is the risk that emanates from the processes that are carried out within the organisation. As you will be aware, there are a myriad of these processes – for example, from the payments systems used by an organisation to the manual processes that are used to open and lock up a branch securely at the start and end of the working day.

Risk is evident when these processes are inefficient or ineffective. A balance will need to be struck between the efficiency and effectiveness of these processes – the cost of providing a watertight process may be prohibitive and thus the organisation may accept that there are some risks inherent in the process – however, these risks must be at an acceptable level for the organisation and the regulator. This balance is evident when you take out car insurance – it may be that you feel that the cost of the policy is prohibitive, so you decide to opt for a greater excess on the policy, which makes the premium affordable for you. By taking this course of action, you are taking on a greater risk – if you have a claim, then you will have to pay a greater excess, but the cost of paying for a lower excess is excessive when compared to the risk involved.

5.7 People risk

It is often said that one of the ways in which an organisation can differentiate itself from the competition is through its people. However, with people comes risk – errors can occur due to a lack of knowledge (either from poor training or inappropriate recruitment and selection); from having inadequate numbers of staff in the right locations at the right time, poor management, and so on.

5.8 Systems risk

Here we are looking at the technology employed by firms to assist in their operations. With technology comes the risk of system failure, data quality and the security of the data held. This last area has been illustrated by the high profile publication of the failure of some organisations to keep confidential information out of the public domain. The banker's duty of confidentiality makes this area even more important for a bank.

5.9 External risk

No organisation operates in a vacuum, therefore external risk will always be an area for consideration – these are the risks that come from the external environment in which the organisation operates. Unfortunately the firm will have little or no control over these events – for example, a loss of external power, extreme weather events, etc – but the effects of external risk can be mitigated by the organisation having contingency plans. Business continuity planning is an example of this. Having such a plan will not prevent the external event from occurring, but if it does occur, then the organisation will have a robust and tested plan to minimise the impact of the event and have the firm's operations up and running again as soon as possible.

There are other external risks to consider – for example, a change in the tax regime, a change of government, money laundering, or the raids that can be carried out on bank branches.

The point was made earlier in this section that whilst the other risk areas are not necessarily exclusive to banking, they are of particular significance to banks. Operational risk applies to every organisation – including banks.

6 The risk management lifecycle

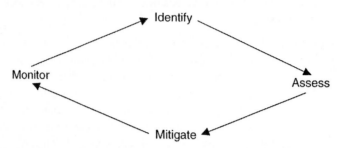

The **risk management lifecycle** starts with the identification of risk and works through to the monitoring of risk.

6.1 Risk identification

It is vital that the management of risk is a pro-active process. Therefore, rather than waiting for the risk event to occur and the organisation then deciding how to deal with it, the business must be constantly appraising both its internal and external environments to identify any risks that it may be facing. The process of risk identification must produce a clear understanding of what these risks are.

This is a critical stage of the process as the business must comprehend the risks that it faces before it can do anything about it. As the organisation operates in a dynamic environment, then the identification of risk must be an on-going process.

There are a number of ways in which risks can be identified in an organisation.

QUICK QUESTION

What do you think these are?

Write your answer here before reading on.

Whilst there are a range of ways in which this can be done, we will look at the following:

- Workshops
- Questionnaires
- Loss data capture and analysis
- Near miss capture and analysis

6.2 Workshops

This technique is often used when the organisation is considering commencing a project or implementing some form of strategic change. Where this is the case, the representatives of the project will come along to give a brief outline of the proposal. The other attendees are there to assist in the identification of any potential risk through the use of their expertise from their specialist areas.

When the meeting has concluded, the outputs should then be assessed using the risk assessment tools and techniques adopted by the organisation. It is quite common to find that there will be an overlap of risk from one part of the business to another, so it is quite likely that some of the risks identified have already been faced by the organisation. For example, if an organisation is opening a new contact centre, one of the risks identified with the new building could be the possibility of injury to staff through slips, trips and falls – however, the organisation would have encountered this risk in other areas of its operation.

6.3 Questionnaires

These can be used to identify high level risks that can then be assessed in more detail. However, careful wording for the questionnaire is required to ensure that all risks are identified and that the questions are not worded in such a way that could lead respondents to a particular outcome.

6.4 Loss data capture and analysis

If a risk has not been identified by the organisation, it can become apparent when it causes a loss to the business. Whilst this is an unsatisfactory state of affairs, steps can now be taken to ensure that there is no repetition of the situation. When this happens, the organisation must identify what the cause of the loss was – in effect risk identification is being carried out retrospectively, but this should help avoid a repetition of the event and thus a further loss.

6.5 Near miss analysis and experience

In the last heading, risk identification occurred retrospectively after a loss has occurred. There is also the potential for retrospective risk identification to happen when the business has not suffered a loss, but instead there has been a near miss.

You can relate this to your driving experience – you may alter your style of driving as a result of an accident (this would fall into the Loss data Capture and Analysis heading); but you may also alter your driving technique as a result of a near miss – perhaps a potential collision that was only narrowly avoided.

Whilst it is expected that organisations will act on losses to avoid a reoccurrence, they tend to be not as efficient in reporting the identification of risks for near misses. To be effective, there should be a near miss reporting requirement that applies to the whole organisation. The willingness of employees to report near misses can be dependent on the culture of the organisation. Often, only one or a handful of people in any business are aware of a near miss – so if it goes unreported, the organisation has lost out on the opportunity of putting steps in place to avoid a repetition of the event – possibly with more serious consequences. However, individuals may choose not to report a near miss if they think there is a possibility that they will suffer some negative consequences as a result of reporting. It is important that the firm develops a culture where near misses can be reported without fall-out for the members of staff concerned.

6.6 Risk assessment

Once the business is clear as to the risks it faces, it then has to decide how likely it is that these risks will occur and if they do occur, what is the likely effect of them on the business? This process needs to start as soon as possible after the risk has been identified as a potential outcome is a change of direction for the business. If we think about a potential change initiative – once we have identified the risks associated with the initiative, we need to assess these risks right away as depending upon the likelihood and impact of each risk occurring, the best decision might be not to proceed with the change. The sooner that this decision is made for the business the better as less time and resources will have been invested in it.

6.7 Cause and effect

When we analyse risk, we need to consider what could cause the risk and, should the risk event occur, then what would the impact – of effect – of this be. Normally, we would expect there to be a number of potential causes for a risk event to occur. For example, the front end system used by tellers in your organisation could fail for a number of reasons.

QUICK QUESTION

Based on your experience what could these causes be?

Write your answer here before reading on.

These causes could be a power failure, a technical problem with the software in the system, or misuse of the system by inappropriately trained staff. No matter what the cause is, the effect is that the system goes down – the effect is a disruption to the levels of customer service provided by the organisation. Ideally the organisation should look to manage the causes of the event – therefore if these do not occur, then the effect will not happen either.

QUICK QUESTION

Looking at the example above, what could the organisation do to influence these causes positively?

Write your answer here before reading on.

There are things that the organisation could do to avoid the technical problems – for example, by monitoring and/or servicing the system appropriately; staffing issues could also be dealt with by better training and supervision of staff using the system. Unfortunately, there is not much that can be done by the business regarding its power supply – this is an external risk.

QUICK QUESTION

Is there anything that the organisation could do regarding the power failure?

Write your answer here before reading on.

Whilst the organisation has no control over the supply of power to its premises, it could come up with a contingency plan should such an event occur.

Whilst we have stated that there can be a number of causes that could make a risk event occur, it is also possible that a risk event could have more than one outcome. In the example above, could result in a loss of customer service, or if the system is being used to produce information for internal reporting in the organisation, then this could also be affected. Finally, if the system failure occurs after close of business and tellers are relying on the system to balance their tills, then they may now need to carry out this procedure manually and if this takes longer to do, overtime payments and loss of goodwill with employees may be the impact.

6.8 Probability

Probability is the likelihood of an event occurring, often expressed as a percentage. For example, 0% would be an impossible event, 50% is an even chance of an event occurring and 100% is a certainty of an event occurring. This can be applied to risk assessment when we are looking to express how likely it is that a risk event could occur. When we look at probability the norm is to look at how often the event has occurred in the past, and we can then estimate how likely it is to happen in the future.

6.9 Mitigation

Having assessed the probability and impact of the risk, the organisation can move on to decide how best to mitigate the risks. The following graph illustrates how these risks could be dealt with (it is called an impact and probability grid):

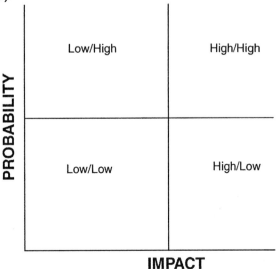

High probability/High impact

These risks must be understood and addressed first – they are the risks to avoid. These are risk events that are likely to happen and when they do occur, will have a significant impact upon the business. It is likely that an organisation would seek to avoid these risks.

Low impact but high probability

Whilst these risks may not represent a high cost to the organisation, the likelihood of occurrence means that they should not be ignored – they could represent a significant cost once all the small impacts are summed. Therefore these risks must be controlled.

High impact but low probability

These are risks that will only occur infrequently, but when they do, the impact will be serious. It is likely that this type of risk would be managed by risk transference, which we will consider shortly.

Low impact/Low probability

It is still worth considering these risks as circumstances can alter and they become more significant. Generally these risks are accepted by organisations. However, it is important not to lose sight of these risk events as their significance could change over time.

However, before moving on to look at these options in more detail, keep in mind that risk cannot always be fully mitigated. Mitigants can reduce a risk to an acceptable level, but an element of risk may remain – this is called residual risk. The definition of residual risk is:

The term used to describe situations where the controls or other risk management tactics in place do not fully mitigate the whole of the risk being experienced. The result is that the business unit will still experience a degree of outstanding risk. The residual risk exposure in a business can be the result of an informed decision or an unintentional situation.

6.10   Risk avoidance

This is where the risk is such a threat to the business that it must simply be avoided. In other words the risk event is beyond the organisation's current risk appetite. An example of **risk avoidance** would be a decision not to kayak due to a fear of water.

An organisation can employ proactive avoidance or abandonment.

Proactive avoidance is where the organisation deems that a risk is so great it will avoid it – for example it may be planning to launch a new product, but changes in the market lead it to abandon its plans as the risks associated with the product launch are now too great.

Risk abandonment occurs when the organisation is already pursuing a particular strategy and it decides to abandon this due to an unacceptable risk. In the example above, the business may have launched its new product before the market changes occur – however once they do, the business then decides to withdraw the product from the market.

Whilst the avoidance of the risk can be viewed positively as the organisation will no longer be able to suffer from the risk event occurring, there is also a negative element – any potential benefits that could accrue from the course of action will now not be available to the company.

6.11   Risk sharing

This is where the overall risk is reduced to an acceptable level by the organisation sharing the risk with another party – for example through a joint venture.

QUICK QUESTION

What is your understanding of a joint venture?

Write your answer here before reading on.

A joint venture is where two or more organisations collaborate to deliver a product or service. By doing so they are sharing the risks (and potential benefits) associated with the venture.

Another example of **risk sharing** is outsourcing if the risk associated with the outsourced activity is shared – this will depend on the contractual nature of the outsource. We considered outsourcing earlier in this chapter. As with risk avoidance there is also a disadvantage to risk sharing – if the risk is shared, then the benefits that accrue from the activity will need to be shared with the other party.

6.12 Risk transfer

Risk transfer is where the risk is transferred to another party who accepts the risk. Risk transference can apply to the risk itself or the financial consequences of the risk. An example of risk transference in financial services is when security companies are hired to transfer cash around the organisation – it is the security company that accepts the risks associated with this activity.

There are a number of ways in which risk can be transferred. Here are two examples:

Leasing and hiring – a leaseholder may require that the asset is returned to them at the end of the leasing period in the same condition as at the start.

Subcontracting – this often occurs when specialist services are needed as part of a larger project or contact.

The financial consequences of risk can also be transferred.

QUICK QUESTION

What is the common way for this to happen?

Write your answer here before reading on.

We have all transferred the financial consequences associated with a risk when we have taken out an insurance policy. However, when such a policy is bought, all it can do is make financial compensation for the risk event – for example, by paying for the repairs on a car after an accident. What the policy cannot do is remove the emotional trauma suffered as a result of the risk event – for example, the hurt and upset that most people feel as a result of their home being burgled. Again, the most that an insurance company can do is make financial compensation for hurt and upset.

6.13 Risk acceptance

There are times when an organisation will feel that whilst risks are present they are worth accepting – possibly due to the potential benefits that could accrue as a result of the activity. It may be that the consequences of the risk are low, or that the likelihood of the risk event occurring is low. You will recall from earlier that when these two likelihoods combine, then there is a greater chance of **risk acceptance**. Risk acceptance also occurs if the risk has initially been larger, but it has been mitigated to a certain level and the organisation feels that the level of residual risk is acceptable – you do this when you take out an insurance policy that has an excess attached to it.

6.14 Risk reduction

The aim of **risk reduction** is to reduce the chance of the risk event actually occurring, or to reduce the impact of the risk if it does occur.

If we consider each of these in turn, reducing the probability of the risk event occurring before the event actually happens – for example, air traffic control measures are designed to reduce the likelihood of an air collision occurring. An example closer to home could be that when your organisation developed its disaster recovery plan, this may have highlighted particular risk possibilities that the organisation has taken steps to reduce – for example, all of the back office processing may have occurred in one location and thus there was a risk if this building became inaccessible (for example due to flooding). A risk reduction technique could be to have this work carried out in a variety of locations and having the work done there backed up. As a result, if one of the centres becomes inaccessible, then operations can continue as normal from the other locations using the backed up information.

The other strategy under this heading would be to reduce the impact of the risk once the event has occurred.

QUICK QUESTION

Can you think of an example that falls under this heading?

Write your answer here before reading on.

There are a number of examples that you could have quoted:

- A mountaineer being attached to a fixed rope would mean that in the event of a fall, the impact would be minimised as he/she is stall attached to the rope.

- Wearing a seat belt will not prevent a motoring accident from occurring – but if it does occur, then the seatbelt helps to mitigate the negative impact of the crash.

- Having a disaster recover plan will allow the organisation to continue operations in the wake of am major incident.

6.15 Risk retention

An important element of risk acceptance is the concept of **risk retention** which can be a planned or unplanned activity. For example, a bank might have identified a risk using the concepts previously outlined and determined that rather than transfer the risk, the optimal approach is to retain the risk within the organisation but seek to adopt other mitigation approaches to reduce the retained risk to an acceptable level. This is sometimes referred to as 'buying the risk' – so the organisation has decided to accept the level of risk, but has plans in place to mitigate the impact of the risk event should it occur.

You should also bear in mind that if a risk has not been identified, whilst the event could occur, the organisation will not have any mitigating strategies in place – this is unintentionally retained risk.

6.16 Monitoring

The management of risk should be an ongoing process; therefore risk should be monitored on an ongoing basis. This may be in the shape of key risk indicators that tell us if a risk is moving from one of the categories described above to another.

7 Data management

The Data Management Organisation defines data management as '...the development, execution and supervision of plans, policies, programs and practices that control, protect, deliver and enhance the value of data and information assets.'

Due to the nature of their business, banks have always maintained information and data about their customers in a variety of formats. You may be surprised to learn that as recently as the early 1980's certain pieces of information were still being recoded in bank branches with fountain pens. However, developments in technology have radically altered the volume and format of information that is held by banks – this development can partly explain the introduction of data protection legislation after this date. You will read more about this in the Regulation chapter of this study text. Technological developments have not only altered the amount and format of data, but has also changed its accessibility. Until the early 1980's, a lot of information was held at branch level, and due to the storage devices used (bound ledgers) this information was only accessible at its source. If you compare this to current data management arrangements, information can be stored in one part of the organisation, but can be accessed by a wide range of staff (and indeed customers) in a host of locations.

When considering data management, it is perhaps best to think of this data as the collective memory of the bank. Businesses will use a variety of methods for storing data, whilst it is simple to think of this as computer systems, other aspects of it are filing cabinets, notice boards and people. No matter how the data is stored, we need to consider how quickly data can be entered and retrieved from the system, and a number of different systems can be used. These include:

- A transaction processing system – to collect and store data from routine transactions.

- A management information system – which will convert data from the transaction processing system into information that the organisation needs for management purposes – for example, the total amount of deposits and advances in a particular area or perhaps a business unit.

- A decision support system – this will support managerial decision making by providing models to process and analyse data. The risks involved in these models would be subject to the bank's Model Risk Policy.

- Executive information system – which provides information to senior management to inform the strategic management of the business.

- Data mining – which will use statistical analysis to uncover hidden trends and relationships in data.

QUICK QUESTION

What do you think are the desirable attributes for the data stored by an organisation?

Write your answer here before reading on.

These include:

- The ability to share data to allow a number of people to access the data at the same time. If the data is unlikely to change, then this could be achieved simply by printing and distributing multiple copies of the data.

- It must be simple to move the data around the organisation to the people who need it.

- Security – the data must be kept safe and backed up as necessary.

- The information must be reliable and precise.

- Data should be current and up to date.

- The data must be fit for purpose and support the decision making processes that it serves.

7.1 The role of the organisation's people

The staff within the organisation are a key component of the firm's memory. There is a huge amount of information in any organisation that is shared through undocumented and sometimes invisible informal networks – sometimes referred to as the 'grapevine'. 'Metamemory' is the word given to the skill of being able to use the memory of the business – essentially this is about knowing where the relevant information is and how to access it. The standard workflows and procedures used in banks is one way of ensuring consistency and accuracy in the management of information.

7.2 Documents

Reports, email, memos and manuals are communications mediums used in a businesses to manage and share information and data.

7.3 Problems with data management systems

As with any process and system, there are a number of drawbacks associated with the management of data, including:

- Redundancy – the same information may be stored in a number of locations across the business – for example, a customer's address. However, when the customer advises a change of address, how do we ensure that this is captured in all of the right location?

- Lack of data control – if data is managed in different ways by different parts of the organisation, then there is the danger that an inconsistent approach will creep in.

- Poor interfacing will mean that data can be useless to its users.

- Delays – in current operating environments – but decision makers may need to access data quickly. However if the design of the system leads to delay, then this can render the information either stale or dangerously inaccurate due to a change in the operating environment.

- Reality – data must be relevant to the climate in which the firm operates.

- Lack of integration – if the data is spread throughout the organisation, the task of integrating it throughout the firm may be costly and complex.

8 Business process re-engineering

Effective management is dependent on efficient business processes to meet customer and stakeholder needs. A process is defined as 'a set of linked activities that take an input and transforms it to create an output.' Businesses need to constantly change and review the way they work to remain competitive and profitable. As a guide, organisations should adopt a philosophy of continuous improvement, where processes are changed in gradual stages to maximise the success of process improvements. However, sometimes, certain processes may need a rapid and radical overhaul. This may be caused by stakeholder pressure to achieve cost reductions or investment returns, for example. **Business process re-engineering** (BPR) was defined by Hammer & Champy (1993) as:

> 'The fundamental re-thinking and radical re-design of business process to achieve dramatic improvements in critical, contemporary measures of performance, such as cost, quality, service and speed.'

This diagram illustrates the relationship between continuous improvement and breakthrough improvement:

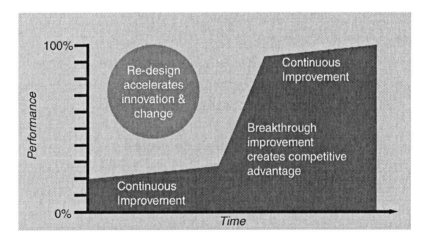

As you can see, small changes occur constantly, but from time to time major change will impact the firm, before returning to a period of incremental change. The important thing to keep in mind is that change is an ongoing process – organisations no longer stand still. Rather they are dynamic and evolving environments.

8.1 The approach to business process re-engineering

1. **Develop the business vision and process objectives**

   The BPR method is driven by a business vision, which implies specific business objectives such as cost reduction, time reduction and output quality improvement.

2. **Identify the business processes to be re-designed**

   Most firms use the high-impact approach, which focuses on the most important processes or those that conflict most with the business vision. A lesser number of firms use the 'exhaustive approach' that attempts to identify all the processes within an organisation and then prioritise them in order of redesign urgency.

3. **Understand and measure the existing processes**

    To avoid the repeating of old mistakes and to provide a baseline for future improvements.

4. **Identify IT levers**

    Awareness of IT capabilities should influence BPR.

5. **Design and build a prototype of the new process**

    The actual design should not be viewed as the end of the BPR process. Rather, it should be viewed as a prototype, with successive iterations. The metaphor of prototype aligns the BPR approach with quick delivery of results and the involvement and satisfaction of customers.

BPR should not be entered into lightly and people may be wary of BPR programmes, as they have sometimes been accompanied by massive redundancy programmes.

Other reasons for criticisms of the approach are as follows:

- BPR focuses on processes and as a result it sometimes becomes very internally focused, at the expense of customers.

- BPR assumes the need to 'wipe the slate clean' and re-design processes, rather than tinker with the existing process.

- Sometimes, gradual and incremental change (such as Kaizen) may be a better approach. The incremental change philosophy is more people-oriented and BPR requires considerable change management skills.

8.2 Total Quality Management (TQM)

There are a number of different approaches to **TQM**, but they have several characteristics in common. They all require organisations to:

- Know their business direction (mission/vision/objectives/values)
- Know their customers
- Know what their customers think of the services/products currently supplied and to be committed to providing products/services, which consistently meet their expectations at the right cost
- Provide good value, relative to available alternatives
- Be committed to finding problem areas and take responsibility to resolve them
- Be committed to pursuing TQM, especially at top management level

The role of employees in TQM is often under-emphasised – they should feel free to experiment and confident to do so. They also need to be fully trained to ensure they are equipped to deal with the new challenges. Managers should equip themselves with a toolkit of creative and problem-solving techniques such as:

- **SWOT and PEST analysis**
- **Brainstorming and nominal group technique**
- **Quality circles**
- **Six sigma**
- Ishikawa/Fishbone/**cause and effect diagrams**
- **6 Thinking Hats**

8.3 SWOT analysis

Strengths: could include what organisation is effective at; well known for; generates its reputation; causes other organisations to learn from them; co-operation with other organisations.

Weaknesses: may include things the organisation does badly at; is ineffective; has poor reputation for; losses, hardships; retention, turnover, sickness; complaints or investigations.

Opportunities: could be future possibilities if some weaknesses are eliminated and probably requires most creative thinking.

Threats: could mean from competitors or from failing to take advantage of opportunities or build on success. Could be due to complacency or taking eye off the ball.

Strengths and weaknesses are internal to the organisation, opportunities and threats are external.

8.4 PEST analysis

This examines the external environment and global factors that can affect organisations. A PEST analysis can provide a quick visual representation of external pressures.

Political factors may include legislation, government policy and may be at a local, regional, national or international level.

Economic factors may include consumer activity, inflation or unemployment. It may cover government policy e.g. taxation changes, transport policy.

Social factors may include changes in the population e.g. lower birth rate may lead to recruitment difficulties. Demographic changes may affect organisations e.g. people may move away from an area for various reasons.

Technological. Managers must be aware of the impact of new technologies, which can be more effective, efficient and reduce costs. Examples may include equipment or improved communication systems.

Recently, two other factors have been added (making it PESTLE analysis):

Legal: The effects of national and legal legislation or regulation.

Environmental: Local, national and global environmental issues.

8.5 How to facilitate SWOT and PEST analyses

You should gather a group of people who are knowledgeable about the area of improvement or are connected to the input/output. Then draw a square on a flipchart or board and divide into 4 quadrants with the SWOT/PEST headings in each (see below). Follow the brainstorm rules described later to generate comments. Use results to focus improvement efforts and further problem-solving techniques.

Strenghts	Weaknesses
Opportunities	Threats

Political	Economic
Social	Technology

8.6 Brainstorming

Brainstorming is a technique for getting a large number of ideas from a small group of people in a short amount of time. To get the best results follow these rules:

No criticism

Participants should contribute ideas without fear of criticism from others. They likewise should suspend judgement on the ideas of others.

Freewheel

The process of brainstorming should promote the free flow of ideas without analysis or evaluation. It allows apparently silly or far-fetched ideas, which may develop into something useful.

Go for quantity

The aim is to get as many different ideas as possible in the allotted time. Everyone should contribute something, however unimportant it may appear to be.

Record

Write down all ideas, even repetitions on a flipchart for all to see. The written words themselves will trigger other ideas for the team.

Cross fertilise

Use other people's ideas as springboards for your own. Building on ideas is an effective way of creating the best ideas.

Incubate

After the allotted time for generating ideas, each person should identify those ideas they find most useful. The team can then select the ideas, which should be developed.

Reverse brainstorm

If the group is finding it difficult to generate ideas or the subject has been explored before, try reversing the objective to aid creativity. When the ideas have been listed, reverse them back to answer the original objective.

For example, if the objective is to increase customer satisfaction, reverse this to how can we ensure our customers complain? From an idea, such as don't answer their emails may come a reversed idea of monitoring/ improving letter response times.

In order to run a brainstorming session, the facilitator should define the problem or issue to be brainstormed. Thereafter the group should shout out suggestions/ideas which the facilitator should scribe onto a flip chart or marker board – this visibility of ideas is important as this may spark good ideas in the minds of other participants. It is useful if the facilitator comes from a different business area than the participants and that they simply carry out the role of facilitator – they do not participate or comment on any of the ideas.

8.7 Nominal group technique (NGT)

A structured form of brainstorming with up to 10 participants and an experienced facilitator (or up to 3-4 groups of up to 10 participants, with a spokesperson for each group and a single facilitator overall)

Underlying principles

NGT is based on three fundamental, research-based principles:

- Nominal Groups are thought to generate better quality ideas than interacting groups typical of classic brainstorming. A nominal group consists of several people (usually gathered in one room) who are prepared to work as a team to resolve a problem. This sharing of ideas (which are anonymously submitted) promotes a sense of involvement and motivation within the group.

- The round robin element provides encouragement and equal opportunities for all members to contribute. Contribution from all participants is encouraged and every individual's idea is given equal standing, whether unique or not.

- Reliable communication requires that the recipient's understanding of a message be checked with the sender, especially in the case of 'new ideas being put forward. Checks for accurate communication are built in to the technique.

Standard procedure

Various forms of the procedure can be undertaken, however, the classical form uses the following steps:

1. Anonymous generation of ideas, in writing, begins with the facilitator stating the problem and giving the participants up to 10 minutes to jot down any initial ideas privately. The facilitator also writes down their own ideas.

2. Round-robin recording of ideas allows each person in turn to read out one idea, which the facilitator writes up on a flip chart for all to view and numbered sequentially. This is repeated going around the groups until all ideas are exhausted and any duplicates are eliminated.

3. Serial discussion then occurs to clarify ideas and check communication is encouraged by the facilitator. Working through each idea systematically asking for questions or comments with a view to developing a shared understanding of an idea. Discussions are calm and controlled to aid clarification of the idea, they are not heated debates.

4. A preliminary anonymous vote on item importance is usually carried out.

5. Further discussion and voting takes place if the voting is not consistent. Steps 3 – 4 can be repeated and any ideas that received votes will be re-discussed for clarification.

8.8 Quality circles and six sigma

A quality circle is a group of people who meet regularly to discuss quality related work problems so that they may examine and generate solutions to these. The circle is empowered to promote and bring the quality improvements through to fruition.

These are credited to so-called quality guru Professor Ishikawa in 1962 and have been in use in various forms ever since – particularly as workshops to facilitate change and improvement.

Quality circles require

- Commitment from senior management, unit management, staff and of course the circle members.

- A team of 5-20 people, who need to participate freely together, to challenge assumptions and existing methods, examine data and explore possibilities.

- They need to be able to call in expertise and ask for training.

- The quality circle needs a budget so they can be responsible for tests and possible pilots.

- They need a skilled team leader who works as a facilitator of team efforts not a dominator.

8.9 Six sigma

This is a name given to an approach to quality first adopted by Motorola in the 1980s. Their manufacturing objective was to achieve as near to zero defects as possible. Sigma derives from the Greek symbol for standard deviation and Motorola decided that the specification range of any part of the product/service should be ±6 the standard deviation of the process.

The six sigma approach holds that improvement initiatives can only be successful if significant resources and training are devoted to their managers. It recommends training groups of practitioners who act as internal consultants to improve processes. They become experts and classed as Master Black Belt, Black Belts and Green Belts (deriving from martial arts classifications).

Master black belt

These are the experts in Six Sigma tools and techniques. Primarily seen as teachers, coaches and mentors to Black Belts and Green Belts. Their skills include quantitative analytical skills and interpersonal skills. This role is likely to be full time.

Black belt

These play a direct role in organising improvement teams and coaching green belts. They will require a minimum of 20-25 days training and carry out at least one major improvement programme over a 3-6 month training period. These roles may also be full-time.

Green belt

Work within improvement teams, usually as team leaders and facilitators. Training will take 10-15 days and may be expected to spend around 20% of their time on improvement projects.

The 5-Stage Six Sigma Improvement Process (DMAIC):

- **Define.** Senior Management define what needs improving.

- **Measure.** Guided by the Black Belt measures the existing process in terms of amounts of defects (this could be human resources – errors, conflict, poor communication etc).

- **Analyse.** Using the data from the measure stage, the group challenges the existing process and ask: why are we doing this?

- **Improve.** All ideas generated by the team are implemented.

- **Control.** Controls are put in place to ensure that the new processes are used in the intended way and become the norm. Once satisfied that the new process is working, the Six Sigma expert leaves the team and moves on.

However the DMAIC concept is a cycle, meaning that once started, the continuous improvement philosophy carries on in that improvement should become part of every person's job.

8.10 Ishikawa/fishbone/cause-and-effect diagram

This is a tool that helps team identify, sort and display possible causes of a specific problem or quality and take corrective action

The basic layout of a cause and effect diagram is as follows:

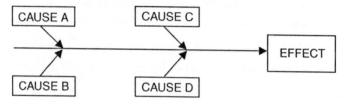

How to create a cause and effect diagram

- Identify and define the effect (fault/problem)

- Draw the spine of the fishbone and create the effect box

- Draw a horizontal arrow pointing to the right on the spine

- Identify the main causes being studied e.g.

    - Methods, materials, machinery and people

    - Policies, procedures, people and plant

    - Environment

- Write the main categories in cause boxes above and below the spine and draw diagonal lines and arrows connecting the box to the spine

- For each major branch identify other factors and add details to the fishbone

- Analyse the diagram and circle the causes you can take action on

Example diagram to show cause-and-effect diagram to identify possible causes of computer downtime:

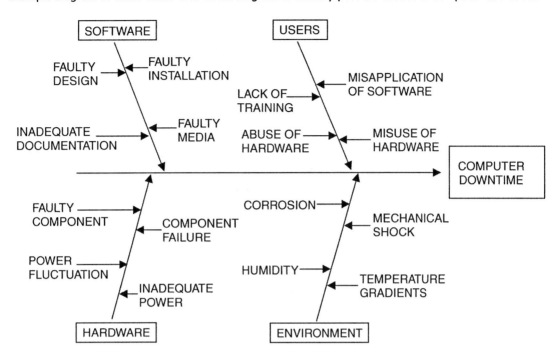

8.11   6 thinking hats

6 Thinking Hats is an important and powerful technique. It is used to look at decisions from a number of important perspectives. This forces you to move outside your habitual thinking style, and helps you to get a more rounded view of a situation.

This tool was created by Edward de Bono in his book 6 Thinking Hats.

Many successful people think from a very rational, positive viewpoint. This is part of the reason that they are successful. Often, though, they may fail to look at a problem from an emotional, intuitive, creative or negative viewpoint. This can mean that they underestimate resistance to plans, fail to make creative leaps and do not make essential contingency plans.

Similarly, pessimists may be excessively defensive, and more emotional people may fail to look at decisions calmly and rationally.

If you look at a problem with the 6 Thinking Hats technique, then you can solve it using all approaches.

How to use the tool

In meetings this tool has the benefit of blocking the confrontations that happen when people with different thinking styles discuss the same problem. It encourages a balanced approach to be taken by the group. Each Thinking Hat is a different style of thinking:

White Hat:
With this thinking hat you focus on the data available. Look at the information you have, and see what you can learn from it. Look for gaps in your knowledge, and either try to fill them or take account of them. This is where you analyse past trends, and try to extrapolate from historical data.

Red Hat:
Wearing the red hat, you look at problems using intuition, gut reaction, and emotion. Red hats should also try to think how other people will react emotionally. This participant must try to understand the responses of people who do not fully know their reasoning.

Black Hat:

Using black hat thinking, look at all the bad points of the decision. Look at it cautiously and defensively. Try to see why it might not work. This is important because it highlights the weak points in a plan. It allows you to eliminate them, alter them, or prepare contingency plans to counter them.

Black Hat thinking helps to make your plans tougher and more resilient. It can also help you to spot fatal flaws and risks before you embark on a course of action. Black Hat thinking is one of the real benefits of this technique, as many successful people get so used to thinking positively that often they cannot see problems in advance. This leaves them under-prepared for difficulties.

Yellow Hat:

The yellow hat helps you to think positively. It is the optimistic viewpoint that helps you to see all the benefits of the decision and the value in it. Yellow Hat thinking helps you to keep going when everything looks gloomy and difficult.

Green Hat:

The Green Hat stands for creativity. This is where you can develop creative solutions to a problem. It is a freewheeling way of thinking, in which there is little criticism of ideas. A whole range of creativity tools can help you here.

Blue Hat:

The Blue Hat stands for process control. This is the hat worn by people chairing meetings. When running into difficulties because ideas are running dry, they may direct activity into Green Hat thinking. When contingency plans are needed, they will ask for Black Hat thinking, etc.

A variant of this technique is to look at problems from the point of view of different professionals (e.g. doctors, architects, sales directors, etc.) or different customers.

Six Thinking Hats is a good technique for looking at the effects of a decision from a number of different points of view. It allows necessary emotion and scepticism to be brought into what would otherwise be purely rational decisions. It opens up the opportunity for creativity within decision-making. The technique also helps, for example, persistently pessimistic people to be positive and creative. Plans developed using the 6 Thinking Hats technique will be sounder and more resilient than would otherwise be the case. It may also help you to avoid public relations mistakes, and spot good reasons not to follow a course of action before you have committed to it.

The technique can also be used to develop team members. Should an individual normally have a positive outlook and so finds it difficult to empathise with more negative members of the team, it can be useful to ask them to take on the black hat role and vice versa. By doing this, you are encouraging individuals to move outside their comfort zone and look at things from a different viewpoint. The result should be a greater awareness of others in the team and their perspectives.

KEY WORDS

Key words in this chapter are given below. There is space to write your own revision notes and to add any other words or phrases that you want to remember.

- External customer
- Internal customer
- Service level agreement
- Outsourcing
- Risk management
- Operational risk
- Risk management lifecycle
- Risk avoidance
- Risk sharing
- Risk transfer
- Risk acceptance
- Risk reduction
- Risk retention
- Business process re-engineering
- Total quality management
- SWOT
- PEST analysis
- Brainstorming
- Nominal group technique
- Quality circles
- Six sigma
- Cause and effect diagram
- Six thinking hats

REVIEW

Now consider the main learning points that were introduced in this chapter.

Go through them and check that you are happy that you fully understand each point.

- Jobs in bank branches have seen a narrowing in the range of responsibilities over recent years.

- Two factors that have influenced the structure of banks were the introduction of automated credit scoring and the establishment of centralised back office processing areas. This has introduced the internal customer concept to banking.

- In recent years banks have bought in specialist services from third party suppliers – this is called outsourcing.

- Risk management seeks to reduce risk to an acceptable level.

- There are a number of types of risk – for example, credit risk, liquidity risk, etc.

- Operational risk is split into process, people, systems and external risk.

- The risk management lifecycle comprises risk identification, assessment, mitigation and monitoring.

- Data management is the development, execution and supervision of plans, policies, programs and practices that control, protect, deliver and enhance the value of data and information assets.

- Total Quality Management techniques include SWOT analysis, PEST analysis, brainstorming, nominal group techniques, quality circles, Six Sigma, cause and effect diagrams and 6 Thinking Hats.

chapter 5

LEADERSHIP AND MANAGEMENT

Contents

Learning outcomes

On completion of this chapter you should be able to:

- recognise and discuss the factors that contribute to the effective leadership and management of a retail banking organisation

- identify the main components of a retail banking strategy

- identify a range of key performance measures in a retail banking operation and critically evaluate a range of tools used to assess and manage performance against these measures

Introduction

In this chapter we will consider the factors that contribute to the effective management and leadership of a retail banking operation. The chapter starts with a discussion around the key differences between leadership and management. We then move on to consider the actions that a successful leader should take, before discussing how the strategic direction of an organisation is formulated and implemented. We then return to more of the operational aspects of managing people – in particular how staff can be coached to raise performance and how this performance is managed. As we live in a period of change, the chapter will conclude with a discussion around the most effective ways to mange change.

1 What is a manager?

QUICK QUESTION

Within your organisation are all managers at the same level?

Write your answer here before reading on.

The answer to this question will, almost certainly, be no. As you will be aware, there are different levels of management and different types of specialist managers within any organisation and they all have specific functions. To start this section we will look at what the common elements of the roles of the manager are.

As there are hierarchical levels in an organisation, so there are managerial levels. Senior managers will spend much of their time thinking of the long term future direction of the business and, although operational managers may also think longer term, they are more concerned with achieving weekly and monthly goals. Team leaders may be more concerned with daily goals. This is a fundamental in the roles of a manager – over what time span does a managers decisions effect? Broadly speaking, the more senior the manager, then the longer the time period their decisions will affect. We will return to this theme later on in the chapter when we look at strategic decisions. Despite this diversity of role and specialisation is it still possible to define the word manager.

QUICK QUESTION

Write down your definition of a manager.

Write your answer here before reading on.

The first person to define management was Henri Fayol (1841 – 1925). He wrote that management is:

To manage is to forecast and plan, to organise, to command, to coordinate and to control.

Whilst more modern writers have put more of emphasis on the need to guide, lead and motivate, there are still many common elements with Fayol's definition.

Naylor defined management in 1999 as:

Management is the process of achieving organisational objectives, within a changing environment, by balancing efficiency, effectiveness and equity, obtaining most from limited resources, and working with and through other people.

Note that Naylor's definition draws in the theme of managing in a changing environment and again we will consider this further later on.

We will now look at what these definitions mean.

Organisational objectives

Most people will agree that effective management is about the achievement of organisational objectives or goals. In order for any planning to take place, then there must be established goals or objectives to work towards. This is one of the important ways in which managers will communicate to the people who report to them. If these people have clearly defined goals to work to, then they are able to plan and coordinate both their work and the work of others. Objectives will start at the top of the organisation with the strategic objectives and then percolate their way down the hierarchy to different areas and levels within the business. Eventually these objectives are percolated to the extent that they become objectives for individual members of staff.

When we think about organising, then we are looking at both time and resources. This can result in designing an organisational structure that defines the relationship between departments and people – this will allow for responsibilities and authority to be allocated to individuals through their job descriptions or specifications. This organisation will also allow work to be delegated and so ensure the unity of command. When devising this structure, the number of individuals who report to the one manager – the **span of control** – should be limited to ensure effective control takes place.

A changing environment

As you will be aware, one of the few constants in the working environment of the 21st century is change. This change impacts on both the organisation and on those who work in it. An important as aspect of a manager's role is to deal with change and help those with whom (s)he comes in contact with to cope successfully with this change.

Balancing efficiency, effectiveness and equity

These are three words that are often freely used when discussing the skills of a manager, but often without much thought as to their real meaning.

QUICK QUESTION

Write down what you understand by the words efficiency, effectiveness and equity.

Write your answer here before reading on.

Efficiency is the measure of how well we can turn inputs into outputs. For example, a member of staff whose job involves high degrees of word processing could have their efficiency measured by typing speed expressed in terms of words per minute. In order to do this we are comparing a specified input to output in the same way as we measure a car's fuel consumption efficiency by talking of its 'miles per litre' where the input of fuel is converted to the output of distance travelled.

Effectiveness, on the other hand is how well we achieve results. In the previous example, let's say that the individual is working in the preparation of legal documents and is able to type 90 words per minute, but their work is riddled with errors, then they are not being terribly effective. Effectiveness therefore is about getting results. There can often be too strong an emphasis on getting the end product in place no matter the cost – for example, a team of engineers may work long hours of overtime in order to get a power line in place and operational by the deadline they have been set. However, by the time the overtime bill has been met, this goal may have been achieved well over budget.

Equity is about fairness to all. For example, the organisation should not lose sight of the people who are affected by its operations. In many sectors, there will be a regulator who is concerned with equity amongst consumers and financial services are no exception.

Obtaining the most from limited resources

Within any organisation there will be a finite amount of resources. Therefore an important part of the manager's role will be the ability to make the best use of the resources at their disposal. Coordination is an important skill to mention here – where resources are limited, we need to be able to coordinate materials, equipment, financial and human resources to ensure that the goals of the organisation are met.

With and through other people

We often read of management being the ability to ...get things done through other people and this indeed is an important aspect of the manager's role. Management is a social process where we need to work with others – either other members of the organisation or people who are external to the company.

Overarching all of this is the ability of the manager to communicate. Communication is the keystone of management – if we communicate well, then we will be able to fulfil this definition of management more effectively.

2   What is a leader?

Most of us know, at an instinctive level, that management and leadership are different. However, understanding just how they differ at a practical level if often elusive. This understanding is essential to fulfil a team leader role and stimulate high performance in teams.

Q U I C K   Q U E S T I O N

What do you think are the differences between management and leadership?

Write your answer here before reading on.

Management is basically about controlling things, being hands on with activities like budgets, timescales, progress etc.   Leadership is more concerned with direction, movement, progress and change. The following quotations might help clarify this:

> Managers do things right – Leaders do the right thing – Warren Bennis.
>
> A real leader faces the music, even when they don't like the tune – Anon.
>
> Leadership is the art of getting someone else to do something you want done because he wants to do it - Dwight Eisenhower.

Q U I C K   Q U E S T I O N

Do you think that this means that leadership is better than management?

Write your answer here before reading on.

This is certainly not the case.

Management activities cannot be ignored. Sound management will underpin successful leadership. Combining management activities with leadership activities will lead to better results. There are a number of activities that may be deemed to be either management activities or leadership activities – a

team meeting, for example, can be a routine management activity or an inspiring leadership activity depending on the way the team leader runs it. The test is how team members feel at the end of it. Do they feel keen or even inspired to do what is necessary?

There is a useful distinction that may be drawn between managers and leaders:

- Management is a **function** that must be exercised in any business.
- Leadership is a **relationship** between the leader and the led that can energise an organisation.

A number of writers over the years have attempted to define leadership – we will look at these later on in the chapter. However, when looking at these definitions there are a number of common elements, around people, influencing, and goals.

It can be difficult at times to be prescriptive about the specific things that a leader should do in order to inspire team members as teams and leaders operate in a variety of situations. This can be borne out in your own experience – you do doubt have experience of working for effective leaders and may well have worked for ineffective leaders.

3   What is an organisation?

Before we move on to look at the functions of a manager, we must reflect on what is meant by an organisation.

QUICK QUESTION

Why do you think that this is necessary?

Write your answer here before reading on.

We need to be clear about what an organisation is because managers exist within organisations. When we look at their role, we see that it is managers who manage the resources of the organisation – the finance, the people, the resources, etc.

QUICK QUESTION

What organisations have you encountered so far today?

Write your answer here before reading on.

There will be many and various answers to this question. The most obvious is the organisation that you work for, coming a close second will be the Chartered Banker Institute by virtue of the fact that you are studying this course. Thereafter, your list may become rather diverse – it could include the organisation that transported you to work today, the library that you are studying in, the radio station that you are listening to and (if it is classical music), the orchestra that are playing at the moment.

Organisations are present in our social, political and work environments and it is impossible to imagine life without them.

QUICK QUESTION

What common factors do organisations share?

Write your answer here before reading on.

Most likely, you have reflected that organisations are made up of a number of people who are all working to a common goal. All of these are present in the following definitions:

An organisation is a social device for efficiently accomplishing through group means some stated purpose.

Katz and Kahn

There are three common features in and organisation – people, objectives and structure. It is the interaction of people in order to achieve objectives that forms the basis of an organisation.

Mullins

The planned coordination of the activities of a number of people for the achievement of some common, explicit purpose or goal, through the division of labour and function and through a hierarchy of authority and responsibility.

Schein

An organisation is a system of cooperative human activities.

Barnard

What do all of these definitions tell us about the common factors of organisations?

Firstly, they tell us that organisations are goal orientated. The performance of the organisation will affect its survival and so this performance needs to be clearly defined – whether in terms of profit, market share, listener figures, waiting lists, etc. If the organisation fails to meet these goals over a period of time, then its very future may be threatened. To remain a member of the organisation may well demand that a certain performance level is attained by the individual. In order to achieve this level of performance, effort has to be coordinated and therefore controlled by someone within the organisation. This leads us onto the second point.

The organisation needs to have a structure. In other words, activities undertaken by individuals within the organisation must be coordinated to achieve the desired outputs of the organisation. This structure should have a clearly defined hierarchy of positions. Each position will have a greater or lesser degree of autonomy and power, resulting in different levels of management. Although there have been great changes in the structure of this organisation over the past 20 years or so, hierarchies are still very much in evidence in organisations – although they may well be much flatter than they were in the past.

Thirdly, there is a social element to the organisation. People will tend to work in groups to achieve the goals of the organisation.

Finally, technical systems will be in evidence. By this we mean that the people within the organisation will need to use their skills, knowledge, expertise and machinery/technology to work towards the goals of the organisation.

4 The functions of management

Whilst there are a variety of definitions covering what different writers feel are the functions of a manager, they do have some common threads. This comes about through an acceptance that the manager is someone who has the responsibility within the organisation of achieving results, not just through their own efforts, but also through others. If there are goals and objectives to achieve, then the manager needs to direct people and other resources towards achieving these goals.

Most writers will agree that there are six main functions of management.

QUICK QUESTION

What do you think these main functions of management are?

Write your answer here before reading on.

We will consider these in turn.

4.1 Planning

Planning implies the establishment of organisation, the breaking down of duties, devising a programme and objectives for a work area and allocating the work amongst the team. It calls for forecasts and demands that managers look ahead and anticipate future events.

4.2 Organising

This involves both time and resources. It can mean designing the structure of the organisation and defining the relationships between individuals and departments, i.e. allocating authority and responsibility within the framework of a job description. It also means delegating work and grouping activities, ensuring unity of command and objectives. As mentioned earlier, the number of people reporting to one manager (span of control) should be limited in number to ensure effective control.

4.3 Problem solving

This involves the manager seeing difficulties and challenges, hopefully before they arise, and planning action to cope with the situation.

4.4 Coordinating

This means the co-ordination of materials, equipment, financial and staff resources to ensure the production of goods or services that the organisation is concerned with. This is crucial where a project or expansion project is involved, as all activities should proceed at a common pace.

4.5 Controlling

This is concerned with evaluating performance and taking steps to bring it into line with plans. It presupposes that plans are already in existence, otherwise there is nothing to control, aim for or measure performance against. From the plans, targets are derived and performance can then be measured against these targets.

Budgets are one of a number of techniques used to control output and expenditure.

4.6 Communicating

Communication was defined by Williamson (1981) as:

> *Communicating is a process whereby messages are transmitted from one person to another.*

Communication is the keystone of managing people as it touches on everything we do. If a manager was to improve their communication skills, then they will delegate better, lead better, motivate better, and coach better and so on.

QUESTION TIME 6

James Smith was appointed to his first team leader post six years ago. He had been an outstanding performer at his last job which required a great deal of technical expertise. You have been his manager for a year and you are disappointed in him as a team leader. He spends as much of his time as possible immersed in the detail and the technical work, and does not interact with his team very much. He manages by writing long e-mails which set out what should be done, the methods to be used, and a clear timescale. If the results are not achieved, the offender is subjected to a public reprimand. James' results are barely adequate because of the rapid turnover of staff in his area.

1. What is your analysis of the current situation?

2. What steps would you take to help James to improve?

Write your answer here then check with the answer at the back of the book.

5 Managerial roles

As well as the functions and processes managers are involved in, it is possible to identify the various roles that they occupy. Mintzberg (1973) classified these into ten different roles, divided into three major groups:

- Interpersonal roles
- Informational roles
- Decisional roles

Interpersonal roles

Interpersonal roles arise from the manager's relations with others. Here the manager can be viewed as a figurehead, representing the organisation and its policies – for example, by signing documents, or distributing awards for high achieving staff at some prestigious function. This role also calls for leadership abilities in that the manager is responsible for the motivation of employees. There is also a role to play in liaising with managers and others from outside the manager's own area of responsibility.

Informational roles

Informational roles arise as the manager has an important role to play communicating in the organisation. This involves the monitoring of information so that the manager can understand how the organisation operates and the influence of the external environment.

The manager will also act as a disseminator of information, passing on information from the environment to the organisation and from senior management to employees. The manager can also act as a spokesperson, communicating information internally to other departments or levels within the organisation and externally to other organisations – for example, with suppliers.

Decisional roles

Decisional roles involve the manager in making decisions about the future of the organisation and the department. In an entrepreneurial role, the manager initiates and plans controlled change by solving problems and taking action to improve the existing situation. Managers also act as a disturbance handlers reacting to involuntary situations and unpredictable events.

The resource allocator role also involves the manager in using formal authority to decide where effort will be expended and in deciding upon the allocation of scarce resources.

The negotiator role involves the manager in negotiating activities with other individuals and organisations – for example, negotiating a new contract with a supplier.

All of these roles can be illustrated by Mintzberg as follows:

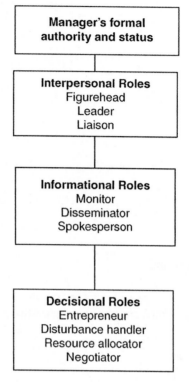

Mintzberg suggests that this is an arbitrary division of the manager's role and that the manager's work does not divide neatly into these categories.

QUICK QUESTION

Using Mintzberg's classification, list some of the jobs that either you or your manager carries out under each heading.

Write your answer here before reading on.

What you have written will vary according to your experience and roles. However, if a manager represents their team at meetings, this is an informational role, decisions about work and staffing would fit into the decisional roles, and cascading information would fit into the interpersonal role.

Braddick suggests the common features are:

- Paperwork
- Telephone calls
- Meetings
- Contacts
- Content – junior management deals with operational problems, whilst a senior manager deals with fewer problems but over a wider basis

QUESTION TIME 7

What do you think leads a manager to be successful?

You could use Mintzberg's description to classify what leads to success.

Write your answer here then check with the answer at the back of the book.

5.1 The role of the manager and the team member

All individuals come to work with certain expectations about what they can gain from the organisation; for example:

- Safe working conditions
- Job security
- Challenging and interesting jobs
- Equitable personnel policies
- Respect

QUICK QUESTION

What distinguishes the manager from the individual?

Write your answer here before reading on.

It is the responsibility of the manager to manage, in other words, get things done through others. It is through the process of managing that the efforts of all the individuals are co-ordinated and directed. Management is concerned with carrying out organisational processes and the execution of work.

The individual in the organisation should direct activities towards the goals management has indicated, and the individual's primary responsibility is for their own actions, whereas managers are responsible for all those in the team.

Management reconciles the needs of the individuals with the requirements of the organisation states Mullins. It is the integrating activity of management that permeates every aspect of the operations of the organisation.

There have been various attempts to study the behaviours which make a manager more effective. Boyatzis (1982) classified five key performance areas where assessment and development programmes could be focused:

Boyatzis' key performance areas:

1. Goal and action management
2. Directing team members
3. Human resource management
4. Leadership
5. Specialist knowledge

---

6 Leadership

Having looked at the difference between leadership and management, along with a description of what a manager does, we are now ready to focus our attentions on what a successful leader does.

As we have already seen, the job of the manager normally involves some leadership ability, but as you may well be aware from your own experience, not all leaders are managers. The difference between leadership and management (although sometimes they may be synonymous) is that management involves co-ordinating activities to achieve organisational goals whereas leadership is more concerned with acting as a guide and motivator for others – although in many situations these two functions are carried out by the same person.

6.1 Teams

As mentioned above, if we are to have a leader, then we also need to have a team or a group to lead.

What is a team?

On average, according to Handy (1976), managers spend 50% of their working day in one team or another. Senior managers can spend as much as 80% of their time in groups. They are an essential feature of working life with most organisations broken up into departments or sections.

Most organisational tasks require the co-ordination of these sub-units, so an understanding and appreciation of the nature and functioning of teams is essential if a manager is to 'manage' effectively.

QUICK QUESTION

What is your definition of a team?

Write your answer here before reading on.

There are many definitions available as to what constitutes a team. Mullins (1989) suggests one essential feature is that its members regard themselves as belonging to a group.

Here are some other definitions that might be of interest to you:

> *A team may be defined as a unified group of people who have their own areas of responsibility within the team, but who need the resources and support of other members of the team to accomplish objectives.*
>
> (Source Mastering People Management Mark Thomas)
>
> *A team is a small number of people with complementary skills who are committed to a common purpose, performance goals and approach for which they hold themselves mutually accountable.*
>
> (Source Katzenbach and Smith)
>
> *Groups develop into teams when their common purpose is understood by all the members.*
>
> (Source Maddux)

6.2 Teams and groups

The terms team and group are often used to mean the same thing – but there are important differences between the two.

- A team comprises of a formal working group of people who are united to achieve a common goal.
- Its success depends on the quality of the combined effort of every team member.
- Effective teams are those that can achieve more together than could be achieved by the individuals working whether alone or as a group.

What makes teams distinct from groups?

- Groups are normally made up of individuals who share something in common, e.g. a trait, or interest but do not necessarily work co-operatively towards a shared aim.

- Teams actively pool their resources, skills and knowledge, and work together supporting one another, interdependently and with a clear understanding of how each member will contribute to the whole.

For example, a group of Olympic sprinters share the desire to achieve their personal best running time. They may train together but the performance of each sprinter is not related to the success of the others. However, a rugby team's success depends on all members training together co-operatively to achieve a collective goal; the performance of one team member impacts directly on the success of their team-mates and the team as a whole.

6.3 Types of teams or groups in organisations

There are two major types of teams or groups in organisations:

- Formal teams
- Informal groups

The formal team

For most people, interacting with other people is a basic human need and this need can be met through working in a team. This is a group created to fulfil specific goals and tasks related to the organisation needs. They can be permanent, for example, the marketing department, or temporary, such as a project team. Normally, the team is judged by both the organisation and those within it by how successful it is in achieving the goals and tasks that it is expected to perform.

In our working environment, we will all be members of at least one **formal team**.

QUICK QUESTION

Why do you think organisation's use teams?

Write your answer here before reading on.

- Effective teamwork can make an enormous contribution to an organisation's productivity and development. As was mentioned above, effective teams outperform the individual efforts of the individuals who comprise the team.

- They can achieve more, to a better quality, more quickly and more efficiently than the most competent individuals can alone.

- When individuals come together as a team, a number of benefits can result.

QUICK QUESTION

What do you think these benefits are?

Write your answer here before reading on.

The benefits of using teams include:

- Lead times for completing tasks can be shortened.

- Close personal relationships can develop which enhance job satisfaction and a personal sense of value and well-being for team members.

- This may result in members becoming more committed to the organisation's aims and thus work harder to produce better results.

- Individuals can extend their own skills and knowledge base by learning from and observing other working practices. For example, department supervisors can share with each other the most effective techniques for managing and motivating their staff.

- Members may be stimulated by performance challenges, and support and inspire one another to achieve more.

- Combining people skills may enable the organisation to extend its range of work, e.g. increase its ability to undertake more projects, or more interesting and challenging projects, or extend the range of products and services provided e.g. Sales and Service will enable the company to attract new as well as service existing customers, or a technical author and a trainer will enable the HR department to develop in-house training courses that are tailor-made to the needs of the company.

- Opportunities to be involved in a wider range of interesting and challenging jobs can increase job satisfaction.

- The risk of failure is reduced through shared responsibility and decision-making. Decisions are more likely to have been considered thoroughly from many different viewpoints.

- Creativity can be enhanced as each team member can draw on the knowledge, skills and experience of others and use them as a sounding board for ideas.

- The skills and working practices of a successful, established team could be transferred to other projects, thereby spreading the rewards of the initial investment of time and energy that team building requires.

The informal group

The **informal group** tends to develop from informal relationships (those which are unnecessary for the organisation), formed to satisfy needs beyond those of doing a job. Research studies indicate that informal relationships and groups are most likely to develop when people meet in the course of other activities outside of work. They usually tend to be horizontal cliques (with people of the same status) but vertical or mixed groups can also be formed. For example, a group of colleagues from different parts of the organisation who have arranged to train for a local half marathon together. Schein (1980) maintains that informal groups almost always arise if the opportunities exist. They can work to the benefit and detriment of the organisation.

QUICK QUESTION

List what you think are the advantages for both the organisation and the individual members of informal groups.

Write your answer here before reading on.

The advantages of informal groups include:

- The group members tend to have a common value system and certain shared views.

- They provide social satisfaction for individuals.

- They aid communication within the organisation, providing an information flow where none usually exists. By belonging to an informal group, networking opportunities for the members exist. The contacts that come about as a result of membership of these groups may be very difficult to replicate in any other format.

- They provide pressure groups demanding action or positive changes within the organisation.

- They provide standards or norms of behaviour for their members. Elton Mayo argued that group norms had more influence on the behaviour of its members than organisational norms.

QUICK QUESTION

List what you think are the disadvantages for both the organisation and the individual members of informal groups.

Write your answer here before reading on.

The disadvantages of informal groups include:

- They can serve a counter-organisational function in that they tend to counteract any coercive tendencies of the organisation.

- They can become too powerful and act as a disruptive force within the organisation.

- They can provide resistance to change and alterations in work patterns.

- The norms and standards for the group can be inconsistent with those of management.

- They provide an active grapevine, spreading rumours throughout the business – particularly at a time of change. These rumours may not be accurate and will tend to become exaggerated as they spread.

- They can generate conflict when they clash with the organisation.

6.4 Why are teams formed?

Teams fulfil a number of formal organisational functions and they can therefore be formed for reasons relating to the work process.

- Teams have productive functions – certain tasks can only be performed through the combined effort of a number of individuals working together. They allow tasks to be completed more efficiently because of the benefits of multiple viewpoints and specialised knowledge.

- Being a member of a team can make work more palatable. The team may encourage co-operation amongst its members in order to modify formal working arrangements sharing or rotating the unpopular jobs.

- Membership of teams can also fulfil other psychological functions – for example, the need for social contact.

- Teams provide an outlet for friendship and offer support and companionship. They can also help in solving work problems and reducing stress. (Maslow acknowledged the social needs of individuals in his hierarchy of needs).

- Teams provide a means of evaluating opinions and attitudes and are a way of confirming one's identity, status, attitude, etc. They give the individual a sense of belonging as well as providing guidelines on acceptable behaviour and acting as a control on behaviour.

Social Exchange Theory maintains that the desire to join and remain with a group or team can be explained in terms of costs (anxiety, irritation, embarrassment) against rewards (increased self esteem, praise and status). Most research seems to conclude that groups fulfil both formal and informal functions, that is, they serve both the organisational and individual's psychological needs.

The next issue that must arise is how an organisation can ensure its groups work as effectively as possible and give maximum benefit to both organisation and individual.

6.5 Effective work teams

Research has revealed that there are certain common factors apparent in effective work teams:

Goals

This is the vision of what the team is all about - why it is there. Before anything else can work, we first have to establish and understand the overall goal of the team. This understanding must be shared by all team members for it to be fully effective.

If everyone shares the same view of the goal it then becomes easier to establish what each team member can contribute to the goal. These contributions are the team roles.

Roles

This is what people do in the team to contribute to the goals of the organisation – this will include the tasks people carry out, but it also encompasses any part each person plays in maintaining the overall effectiveness of the team. Roles can include boundaries of authority and freedom and perceptions of what other team members expect.

For example, one team member might be responsible for a particular part of the safety documentation process, and furthermore be recognised as someone who keeps a level head in a crisis. Both of these roles have an important part to play in how the team operates as a whole.

Only once roles are understood and agreed within a team can the team processes be most effective. If roles are not fully agreed/understood, the following phrases (amongst others!) may be heard:

I thought you were doing that....   That's my job.... etc.

Size

There also tends to be an optimum size in effective work groups. Between five and eight members is considered ideal. This gives enough individuals for there to be variety and multiple viewpoints but people are not inhibited to speak or express their opinion.

Supportiveness

Groups whose members are supportive of others will also be more effective. Constructive criticism can be helpful to the progress of the group whereas destructive and excessively critical comments will destroy rapport and support among members.

Processes

These are how the team does things. Team processes can include the frequency, content and structure of team meetings, how decisions are made in the absence of any individual, or the ways in which decisions and information are communicated. Team processes will be affected by how the leader operates. These will have different effects on how decisions are made, and by whom, and how information is communicated.

The way in which the team processes are carried out will have a bearing on the relationships within a team.

Relationships

Relationships within a team are based on who thinks what of whom, and the extent to which any one team member respects and understands another. Differing beliefs, values and needs of individuals, and how these are dealt with will also affect relationships within a team. It is important to note that a difficulty between two or more team members may have its origin further up the hierarchy. For example, confusion of team roles may result in one team member resenting another for not doing their job or overstepping the mark. The underlying difficulty here is not that the team members dislike one another, but that the individual roles have not been agreed, which leads to misunderstandings.

Mutual respect and understanding for individuals within a team means that more of the team members' energy is spent in achieving the team goals rather than nursing personal differences.

Cohesiveness

The more effective team has similarities amongst its members in terms of background, status, objectives, norms and values. Similarity in levels of skill and ability also leads to greater cohesiveness. If a team fails to achieve its goals because of a lack of resources, either physical or material, then it develops a sense of failure and is unable to support and strengthen its membership.

6.6   Team members and their roles

Belbin Team Roles was designed by Dr Meredith Belbin who defined a team role as:

A tendency to behave, contribute and interrelate with others in a particular way.

Belbin did a great deal of work on the effectiveness of teams. He identified nine key roles for team effectiveness. He believed that for a team to be effective they needed to have all of the nine roles. However, this may make it seem that it is impossible to have an effective team if there are less than nine team members – however, it is possible for one person to take on more than one role.

The roles identified by Belbin are:

- Implementers
- Team workers
- Shapers
- Resource investigators
- Completer-Finishers
- Plants
- Monitor evaluators
- Coordinators
- Specialists

We will look at each role in turn – you will see that there is no ideal role, rather they complement one another. Belbin argues that it is when all of these roles are in evidence then we have an effective team.

Implementers

Characteristics – Implementers have practical common sense and a good deal of self-control and discipline. They favour hard work and tackle problems in a systematic fashion. On a wider front the implementer is typically a person whose loyalty and interest lie with the organisation and who is less concerned with the pursuit of self-interest. However, the implementer may lack spontaneity and show signs of rigidity.

Function – the implementer is useful to an organisation because of their reliability and capacity for application. They succeed because they are efficient and because they have a sense of what is feasible and relevant. It is said that many executives only do the jobs they wish to do and neglect those tasks, which they find distasteful. By contrast, an implementer will do what needs to be done. Good implementers often progress to high management positions by good organisational skills and competency in tackling necessary tasks.

Team workers

Characteristics – Team workers are the most supportive members of a team. They are mild, sociable and concerned about others. They have a great capacity for flexibility and adapting to different situations and people. They are perceptive and diplomatic. They are good listeners and are popular members of a team. They operate with sensitivity at work, but may be indecisive in crunch situations.

Function – the role of the team worker is to prevent interpersonal problems arising within a team and thus allows all team members to contribute effectively. Not liking friction, they will go to great lengths to avoid it. It is not uncommon for team workers to become senior leaders especially if shapers dominate team leaders. This creates a climate in which the diplomatic and perceptive skills of a teamworker become real assets, especially under a managerial regime where conflicts are liable to arise or to be artificially suppressed. Team worker leaders are seen as a threat to no one and therefore the most accepted and favoured people to serve under. Team workers have a lubricating effect on teams. Morale is better and people seem to co-operate better when they are around.

Shapers

Characteristics – Shapers are highly motivated people with a lot of nervous energy and a great need for achievement. Usually they are aggressive extroverts and possess strong drive. Shapers like to challenge others and their concern is to win. They like to lead and to push others into action. If obstacles arise, they will find a way round. Headstrong and assertive, they tend to show strong emotional response to any form of disappointment or frustration. Shapers are single-minded and argumentative and may lack interpersonal understanding. Theirs is the most competitive team role.

Function – Shapers generally make good leaders because they generate action and thrive under pressure. They are excellent at sparking life into a team and are very useful in teams where political complications are apt to slow things down; shapers are inclined to rise above problems of this kind and forge ahead regardless. They are well suited to making necessary changes and do not mind taking unpopular decisions. As the name implies, they try to impose some shape or pattern on group discussion or activities. They are probably the most effective members of a team in guaranteeing positive action.

Resource investigators

Characteristics – Resource investigators are often enthusiastic, quick off the mark extroverts. They are good at communicating with people both inside and outside the organisation. They are natural negotiators and are adept at exploring new opportunities and developing contacts. Although not a great source of original ideas, the resource investigator is effective when it comes to picking up other people's ideas and developing them. As the name suggests, they are skilled at finding out what is available and what can be done. They usually receive a warm reception from others because of their own outgoing nature.

Resource investigators are relaxed personalities with a strong inquisitive sense and a readiness to see the possibilities in anything new. However, unless they remain stimulated by others, their enthusiasm fades rapidly.

Function – are good at exploring and reporting back on ideas, developments or resources outside the group. They are the best people to set up external contacts and to carry out any subsequent negotiations. They have an ability to think on their feet and to probe others for information.

Completer-Finishers

Characteristics – Completer-Finishers have a great capacity for follow through and attention to detail. They are unlikely to start anything that they cannot finish. They are motivated by internal anxiety, yet outwardly they may appear unruffled. Typically, they are introverted and require little in the way of external stimulus or incentive. Completer finishers can be intolerant of those with a casual disposition. They are not often keen on delegating; preferring to tackle all tasks themselves.

Function – completer finishers are invaluable where tasks demand close concentration and a high degree of accuracy. They foster a sense of urgency within a team and are good at meeting schedules and deadlines. In management they excel by the high standards to which they aspire, and by their concern for precision, attention to detail and follow-through.

Plants

Characteristics – Plants are innovators and inventors and can be highly creative. They provide the seeds and ideas from which major developments spring. Usually they prefer to operate by themselves at some distance from the other members of the team, using their imagination and often working in an unorthodox way. They tend to be introverted and react strongly to criticism and praise. Their ideas may often be radical and may lack practical constraint.

They are independent, clever and original and may be weak in communicating with other people on a different wavelength.

Function – The main use of a plant is to generate new proposals and to solve complex problems. Plants are often needed in the initial stages of a project or when a project is failing to progress. Plants have usually made their mark as founders of companies or as originators of new products.

Too many plants in the one organisation, however, may be counter productive, as they tend to spend their time reinforcing their own ideas and engaging each other in combat.

Monitor evaluators

Characteristics – Monitor evaluators are serious-minded, prudent individuals with a built-in immunity from being over-enthusiastic. They are slow in making decisions preferring to think things over. Usually

they have a high critical thinking ability. They have a capacity for shrewd judgements that take all factors into account. A good monitor evaluator is seldom wrong.

Function – monitor evaluators are best suited to analysing problems and evaluating ideas and suggestions. They are very good at weighing up the pros and cons of options. To many outsiders the monitor evaluator may appear as dry, boring or even over critical. Some people are surprised that they become leaders. Nevertheless, many monitor evaluators occupy strategic posts or thrive in high-level appointments. In some jobs success or failure hinges on a relatively small number of crunch decisions. This is ideal territory for a monitor evaluator; for the person who is never wrong is the one who scores in the end.

Coordinators

Previously, this role was described as Chairman.

Characteristics – the distinguishing feature of co-ordinators is their ability to cause others to work towards shared goals. Mature, trusting and confident, they delegate readily. In interpersonal relations they are quick to spot individual talents and to use them in the pursuit of group objectives. While coordinators are not necessarily the most insightful members of a team, they have a broad and worldly outlook and generally command respect.

Function – coordinators are well placed when put in charge of a team of people with diverse skills and personal characteristics. They perform better in dealing with colleagues of near or equal rank than in directing junior colleagues. Their motto might well be 'consultation with control' and they usually believe in tackling problems calmly. In some companies coordinators are inclined to clash with shapers due to their contrasting management styles.

Specialists

Characteristics – Specialists are dedicated individuals who pride themselves on acquiring technical skills and specialised knowledge. Their priorities centre on maintaining professional standards and on furthering and defending their own field. While they show great pride in their own subject, they usually lack interest in other people's subjects. Eventually, the specialist becomes the expert by sheer commitment along a narrow front. There are few people who have either the single mindedness or the aptitude to become a first class specialist.

A lot of people get confused about the Specialist role and tend to think of it in terms of a person's function rather than behaviour. This is particularly so at a senior level, for example, the production or operations director may regard the finance director as a Specialist. The true behavioural Specialist however is driven by the pursuit of knowledge and information. These people just love the process of learning. It pervades everything they do and they want to go into things very deeply, thus everyone and not just those who are impressed by their functional expertise will see them as truly knowledgeable.

Function – specialists have an indispensable part to play in some teams, for they provide the rare skill upon which the firm's service or product is based. As managers, they command support because they know more about their subject than anyone else and can usually be called upon to make decisions based on in-depth experience.

7 Stages of team development

We can continue our study of roles by looking at the **stages of team development**. Tuckman developed this theory, which seeks to explain the stages that a team will travel through from its inception to maturity. These stages are listed as:

- Forming
- Storming
- Norming
- Performing

7.1 Forming

This is the bringing together of a number of individuals who formulate the initial objectives of the team. At this stage, leaders, patterns of behaviour and roles begin to emerge. Members are attempting to create their identity within the team.

At this stage of development, the team typically will:

- Interact formally, cautiously and warily – as they do not know one another well at this stage
- Experience confusion concerning individual roles within the team – who does what in the team,
- Try to get to know one another – albeit at a fairly superficial level
- Tend to be guarded and reserved, keeping opinions to themselves – until they feel more comfortable later on in the stages of development
- Not involve themselves or participate much in group activities
- Need a lot of direction, guidance and reassurance
- Focus on self instead of team issues

QUICK QUESTION

What do you think should be the team leader's interventions at the forming stage?

Write your answer here before reading on.

At the forming stage, the team leader should seek to:

- Establish clear team direction and goals – to make team members feel more comfortable as they can start to see where they, as individuals, fit into the team
- Set definite personal objectives, roles and responsibilities, and clarify expectations
- Promote warm, informal, non-critical relationships
- Provide opportunities for asking questions and clarification
- Refocus attention from social and onto task-based issues

7.2 Storming

As people begin to get to know one another, they start to present their views to the team and disagreements and arguments begin to occur. It could mean conflict and the eventual collapse of the team, but if this stage is successfully passed, then new objectives and operating procedures for the team can be established.

At this stage of development, the team typically will:

- Experience conflict, confusion, frustration, anger
- Withdraw/be unwilling to participate in the activities of the team
- Focus on personal power and status issues
- Demonstrate competitive behaviours
- Voice open expressions of dissatisfaction

Personal relationships can be very strained at this stage of development, and often there are open expressions of dissatisfaction with the leader.

QUICK QUESTION

What do you think should be the team leader's interventions at the storming stage?

Write your answer here before reading on.

At the storming stage, the team leader should seek to:

- Refocus attention onto objectives
- Redefine roles
- Provide opportunities for positive feedback and discussion
- Identify conflict and deal with it quickly, calmly and constructively
- Promore and develop procedures to guide team interactions, values and good communications

However, it is important that the leader allow the team to storm. This is a stage that the team needs to work through in order to mature. There is a danger that if the leader is uncomfortable with conflict, then they may be tempted to sweep the behaviours of this stage under the carpet. Unfortunately, by doing this, the leader is simply storing up trouble for later – as the team will probably regress to this stage before it can move onto maturity.

7.3 Norming

As the conflict of the storming stage is resolved, new guidelines and standards of behaviour will be established. The norms of the team govern members' behaviour but not their thoughts. They are standards of behaviour to which members will conform and are unique to each group – its culture.

Norms are especially developed for those behaviours seen as important by the team. Norms are passed on from member to member, and often initiating behaviours help to determine the later trends; for example, the person who initially assumes leadership of the group will eventually be appointed Coordinator.

Norms can sometimes be changed or introduced by an important incident which then sets a pattern. Norms could also be regarded as 'organisational legislation'; they do not have the force of law but they still restrict behaviour. For instance, if a key member of a group works long hours and at weekends, that behaviour can spread and permeate through the group. Similarly, the amount of overtime can be established as a set amount each week.

At this stage of development, the team typically will:

- Strive for a sense of achievement and maintenance of a sense of group/belonging
- Be tolerant and accepting of one another
- Agree on procedures and processes and adhere to these
- Focus on mutual support, encouragement and harmony
- Participate in the decision-making and problem-solving process

QUICK QUESTION

What do you think should be the team leader's interventions at the norming stage?

Write your answer here before reading on.

At the norming stage, the team leader should seek to:

- Encourage additional involvement and participation from all team members in the decision making, objective setting and action planning process
- Practise a range of problem solving techniques to enable the team to accept more demanding projects
- Provide increasing opportunities for giving and receiving feedback, progress reporting and the expression of opinions
- Continue to set ever-more challenging objectives to increase the team's creative responses and innovation
- Elicit the team's opinion and reach consensus rather than imposing decisions from outside
- Reiterate and clarify procedures that encourage give and take and promote tolerance and understanding

7.4 Performing

When the group has successfully progressed through the three earlier stages, it will have created the cohesiveness to operate effectively as a team. At this stage, the team will finally be able to concentrate on the achievement of its objectives.

At this stage of development, the team typically will:

- Work together with energy and creativity
- Enjoy high levels of trust, tolerance, respect
- Have high levels of involvement and participation
- Make decisions by consensus
- Have high productivity and commitment
- Have a strong sense of team spirit, identity and pride
- Be prepared to take risks

QUICK QUESTION

What do you think should be the team leader's interventions at the performing stage?

Write your answer here before reading on.

At the performing stage, the team leader should seek to:

- Identify appropriate actions to tackle the factors that diminish performance
- Actively confront issues and develop procedures to overcome these issues
- Seek out new challenges that will demand sharper decision making skills and stimulate creative thought and innovation
- Review procedures, self assessment, evaluation and feedback of the team
- Recognise and reward the team's individual and collective successes
- Focus on opportunities for personal development of each team member

Whilst the stages of team development can appear to be an incremental process, it must also be borne in mind that it is possible for teams to regress through the stages of development. For example, a team may be at the norming stage of development, but if there are changes in the personnel of the team, it may be that they team dynamic is affected in such a way that the team moves back to the forming stage. Similarly, should the task(s) that the team is expected to accomplish alter in a dramatic fashion, then this may also impact on the stage that the team is at.

In recent years, there has been a move to introduce a final stage to this model – 'mourning'. This occurs when the team breaks up and members reflect upon their experiences and feel loss for the team and their colleagues. This can be particularly relevant for a project team, which, by its very nature, will only be created for a specific period of time. Once the project is completed, it is common for some team members to feel this sense of loss.

8 Leadership effectiveness

An issue which has concerned organisational theorists is why some leaders are effective and others ineffective. You may well have experience of this from your own working life.

QUICK QUESTION

What is it that makes for an effective leader?

Write your answer here before reading on.

A popular leader is not always an effective one. This person can sometimes hinder the performance of a team by always putting the needs of the individual (or a number of individuals) first.

An effective leader is often the one who balances the needs of the team, individual and task that has to be completed.

There are three major approaches to leadership effectiveness, corresponding broadly to historical phases:

■　Trait approach
■　Style approach
■　Contingency approach

We will look at these in turn.

8.1　Trait approach

This approach is the earliest attempt at explaining why some people are successful as leaders and others are not. It focuses on the individual occupying the post, not on the job itself.

The **trait approach** suggests that leaders have certain qualities or traits, which are innate and not easily developed or acquired, and this distinguishes them from their followers. Attention should therefore be directed to selecting as leaders those people who possess these qualities, since the characteristics cannot be developed or encouraged through training. In other words – we are either born with the ability to lead or without the ability to lead, and there is nothing that we can do about it.

QUICK QUESTION

What do you think are the traits of a successful leader?

Write your answer here before reading on.

Researchers have found it difficult to identify the traits likely to lead to leadership effectiveness. Among the many that have been suggested are size, energy, integrity, decisiveness, knowledge, wisdom and imagination.

Certain studies have cited significant correlations between some traits and leadership effectiveness. Ghiselli (1963) found intelligence, ability, initiative, self assurance and individuality important. Stogdill (1974) found intelligence, scholarship, dependability, responsibility, originality, social improvement and socio-economic status important in distinguishing leaders from non-leaders.

QUICK QUESTION

What do you think are the drawbacks to the trait approach?

Write your answer here before reading on.

There are a number of problems associated with this approach:

- It may be that effective leaders learned to develop these qualities after becoming leaders and the ability to respond to the situation is the key trait.

- There is not much agreement among researchers as to which characteristics are important.

- This approach does not help in the development and training of future leaders.

8.2   Style approach

The **style approach** introduced the concept that managers adopt very different methods when motivating staff and completing a task. These styles range from authoritarian to democratic.

Douglas McGregor summed up these two extremes in his **Theory X** (the authoritarian) and his **Theory Y** (the democratic). McGregor believed Theory Y was more appropriate for the modern manager.

The traditional approach to leadership and encouraging a satisfactory level of employee involvement and effort is expressed in:

Theory X

- The average person has an inherent dislike of work.

- Because of this most people must be coerced, controlled, threatened with punishment to get them to put adequate effort toward the achievement of organisational goals.

- The average person prefers to be directed, wishes to avoid responsibility, has relatively little ambition and wants security above all.

Fortunately, according to Theory X, not all employees are like this. There are some superior people, who can assume authority and control (those destined to be managers).

This approach can be summarised: control them and knock them into shape. These views can also be summarised as the 'carrot and stick' approach to management with incentives and sanctions combined.

A more modern approach to management is expressed in:

Theory Y

- Work is as natural as play or rest.

- The average person not only accepts but seeks responsibility.

- In modern industrial life people's potential is only partially utilised.

- External control and the threat of punishment are not the only means of bringing about effort towards organisational objectives.

The style approach suggested that certain leaders were effective because of the style they adopted. There are a number of theorists who could be said to support this approach.

White and Lippitt Iowa studies

Their research was carried out in a boys' summer camp. The group leaders adopted and changed leadership styles, from authoritarian to democratic and laissez faire.

- Authoritarian – all policies were determined by the leader. The leader dictated the jobs to be done by each member and was personal in praise and criticism.

- Democratic – all policies were determined by joint discussion between the leader and the group. The division of tasks was determined by the group and the leader was objective in his praise and criticism.

- Laissez Faire – the group alone decided the policies if any and the way tasks were to be divided. The leader gave only occasional comments on performance.

Overall, the democratic style proved to be most effective in terms of group morale and productivity.

Tannenbaum and Schmidt

Tannenbaum and Schmidt developed a continuum of leadership styles ranging from boss-centred leadership (authoritarian) to employee-centred leadership (democratic). The continuum also includes the degree of authority used by a manager and the degree of freedom for team members.

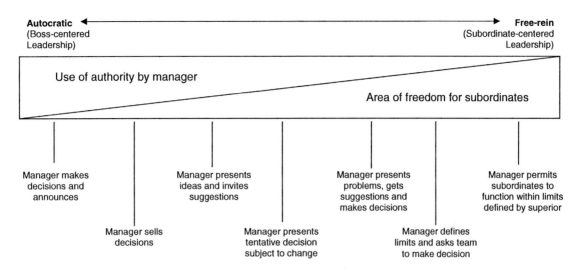

This continuum could also be summarised as tells, sells, consults.

Tannenbaum and Schmidt suggest that there are certain factors which will help to determine what type of leadership style is most appropriate:

- The manager

    - Security in their position and with the team
    - Leadership style preferences and comfort zone
    - Confidence in team members
    - Value systems

- The team members

    - Necessary knowledge and experience
    - Understanding of the organisation
    - Willingness to accept responsibility
    - Need for independence
    - Interest

The most successful managers are those who can assess the situation and respond to it adopting the most suitable style to match the circumstances.

The Ashridge studies

A series of studies at Ashridge College in the 1960s/1970s identified four styles of management (similar to the Tannenbaum and Schmidt continuum):

- The tells style – the manager makes decisions and announces them.

- The sells style – the manager makes their own decisions but rather than announce them to the team, they try to persuade the team to accept them.

- The consults style – the manager does not make the decision until they have presented the problem to the group and heard their advice and suggestions.

- Joins style – the manager delegates to a group (including the manager) the right to make decisions. The manager indicates the limits within which the decisions must be made.

QUICK QUESTION

Each style has a number of advantages and disadvantages. List what you think these are for each style.

Write your answer here before reading on.

Tells style

Advantages:

- Decisions are clear cut and rapid.
- Everyone knows who is boss.
- Things get done.
- Orderly atmosphere.
- Suitable in a crisis where time is at a premium.

Disadvantages:

- Little incentive rests with individuals.
- Work is often uninteresting as manager does not delegate.
- People do not innovate or take risks because of fear of punishment.
- Encourages yes people.
- Can result in low motivation and high turnover.

Sells style

Advantages:

- Similar to tell but more pleasant relationships between managers and staff.

Disadvantages:

- Many employees do not like being treated as children.
- Employees like independence and autonomy.
- Can also result in low motivation and high turnover.

Consults style

Advantages:

- People feel involved.
- People feel committed.
- Employees have opportunity of learning through discussion and making mistakes.
- Motivates people.

Disadvantages:

- Decisions take longer.

- Sometimes employees have nothing to contribute because the decision does not allow it or they do not have the knowledge.

- Can be difficult to obtain consensus within the group.

Joins style

Advantages:

- Everyone involved
- Everyone committed
- High morale
- Open atmosphere
- Stimulates learning

Disadvantages:

- Decision making slow
- Ambiguity about leadership
- Sometimes, compromise decision taken, which may not be the best decision – in order to keep the team happy
- Time sometimes wasted because of unnecessary discussion

A survey of style in a large multinational business revealed that the consultative type was most often preferred, although this varied according to the different categories of employee. Unlike Blake, McGregor, and Likert, the Ashridge researchers do not suggest an ideal style – it depends on circumstances they argue.

8.3 Contingency approach

The latest thoughts on effective leadership belong to what is termed the 'contingency school' and are developed from the concept that the most effective leaders have the ability to adapt their style according to the situation.

Perhaps one of the best known theories within the **contingency approach** is Fiedler's contingency theory.

Fiedler's contingency theory

Fiedler (1967) classifies a leader's orientation in terms of whether they enjoy working with others – they then have a high Least Preferred Co-worker (LPC) score – or whether they are more production orientated – a low Least Preferred Co-worker (LPC) score.

A questionnaire is issued to potential and existing leaders which, when completed, indicates whether they enjoy working with others (i.e. a high LPC score) or whether they dislike working with others (i.e. a low LPC score).

Fielder also attempts to identify key features in the situation as described below.

1. Position of power:

   The more formal the leaders position the greater the range of rewards and punishments at their disposal – the power is judged as weak or strong.

2. Task structure:

   A high degree of task structure gives a more favourable situation for the leader as it means the leader can more easily monitor and influence the team member's behaviour.

3. Leader – member relations:

   Is the relationship between a leader and the followers good?

   All these factors are combined in Fiedler's contingency model indicating which situations are favourable to a particular type of leader.

The general pattern of results of research on Fiedler's contingency theory

When the situation is very favourable (good leader-member relations, structured task, a strong position of power) or very unfavourable (poor leader member relations, unstructured task, weak position of power) then a task orientated leader (low LPC score) with a directive, controlling style will be more effective.

When the situation is moderately favourable, then a participative approach (a high LPC score) will be more effective. Fiedler concludes that leadership style will vary according to the situation and that leadership effectiveness may be improved by changing the leadership situation. The position of power, task structure and leader-member relations can all be changed to make them compatible with the characteristics of the leader.

8.4 Action centred leadership

John Adair developed his approach in training leaders at Sandhurst with what is known as '**action centred leadership**'.

The effectiveness of the leader is dependent on meeting three areas of need within the work group:

- The task – as mentioned earlier in this chapter, teams operate within organisations to achieve certain tasks. Therefore effort and attention must be directed towards those things that help the team achieve its task.

- The team – the leader must also look at ways of bringing the team together to operate as a cohesive unit, building team morale and developing a feeling of belonging.

- The individual – teams are made up of individuals and the leader must ensure that the needs of the individuals within the team are being met.

This relationship can be illustrated diagrammatically:

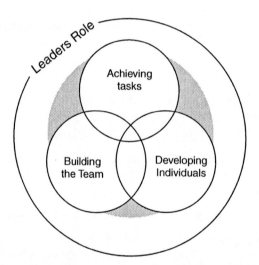

For the leader to be successful, then equal attention must be paid to all of these areas. If too much focus is put on one area, then this will cause problems in other areas. For example, if a leader is too task focussed and does not give due attention to the team and the individuals within the team, then they will be perceived as being very autocratic. As a result, the team may well become disillusioned and alienated from the leader, and so their commitment to achieving the task will diminish. A further example could be a situation where the leader devotes too much time and resource to one individual within the team, the consequence being a reduction in the loyalty of the other team members.

However, there will be situations where it is in the best interests of the team and the organisation for the leader to spend a disproportionate amount of time on one of these three areas – with the proviso that this increased focus is only for a short period of time.

QUICK QUESTION

Write down some circumstances where you feel this course of action would be appropriate.

Write your answer here before reading on.

Situations where increased attention to one of the three areas would include:

- At the times of year when quarterly reviews and annual appraisals are due, the team leader will have a greater focus on the individual.

- If a team is having an awayday teambuilding event, the focus will be on the team.

- If there is a backlog of work and pressure is on to clear this quickly, then the focus will be on the task.

QUESTION TIME 8

George Boxer joined the bank when he left school. By persistent hard work, he became branch manager at the age of 50. He says he came up the hard way and thinks that young people today have a very easy life – but not in his branch. No one comes late or goes early. No one gets away with poor work. If a mistake is made, a reprimand swiftly follows.

1. What are the possible consequences of this style of management?

2. What other possible styles would you draw to George's attention?

Write your answer here then check with the answer at the back of the book.

9   Leadership and interpersonal relationships

A leader can be appointed, selected or chosen informally. Attempted leadership occurs when one in the group tries to exert influence over others. You may have experienced this on a leadership training course where during the practical sessions one course participant will try to exert influence over his/her fellow participants. Successful leadership occurs when influence brings about the behaviour and results intended by the leader. Effective leadership occurs when it results in functional behaviour and the achievement of team goals.

Within an organisation, the leadership influence will be dependent on the type of power the leader can exercise over others. This exercise of power is a social process and explains how different people can influence the behaviour of others. There are five main sources of power as identified by French and Raven:

- Reward power – based on fact and on the team members' perception that the leader has the ability and resources to obtain rewards for those who comply, e.g. pay, promotion.

- Coercive power – based on the fact and the team members' perception that the leader has the ability to punish those who do not comply.

- Referent power – based on the team members' identification with the leader. The leader exercises influence because of perceived attractiveness – charisma. A manager may not be able to reward subordinates but can still command respect.

- Expert power – based on the team members' perception of the leader as someone who is competent and has special knowledge.

- Legitimate power – based on the leader's position of authority in the organisation.

Another category of power defined by other writers is 'political power', which is derived from knowing how things work, in other words, the politics of the organisation.

QUICK QUESTION

What power bases do you need in order to do your job successfully?

Write your answer here before reading on.

Your power bases will depend on your job and position, but you will probably have at least expert power.

The sources of power are based on the team members' perception of the leader. If suppliers believe a manager has the power to withdraw an order, then the manager can exercise considerable influence even though they may not have this power in reality.

Leadership is dynamic behaviour because it is constantly changing and depends on:

- The characteristics of each leader
- The attitude, needs and characteristics of the followers
- The nature of the organisation – its purpose and structure
- The environment

McGregor, who cites these variables, says leadership is not dependent on just the individual but links many factors.

A leader can also act as a model for his team –attitude, energy, etc can set a pattern and standard for others to follow. The leader is also a representative of the team in the eyes of others – they are the link in the organisation between the team and others. Team members rely on their leader to act as the mouthpiece and occupy a representative role to other parties.

10 Team decision making

QUICK QUESTION

Define decision making.

Write your answer here before reading on.

Decision making is the act of choosing from a range of alternatives. Whilst this may seem a simple enough concept, however, there are often a range of factors to be taken into account when making the decision, and often there will be a time pressure impacting upon the decision.

10.1 The decision making process

When making any decision, we need to consider the following.

- Define and clarify the problem – do we need to act, or is the problem not as important an issues as it first appeared? If so, do we need to act now or would it be better to act at a later date? Is the matter urgent, important or both?

- Gather all the facts about the problem and understand their causes.

- Think about the options and solutions that are available to you.

- Consider and compare the advantages and disadvantages of each option – consult if necessary.

- Pick the best option – avoid vagueness or compromise decisions that do not get to the root of the problem.

- Communicate the decision and the rationale behind it to those involved and affected, and follow up to ensure proper and effective implementation.

Whilst the definition of decisions may make us think that each decision is taken in isolation, this is not usually the case. You will often come across situations where one decision will impact upon another, thus producing a complex operating framework. We also have to consider the long term effect of the decisions that we are making – for example, will the decision tie the business unit into using a supplier of specialist services for a long period of time?

We also need to give thought as to whether the decision is best made by one person – who could either be the team leader or a team member depending upon the decision, the levels of expertise held by the respective parties and development needs.

QUICK QUESTION

What do you think are the disadvantages of group decision making?

Write your answer here before reading on.

The disadvantages of group decision making are:

- It can be costly as we are paying salary costs of a larger number of people who are making the decision.

- It can be time consuming by the time everyone in the group has discussed their position.

- It can create conflict if there are opposing views and individuals are not willing to move their positions. The alternative to this may be that the issue is fudged in order to avoid conflict and as a result the quality of the final decision is poor.

- Group decision making may not be appropriate for confidential decisions – for example, around staffing issues.

- Group decisions may be riskier than those made by individuals and it may be difficult to assign accountability for the decision.

QUICK QUESTION

What do you think are the advantages of individual decision making?

Write your answer here before reading on.

The advantages of individual decision making are:

- It is cheap as only one person is involved.
- It is quick.
- It is confidential.

However, when comparing group and individual decision making, we must always keep in mind that a major advantage to group decision making is that it gives us multiple viewpoints and a wide range of experience and expertise to inform the decision.

The final choice over which method we use is determined by the time available, as well as the need for specialisation and confidentiality. Other factors that could influence the choice are whether we are looking at a routine or non routine decision and the expense involved.

11 Dealing with conflict

Conflict is unavoidable when working with other people. Therefore, as a team leader, focus should not be on avoiding conflict – remember when we discussed the stages of team development, the point was made that in the storming stage, it is important that the leader allows the team to work through the conflict that will inevitably arise at this stage – indeed if the leader tries to avoid the conflict, all that will happen is that the conflict is delayed.

However, it is possible to approach the dealing with conflict in a way that makes use of conflict as a means of building trust, creating innovative solutions to problems, and strengthening relationships – both within the team and with outside parties. However, either avoiding conflict or approaching resolution adversarially, will destroy the essence of true community: interdependence based on trust.

As a team leader, there are two different types of conflict to deal with:

- Conflict that occurs within the team
- Conflict between the team and external parties

We will look at both of these situations.

11.1 Conflict within the team

There are a number of signs of conflict within a team. These are:

- A withdrawal – partly or completely – from the team and its aims. This could be evidenced by an individual whose behaviours change from those supporting and participating in the activities of the team, to a situation where they become withdrawn.

- A lack of participation and involvement from the individual/individuals.

- A lack of commitment to the task or its outcomes. Here the individual may only be concerned with the direct work that he/she carries out and has no concern as to how this contributes to the success of the team as a whole, or views success and failure being based purely on their own efforts, rather than the success or failure of the team.

- Unwillingness to share and cooperate with others – perhaps a more experienced member of the team who is unwilling to share their experience with the rest of the team.

- Sabotage – either directly or indirectly – of colleagues work. This may have come about as a result of a decision being taken by voting, rather than from an attempt by the leader to gain a consensus decision. As a result of this, those team members who perceive that they have 'lost' the vote may take steps – consciously or subconsciously to undermine the work of their colleagues. This can result in the disenfranchised team members being able to demonstrate to the rest of the team that they were right all along by sabotaging the outcome of the decision.

- Underachievement – a team member who has been performing well and their performance level suddenly drops.

- Counter productive expressions of strong emotion – often during team discussions when emotional and negative comments are expressed with a great deal of feeling.

QUICK QUESTION

What options does the team leader have when dealing with conflict?

Write your answer here before reading on.

When dealing with conflict, the team leader may act in the following ways.

- **Avoid the conflict** – here the leader seeks to avoid the conflict, usually in the hope that it will go away. If the conflict is insignificant, and there are more pressing issues for the leader to deal with, then this may be an option. However, there is always a danger here that the leader is sending a message to the team that they are not interested in team issues – in other words, they are task focussed. It may also be that if the conflict is avoided, the situation merely gets worse, until it reaches the point where the leader must take action.

- **Accommodate the conflict** – here the leader acts in a passive way in the hope that by giving those people involved in the conflict what they want, then the situation will be resolved. However, what about a situation where there are conflicting positions within the team, and it is not possible to give both parties what they are looking for – for example, two members of staff wanting to go on holiday at a busy time of year when the business can only release one of them? Another danger with this approach is that if one person is accommodated at the moment, then they may look for something more to accommodate them the next time there is conflict.

- **Confront the conflict** (competition) – whilst the last tactic was termed a passive approach, this one is seen as an aggressive way to deal with conflict. Here the team leader seeks to meet the conflict head on – although an outcome of this is that there will be 'winners and losers'. The question then remains – how do we get the team back onto a harmonious working relationship afterwards? A consequence may be that those who deem themselves to be losers will store up their resentment and work in counter productive ways afterwards.

- **Compromise** – seek to find a middle ground that all parties to the conflict are able to live with. However, this begs the question that has been asked elsewhere in this study text – is the popular decision always the best decision? In this situation, it may be that the leader's attention and effort is on ways to keep everyone happy, rather than thinking about the best solution for the team as a whole.

- **Collaborate** – this is the most fruitful approach. The problem is viewed in a positive light and as seen as a learning opportunity that the team is able to use to grow. The use of problem solving techniques – such as brainstorming may allow for a creative solution to be found – one that may not have become apparent if one of the less useful problem solving approaches had been used.

These approaches are summarised in this diagram:

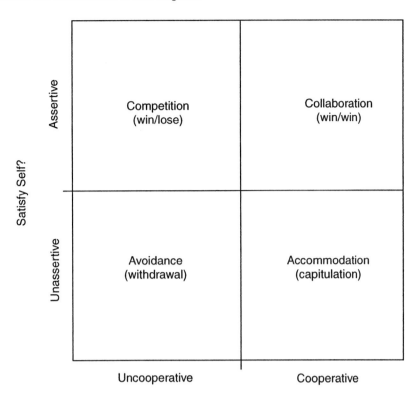

QUICK QUESTION

How should we deal with conflict?

Write your answer here before reading on.

Conflict should be dealt with in the following ways.

- Generate an open, trusting atmosphere where people feel safe to disagree with each other and react rationally actively listening to the opinions expressed. Remember that conflict can be looked upon negatively, as something to be avoided, or positively, where we use the conflict as a mechanism that allows the team to express opinions and feelings in an open and non-threatening manner, and thus move forward.

- Establish ground rules that allow each person's opinion to be shared and discussed constructively. Once the team know what the rules are for this discussion, then there is less likely to be aggressive behaviour – for example, talking over one another – during the discussion.

- Be open to yourself being a party in the conflict – Is your style contributing to/ creating the conflict? If this is the case, what action will you take to change?

- Bring the conflict into the open – encourage people to express their opinions fully. This is the only way in which the parties to the conflict are going to find out what effect their actions are having on others. Often this awareness can be enough to solve the conflict.

- Focus on facts and specifics rather than emotions – depersonalise the issue – in conflict, problems tend to get generalised and are therefore harder to solve. However, once we know what facts we are dealing with, it will be easier for people to accommodate the needs of others.

- Explore and try to identify the root cause and what each party is trying to achieve. By using probing and reflective questions, we can get to the root of the issue. Once we know what we are dealing with, it is much easier to deal with it.

- Use positive and constructive feedback to techniques to evaluate and value each person's contribution.

- Encourage the people involved to look for new elements in the situation and put themselves in the other person's shoes. By acting as a metaphorical mirror, we can let individuals and groups within the team see how others are feeling.

- Aim to reach agreement on a step forward, however small. The hardest part of this working o a solution can be the first step. Once progress has started, it can be easier to move forward.

- Emphasise the positive results of dealing with conflict in a healthy way. This will mean that those responsible for the conflict do not feel guilty about bringing it about. It can also make future conflicts easier to raise – but if conflict is a way for the team to grow, this should be perceived as a positive.

- Conflict – when properly handled – is a way in which we can appreciate other peoples' points of view and can grow as a team.

Good communication skills on the part of the manager can help to resolve conflict. This can be done by:

- Diffusing the emotion, whether that is anger, silent resentment or other evidence of distress.

- Polite (and sensitive) questioning can help to find the real source of the conflict.

- Team members might argue about one issue when the real difficulty lies with role confusion.

- Summarise and clarify each person's point of view.

- Establish how much it matters so that the people involved can decide for themselves whether the conflict is still worth pursuing.

When dealing with conflict, we may need to deal with a person who is angry. Here are some pointers for dealing with this type of situation:

- Listen until the burst of emotion is ended. Do not interrupt the person, or try to guess what the issue is – let them tell you. This can allow the person to expend energy, which can make them feel better and more amenable to a solution. On the other hand, if you interrupt at this stage, you are likely to exacerbate the situation by making the person feel angry. It may also look as though you have pre-judged the issue and want to introduce a solution too quickly.

- Encourage the rest of the team to listen and stop them interrupting. This is due to the points made above and lets the person see that their concerns are being taken seriously by all of the team.

- Begin calming the situation by acknowledging that you have heard and recognise the feelings of anger. Here you are showing empathy – perhaps by reflecting back the emotions that you are observing. This can start to take the sting out of the situation and begin to move to solution mode.

- When the person has calmed down, treat them calmly and with respect – and so you begin to deal with the problem. Thus we are dealing with issues and not personalities.

- Shift the focus away from the outburst – often the person involved will acknowledge that the anger was exaggerated and be embarrassed, even apologetic about the situation.

11.2   Conflict between the team and other parties

Whilst we have focussed on relationships and conflict within a team, there are times when the relationships between and team and other, external parties can generate conflict. You may well have personal experience of this where conflict has arisen between your team and another team within the organisation – for example, an internal supplier – or the conflict may be with an external party. Conflict within the organisation may often arise due to the different roles that are carried out by teams, by confusion over roles (who is meant to do what within the business) or personality clashes between individuals from our team and another.

Frequent examples of intergroup conflict caused by roles, as mentioned above, are given in research. One well known experiment was that conducted by Sherif and Sherif (1961) in a boys' summer camp. A camp was organised so that two teams would form and become competitive, seeing each other in opposing roles. Other research has replicated the results. Each team begins to view the other as the enemy, distorting perceptions, seeing only their own strengths, not weaknesses, and seeing only the worst parts of the other team. Hostility increases whilst communication decreases and the conflict is thus allowed to increase. This may sound familiar to you from your experience of working in teams either at work or in a non-work environment.

Intergroup problems arise not only out of direct competition between clearly defined teams. They are also intrinsic in organisations and society, because of the basis on which society is organised. There are potential intergroup problems between men and women, older and younger generations, different faith groups, higher and lower status (this status may be real or perceived), black and white. Any occupational or social group will develop in group feelings and define itself.

QUICK QUESTION

Do you think that conflict between different teams and groups is necessarily a bad thing?

Write your answer here before reading on.

Intergroup conflict can be desirable in certain situations. Each group becomes more tightly knit and elicits greater loyalty from its members, and the group tends to become more highly structured and organised, as well as more task orientated. This technique can been seen in a number of football coaches, who instil a feeling within their team that the world is against them and that they are the subject of undeserved bias – for example, a negative press. This can have the effect of unifying the team and motivating them to drive on in the achievement of the overall goal. Alex Fergusson the ex-manager of Manchester United is a classic example of this approach.

The negative consequences of conflict, especially the lack of co-operation between groups and teams, can sometimes outweigh the gains and management may try to find ways of reducing tension. The conflict basically arises from a lack of agreement on the goals and role of each group and so the first step must be to establish this agreement and get the two sides working together.

The basic strategy recommended by theorists, therefore, is to locate the goals competing groups can agree on and establish valid communication.

QUICK QUESTION

How do you think intergroup conflict can be resolved?

Write your answer here before reading on.

There are several techniques that try to resolve intergroup conflict. As you study these, reflect on your own experience of when these techniques have been used successfully

Establish a super-ordinate goal

Find a goal all parties can aim for and that will require increased communication. Once people start talking to one another, many of the barriers may start to come down, and individuals can see that they have more in common than they thought previously. Even if they do not have a lot in common, by communicating better with each other, they are in an improved position to understand and empathise with the other team, and this can lead to a greater acceptance of each other.

Intergroup training

This involves bringing in an external agent – for example a consultant, or even a facilitator from another part of the business to try and reduce conflict. The competing parties are brought into the training setting with common goals and asked to discuss and make a list of perceptions of the other parties. These perceptions are then shared between the parties and, after private individual group discussion and reflection, there is a shared discussion on how to manage conflict.

Locate a common enemy

Harmony can sometimes be established by bringing both parties together to fight off an enemy. For instance, a common conflict within a bank can be between the credit and marketing departments. This can bring about perceptions from credit that marketing are simply trying to sell products without a rigorous credit assessment process – thus increasing the probability of future bad debts. Marketing, on the other hand, may feel that the credit area is risk averse and not willing to try to grow the business.

This type of conflict can be reduced if both parties come to the realisation that they are both trying to do their best for the same organisation, and so they can start to work together to compete against other organisations in the same market.

Brining the leaders of the parties together

Once the conflict between the leaders is resolved, they can positively influence the actions of their own people to work together and reduce the conflict.

Reallocation or restructuring of tasks and responsibilities

Parties will no longer be competing for resources – so if this is the root cause of the conflict, then the conflict has been removed.

What can an organisation do to reduce the instances of intergroup conflict?

Write your answer here before reading on.

The division of the workforce into functional or specialist groups is the ideal situation for intergroup conflict to occur. The possibility of it occurring can be reduced by:

- Relatively greater emphasis being given to total organisational effectiveness. For example, by giving greater emphasis to the goals, aims and mission of the organisation. There can also be a link here with performance management – whereby individual and team objectives are linked to the overall aims of the organisation. Thus, if individuals and teams have a clear line of sight as to how their efforts contribute to the overall aims of the organisation, then there is a greater feeling of belonging to the organisation, as opposed to a department or area

- A high degree of interaction encouraged between groups to break down personal barriers and perceptions.

- Frequent rotation of staff between departments encouraged to stimulate a high degree of understanding.

- Win-lose situations avoided and groups not having to compete for scarce resources; rewards should be shared between departments.

Conflict can occur on both an interpersonal and intergroup level and although there may be some positive benefits from a conflict situation, there are also many negative results. Some researchers would claim that, rather than having to resolve a conflict situation, it is better to avoid it altogether, whilst others will claim that conflict is a necessary way for both the organisation and teams to develop to mature, performing businesses.

12   Strategic management

Up until now, our focus has been on management at an operational level, and we will return to this theme later on in the chapter. However, for the moment, our focus will change to decision making and direction setting at the top of the organisation – in other words, strategy. We will start by considering how strategic decisions are made within an organisation, the levels at which these decisions are made and the key differences between strategic and operational management. Then we will examine of the process for making strategic decisions. In the next part of this section we will consider the purpose and nature of organisational objectives and why these need to be set, before considering some of these high level documents.

12.1   What makes a decision strategic?

QUICK QUESTION

List what you think are the characteristics of a strategic decision.

Write your answer here before reading on.

There are a number of characteristics associated with decision making that let us determine whether the decision is operational or strategic.

The first area to think about is whether the decision is likely to affect the long term bearing of the organisation – if the answer to this question is yes, and then we are likely to be looking at a strategic decision.

Secondly, a strategic decision will usually come about if the company attempting to gain some competitive advantage through the decision. For example, is the company trying to steal a march on the competition, by making a move before they do? An example of this would be where a bank decides to invest in the development of an innovative product – for example, when National Australia Group introduced the Current Account Mortgage. This gave the organisation a unique product to offer the market at that time, and so they gained a competitive advantage – at least until other organisations developed similar products.

Strategic decisions are likely to be concerned with the range of activities that an organisation is engaged in. For example, does the company specialise in one area of operations, or do they spread their activities over a number of areas? This is a vital decision for any organisation as the range of activities is central to any organisation's strategic direction. When looking at the range of an organisation's activities, we should also think in terms of geography – for example, does the company wish to operate on global, European or domestic areas? Again, this decision will be central to the strategic direction of the company.

Strategic decisions are also about matching the activities and resources of the organisation to the environment within which it operates – this is what we mean by '**strategic fit**'. Strategic fit seeks to best position the organisation by identifying the opportunities that are available to the company within the environment within which it operates and making plans to grasp these opportunities. When financial services organisations made decisions as to how they could best use the internet to maintain and develop their business, these were decisions around strategic fit. The internet was part of the environment within which firms were operating and it presented new opportunities for both established and new players in the market to exploit.

When we look at strategic decisions, we can also look at what is called '**strategic stretch**'. This is where an organisation seeks to stretch its resources to allow it to obtain competitive advantage or to create fresh opportunities.

Strategic decisions may well result in major resource changes for the organisation. For example, when banks had to make decisions as to whether they would develop back office processing centres. This decision had major resourcing requirements in that these new processing centres had to be built and staffed – however, there was also a resourcing implication for the branch network as a number of tasks that had traditionally been carried out there were now done at the processing centres and so the amount of staff required in branches was subsequently reduced. Finally, this reduction in the number of staff required in branches also had an effect on the space required and many branches were refurbished with the removal of bandit screens, the creation of high security business cash areas and the creation of more space for customer interviews.

As we are starting to see in this analysis, strategic decisions will have an impact on operational decisions. Strategic decisions are looking at the direction, resources and opportunities of an organisation. However, the implementation of these decisions will affect the operational areas of the organisation – indeed it is at the operational level that the benefits of the strategic decisions are realised. Therefore, if the operational aspects of the business are not in line with the strategy, then it is unlikely that the strategic decisions will come to a successful conclusion. For example, a bank could decide to implement a new computer system to make it easier for staff to identify additional products that could be of benefit to customers who are taking out loans. However, if the front end staff are poorly motivated it is unlikely that the firm will obtain any advantage from the strategic decision.

The strategic direction of any organisation is not just affected by the environment within which the organisation operates – it is also affected by the ideals and outlook of those people within the organisation who yield power. For example, do those who have power in the company seek expansion through acquisition or organic growth?

Having looked at what constitutes a strategic decision, we need to turn our attention to what we actually mean by strategy.

QUICK QUESTION

How would you define strategy?

Write your answer here before reading on.

Chambers Twenty First Century Dictionary defines strategy as a long term plan for future success or development.

Whilst this definition is certainly not at odds with what we have discussed so far in this chapter, it would be useful to flesh this out a little. Johnson and Scholes in Exploring Corporate Strategy define strategy as '…the direction and scope of an organisation over the long term, which achieves advantage for the organisation through its configuration of resources within a changing environment and to fulfil stakeholder expectations.'

QUICK QUESTION

Reflecting on Johnson and Scholes definition of strategy, what do you think are the implications of this for strategic decisions?

Write your answer here before reading on.

The consequences of this definition on strategic decisions are:

- It is likely that strategic decisions will be complex. We are looking at big decisions that will have far reaching effects on the organisation. Therefore, unless we are looking at a very small organisation, operating in a tight geographical market, it is likely that these decisions will be complex and far reaching.

- It is also likely that strategic decisions will be made in periods of change and uncertainty. As a result, it is unlikely that those making the decisions will be able to forecast with certainly what the full consequences of the decision will be – thus increasing the risk associated with the decision.

- When making a strategic decision, it is likely that it will have an impact in a number of areas of the organisation. Therefore there is a need for collaboration and cooperation in different parts of the company.

- Strategic decisions may affect relationships beyond the organisation – it may result in a change of suppliers or a change in the way in which third parties are used by the organisation. An example of this would be if the company decides to concentrate on its core business activities and strip out non-core activities – for example, payroll or purchasing. The result of this decision would be that the firm would need to develop a network of suppliers who can provide these outsourced services as and when required.

- Finally, in most cases, strategic decisions will result in changes within the organisation. As we have seen, strategic decisions will affect the direction of the organisation and so it is unlikely that any decision of this magnitude would not result in change to the organisation.

13 The levels of strategy

Strategy is not just something that we see at the top of an organisation – rather there is evidence of it throughout a company. As mentioned earlier, strategy may be seen at the following levels within the organisation:

- Corporate level
- Business unit level
- Operational level

We will look at each of these areas in turn.

At the corporate level, we are looking at decisions that will affect the direction of the organisation. These are decisions that are made at the highest level and are about the fundamental aspects of the organisations operations – for example, in which geographical regions will the company operate?, what range of products and/or services will the company offer?, what is the growth strategy of the organisation, the types of business units that will be contained within the organisation, etc.

The next level down is the business unit level. Here we are looking at how the organisation will be able to compete in its chosen markets and how it is able to gain competitive advantage over the field. To do this, the business unit level of strategy will look at the development of particular products and services. Therefore, whilst the corporate level is looking at the organisation as a whole, the business unit level is concerned with a lower level of the organisation. What then constitutes this business level? The business level is a part of an organisation that offers products and services that are different to those offered by other business units in the company. An example would be the split in many financial services firms between business banking and retail banking. Whilst there may be some similarities between these areas, the products that are offered by each business unit are quite different. Another example would be where a financial services organisation has a number of different banks within its group – possibly these are regional banks. In this scenario, the regional banks are business units. It is also possible to look at business units as being parts of the business that offer different types of products and services – say asset finance.

The final level to look at is the operational level. Here we are looking at those parts of the organisation that implement the strategies that have been developed by both corporate and business unit strategy teams.

14 Strategic management versus operational management

QUICK QUESTION

What do you think are the differences between strategic management and operational management?

Write your answer here before reading on.

When we think of an operational manager, we tend to think of a person who is involved in implementing the decisions of those made in other parts of the organisation – in other words, this person is faced with challenges of operational control. This could be the management of staff in a branch to achieve their targets, or managing staff in a processing centre to process the desired volumes of work on time and at the correct quality. These managers will still have decisions to make, but these decisions must be made in accordance with an existing, pre-determined strategy.

Strategic management involves painting on a much larger canvass than operational management. Strategic management involves looking at more complex situations and looking at organisation-wide issues. This can pose a problem for those organisations that seek to promote from within to strategic management roles – if they are promoting operational managers, then these people will still tend to think in terms of their previous area of expertise – but to be an effective strategic manager, it is vital to be able to look at the bigger picture and being able to take an analytical approach to the issues.

However, to think of strategic management solely in terms of making the strategic decision is to ignore a vital part of the strategic manager's role – that is the ability to see that the strategy decided upon is actually put into action. Therefore, strategic management is not just about understanding the strategy of the organisation and making decisions around this, it is also about being able to transfer this strategy into action.

15   The process of strategic management

There are three stages to the process which we will introduce now and expand on in subsequent chapters. These three stages are:

- Strategic analysis
- Strategic choice
- Strategic action

We will look at each of these in turn.

15.1   Strategic analysis

At the **strategic analysis** stage, we are looking at how the strategy may be affected by the external environment, organisational resources, and the influence of key **stakeholders**. Here we are looking at how changes to the environment will affect the organisation. We also need to consider what resources the organisation has that will give it a competitive advantage or gain new opportunities. Finally, we need to think about how the stakeholders in the organisation and their aspirations will affect the growth of the organisation.

When we carry out this analysis, we need to consider the opportunities and threats that are presented to the organisation by the environment, and what are the resources that the organisation possesses that will allow it to rise to the challenges, as well as thinking about the expectations of the key stakeholders.

QUICK QUESTION

What factors do you think will make up the environment?

Write your answer here before reading on.

The organisation exists within an environment consisting of political and legal, economic, social and technological factors – this is sometimes referred to as PESTEL. You will recall that this model was outlined in the previous chapter.

As you can imagine this environment is not static – it is constantly changing and the organisation has to change to adapt to these altered circumstances. However, these changes are not always negative – they may present opportunities to the organisation, although they may also present threats.

The resources that the organisation possesses comprise its strategic capability. Whilst when we looked at the environment we were looking outside the organisation, we also need to be aware of the internal influences that can affect strategic thinking. Therefore, we need to think of the strengths and weaknesses that the organisation possesses as part of this internal analysis.

There are a number of factors that affect the organisation's purpose. Here we can ask who the organisation is there to serve and how are the managers of the organisation held responsible for the achievement of this? Also, the different stakeholders within the organisation will have different expectations on what they require from management. If there are differences of expectations amongst different stakeholder groups, then it is that group or groups who have the greatest power who will win the day. Recognising this can be an important way of understanding why an organisation follows the strategic path that it does.

When carrying out a strategic analysis, we should also give thought to the ethical considerations that can explain why managers and organisations act in the way that they do.

To summarise this section, when carrying out a strategic analysis of an organisation, we need to look at the environment, strategic capability, expectations and political and ethical environment that prevails within the organisation in order to see the fullest picture of the company. When doing this, we also need to think about what is likely to happen in the future – is the current analysis likely to be sustained in the future or will it be likely to change, and if so, in what ways?

15.2 Strategic choice

By **strategic choice** we mean understanding the future strategy both at corporate and business unit level. It is also about understanding the options available to develop this strategy.

You will recall that at the highest level of the organisation, there is the corporate strategy. This will look at the organisation as a whole and to allow the corporate centre to add value to the organisation; this level may look to see if there is the opportunity to create synergy between different parts of the business. This may not be apparent to those working at the business unit level as the synergies may only be seen by those with a perspective of the whole organisation. Issues about the value (or otherwise) of the corporate centre are referred to as 'corporate parenting'.

 A further area of strategic choice is deciding how the strategy will be developed. Some organisations may choose to grow through following a policy of mergers and acquisitions, whilst others may choose to further develop the business that they already have. When making this choice, the organisation must decide if the strategy is congruent with the strategic position of the organisation, and how feasible it is in terms of the current and future resources of the organisation, as well considering how this fits in with the expectations of the stakeholders.

15.3 Strategic action

As with any planning process, strategic planning will serve no useful purpose if it stops when the plan has been formulated. To be effective, the plan must be translated into action. Therefore, **strategic action** is concerned with seeing that the strategy chosen is working in practice.

When looking at this section of the process we need to firstly consider if the structure of the organisation is the right one to support the strategy. When looking at this, we should be considering, as well as the structure, the processes, the boundaries and the relationships within the company.

We should also be concerned with how well the different resources and areas of the organisation will support the strategy – or has the new strategy been developed building on the current resources available in the company?

As we mentioned earlier, strategic decisions will almost certainly bring about change within the organisation. So, when we are looking at strategic action, we should also think about the change management processes that are present in the organisation.

16 Developments in the study of strategy

The start of the study of strategy occurred in the 1960s. This took the form of business policy courses that were run at institutions such as Harvard University. The view at that time was that strategy was the responsibility of the chief executive. Therefore these courses would be run along the lines of 'What would you do if you were in charge of such and such a company?' This case study approach had little foundation in theory or research – rather it would follow a common sense approach, based on the experience of senior executives.

In the 1960s and 1970s there developed a series of books on corporate planning – with a view to identifying the influences on an organisation and seeking to determine how these would present opportunities or threats to the organisation. This approach felt that there were highly systemised approaches to planning that should be followed. The view at that time was that if managers knew as much as they could about their organisation and its environment then they could make the best decisions.

Both of these approaches were criticised and an increasing amount of research was carried out into how we should learn about strategy. Much of this took the form of looking for the evidence to link the financial performance of an organisation with the strategy that it followed. It was felt that by learning the lessons of the past, managers could make the best decisions for the future.

The counter argument to this was the view that due to the complexities that exist in the real world, it is futile to predict the future by carefully analysing the past. Instead, we should accept that decisions should be made based on the experience of the manager, knowledge of the environment within which the manager operates. The evidence for this was how strategies were adapted and developed within organisations. The argument was that time could be better spent understanding the processes of managerial decision making in the reality of the environment within which these decisions are made.

There has also been a view that managers should take strategic decisions based on analysis and planning – however there is a danger that personal bias and cultural influences can affect decisions too. A counter argument is the view that organisations are akin to living organisms and that they change to adapt to the environment that they find themselves to be in.

17 Organisational mission and objectives

QUICK QUESTION

Why do you think the objectives of an organisation are of fundamental importance?

Write your answer here before reading on.

The objectives of any organisation are so important as they will determine the values of the organisation, the direction that the organisation moves in, the skills and competencies that it seeks to develop, and the

measures that it will put in place to determine whether or not both the organisation and its people have been successful.

You will no doubt have first hand knowledge of objectives through the performance objectives that you have as a result of your organisation's **performance management system**. This very fact underlines one of the fundamental problems that can arise from objectives.

QUICK QUESTION

What is the longest term of your current objectives?

Write your answer here before reading on.

The answer to this question may vary from person to person – however, it is extremely unlikely that any of your objectives has been set for more than one year. Most performance objectives are set with staff at the start of the organisation's financial year, and whilst some may have a delivery date at some point during the year, for most employees, the majority of these objectives will have a completion date at the end of the organisation's financial year. This tells us one of the basic difficulties that can arise with objectives – they tend to encourage a short term view. As we discussed in the last section, strategic decisions tend to be decisions that are taken looking at the longer term view.

QUICK QUESTION

How would you define an objective?

Write your answer here before reading on.

An objective is a statement of certain outcomes that the organisation has to achieve. All organisations will use set criteria to measure success over the range of their performance. However, there is a danger that either the organisation, or the people within it, only focus on one or a couple of these areas. In this section we will look at a range of areas that organisations will look to when either targeting, or assessing performance.

QUICK QUESTION

Why do you think organisations have objectives?

Write your answer here before reading on.

Objectives serve a number of purposes. These are:

- To give the organisation a sense of direction
- To give a focus for decision making
- To motivate employees
- To be used as a controlling mechanism

We will now look at each of these.

17.1 A sense of direction

If the organisation has a set of objectives, these give the employees a sense of where the organisation is going. If these do not exist, different managers may act in different ways even in the same set of circumstances.

17.2 A focus for decision making

Good objectives lead to good plans. In any situation, if we know what the end game is, then we are going to be in a better position to plan how we are going to get there. If the objectives are weighted, then we know what the priority of them is, as well as how much resource should be allocated to each.

Objectives also help with the decision making process. As mentioned, if objectives are weighted and prioritised, then those within the organisation can make decisions with this information in mind. In addition, the objectives themselves can help decision making. For example, if there is an objective around the proportion of revenue that can be directed towards capital expenditure, then this information will be used by the organisation when allocating resources to capital projects.

17.3 To motivate employees

Having objectives and a sense of purpose will help employees to know where the organisation is heading and what role they can play in this. A source of dissatisfaction amongst employees can be a lack of information about where the organisation is going as this can breed a feeling of uncertainty. Objectives help overcome this.

17.4   As a controlling mechanism

As objectives are used to spell out what the expectation of performance is, they can also be used at the end of the period to measure the performance. If the objectives are written clearly and include performance measurements, then it should be a simple task to see if performance has measured up to expectation. An added advantage is that it should be easy for all parties to see what this measurement is.

QUICK QUESTION

What problems do you think there are with objectives?

Write your answer here before reading on.

17.5   Problems with objectives

There can be a number of problems associated with objectives. They may cause problems of conflict between one objective and another, there could be difficulty with measurement, or the objective could be looked upon as an end in itself.

Conflict between objectives

As you will see in the next section, objectives are set in a number of areas so that the organisation can take a balanced view on its activities and direction. However, this can pose a difficulty in that it can be a challenge for those at all levels in the organisation to keep a satisfactory focus on all of these competing areas.

Measurement

It has been mentioned that good objectives will have some form of measurement tool contained within them. However, in some areas it may either prove difficult to agree on a satisfactory measurement tool, or it could be that the measurement tool itself is flawed. For example, an employee satisfaction survey score could be used as a measurement tool, but depending upon the survey, this could be a subjective measurement.

Also, as objectives cascade down the organisation, from strategic to operational levels, it may be that some employees become adept at 'working the system' and forcing through a measurement tool with a level of measurement that will allow them to show that they are delivering a high level performance, when this has not actually been the case.

Objectives being looked upon as an end in themselves

Again this can be a problem as objectives are cascaded down the organisation. This can be a particular problem when the objectives become the basis of rewarding employees by way of annual increments and one-off bonuses. The situation could arise where the employees feel that they are going to do well given their current set of objectives, but due to changing circumstances, some of the areas covered by their objectives are no longer contributing value to the business. Rather than have these objectives changed to more relevant ones, there may be a temptation for the individual to continue working towards the old objectives in the expectation of financial reward.

QUICK QUESTION

What do you think are the areas in which objectives would be set?

Write your answer here before reading on.

The areas that we are going to look at are:

- Profitability
- Growth
- Shareholder value
- Customer satisfaction

17.6 Profitability

As banks are in business to make a profit, it makes sense that objectives are set in this area. It may be that this type of objective is set in terms of a certain amount of profit to be earned within a certain period, but it is more common to find that this type of objective is focussed around some form of ratio. You may be familiar with these from other studies. They could be Earnings per Share, Return on Capital Employed, or Return on Shareholders Funds.

Whilst this measure is both popular and fundamental to the business, there are a number of drawbacks associated with it. For example, profit calculation is not an absolute science. Again, if you have some knowledge of accounting, you will know that there is scope for (quite legitimate) differences in treatment of depreciating assets, valuation of stock, research and development expenditure, etc. Therefore, the profit figure that is reported for an organisation is not necessarily the only figure that could have been produced for that organisation in that year.

You should also keep in mind that when measuring performance, we must always look to the past to find reported profits, rather than looking at the potential of the organisation.

17.7 Growth

Growth is also seen as a key performance indicator in western companies.

Growth may be achieved by acquiring other organisations, or by developing the current business further – or by a combination of these strategies. You will find that where an organisation is achieving rapid rates of growth, this will be achieved by acquisitions. In the 1998 JJB Sports expanded rapidly by their acquisition of a major competitor – Sports Division.

As the concentration of capital continues and organisations grow further, there is a feeling in some organisations that unless they are one of the major players in their market, then they are unlikely to survive – therefore they pay high priority to growth objectives.

We can also see a link between growth and the profit objective – it is common to find accounting conventions that allow the cost of acquiring new companies to be excluded from the Profit and Loss statement. This will have the effect of inflating the reported profit figure and having a correspondingly positive effect on the profit ratios that were mentioned above. However, if the company chooses to grow by developing its existing business, then the costs of this will be charged against profit as they are incurred, having a negative effect on the profit figure reported and with it the measures of profitability.

Experience has taught us that those organisations that grow too quickly are not able to sustain this performance. Any very rapid growth, without the backing of adequate capital will result in the organisation overtrading and experiencing the subsequent difficulties. When this occurs, the value of the organisation's shares will no doubt come under pressure. This has been seen with the 'dot.com' companies that enjoyed rapid growth in the 1990s, experienced rapid declines in the early part of the new millennium. Key stakeholders were left to feel the brunt of this, with shareholders seeing the value of their investments fall, staff suffering redundancy and those who were left, low morale, and some creditors did not gain full payment of their debts. Closer to home, the Independent Commission on Banking has recommended that the investment and retail banking operations of our banks should be separated.

17.8 Shareholder value

As any limited company is owned by its shareholders, it is a logical conclusion that the organisation should be looking to maximise the return for this group of stakeholders. This could be by way of dividend income, by capital growth in the value of their shares, or by a combination of the two. Therefore, if the organisation is looking to make an investment, it should only do so if the return is going to be greater than that to be gained were the shareholders to invest their money elsewhere.

If the organisation is seeking to set a strategy to bring about shareholder value, then this is likely to look very different from a strategy that is designed to bring about profitability or growth. The reason for this is that the stockmarket may take a very sceptical view of an organisation that is looking to grow rapidly through acquisition – as a result, this reaction of the market will result in the organisation's share price declining.

There can be a difficulty with looking solely at maximising shareholder value in that it will not motivate employees – unless they are also shareholders. It might be better to think of shareholder value as a benefit that will result from other objectives being achieved and so the business prospers.

There can be a danger that if the organisation focuses on shareholder value, then there is the possibility that it will fall into the same trap as outlined when looking at profitability – there will be a short term focus, with managers seeking to cut costs, rather than taking advantage of the opportunities that are being presented to them by a changing environment.

17.9 Customer satisfaction

Whilst it is the shareholders who own the company, if the customer is not willing to do business with the company, then there will not be any profit or growth generated for the shareholders. In the present competitive world, customer loyalty to any one organisation is eroding – this is prevalent in the financial services sector. In the past customers would be more likely to remain loyal to the one organisation – 60% of retired customers have never changed their bank. However, as you will no doubt be aware, customers are now far more likely to switch from one financial services organisation to another, and split banking, where the customer uses a number of organisations to meet their needs is now more prevalent than it was in the past.

As a result, most organisations will look to keep existing customers happy and seek to win new business through customer satisfaction. Organisations will now carry out customer satisfaction surveys, with the aim being to build long lasting and fruitful customer relationships.

An additional benefit is that satisfied customers are more likely to spread positive word of mouth about the organisation and be willing to give the organisation referral business – an important consideration is we are looking to build our business.

17.10 Other objectives

The objectives that we have looked at thus far are not the only ones that organisations use. You may be aware in your organisation of operational objectives that focus on quality and output. These are especially prevalent in back office and call centre environments where volumes are important but quality is another measure of customer satisfaction.

Some companies may also have learning objectives as it is only by learning and adapting to change that organisations will be able to prosper in today's fast changing environment.

There could also be objectives within your organisation for levels of staff satisfaction. The notion here is that it is only motivated and satisfied employees that are able, in turn, to deliver customer satisfaction.

When we look at these areas for objectives, we can see that it is necessary to have a range of objectives if the organisation is to survive in the long term. If too much focus is put on one area, it may yield short term success, but this unbalanced approach will bring about problems in the longer term – profit levels will not be sustained, or cutting budgets will limit investment in training or marketing with the attendant long term consequences.

18 The key stakeholders and their interests

As we discussed in the last section, the major problem with looking at these objectives is that they tend to appeal to only one group of stakeholders. However, as we have discussed, to be successful, the organisation needs to be able to satisfy the needs of a wide range of stakeholders. This has already been discussed, but in this section, we will be more specific and will look at who these stakeholders are, and what needs they have.

It is likely to be impossible to meet fully the needs of all of these groups – however, the good news is that stakeholders do not tend to look to have all of these needs fully satisfied – instead, they will usually look to have 'reasonable returns'. An additional positive is that most of these groups' expectations will be based on what returns they have had in the past. Therefore, the organisation is operating in an acceptance zone – in other words, this is the level within which the organisation is satisfying the needs of all the stakeholders. Problems will arise if the organisation moves outside this zone, either by falling below the expectation level, or by exceeding the level. The reason for problems arising if performance is exceeded is that this will no doubt lead to a decline in performance in another area. For example, giving employees an annual increment beyond that which the organisation can afford will cause profit to fall proportionately and thus reduce the satisfaction of shareholders.

QUICK QUESTION

Who do you think are the stakeholders in an organisation?

Write your answer here before reading on.

The major stakeholders in most organisations are:

- Shareholders
- Customers
- Creditors
- Managers
- Employees

You may have identified some other groups, but these are the major ones. However, stakeholder groups and their focus/influence will change with both time and events. For example, a major stakeholder of RBS at the moment is the UK government, due to their shareholding in the organisation. However, prior to the banking crisis, whilst it could be argued that the government was a stakeholder in RBS due to the influence of the bank in the economy, the focus of this stakeholding has changed dramatically.

18.1 Shareholders

As we discussed earlier, these are very obvious stakeholders as they are the owners of the organisation. Their interests will be the returns that they make from the organisation both in terms of dividend and share value growth. Whilst this group do have the power to change the management of the organisation, this is now unlikely to happen, as most investors are 'institutional investors' – for example, pension funds who will take very large shareholdings in companies. If they are unhappy with the performance of the company, they are not terribly likely to change the company's management – rather they will simply dispose of their shareholding.

As a result of this, it is unlikely that a company will seek to maximise shareholder value – rather they will operate within acceptable parameters.

This power of shareholders is unlikely to be used, but it can happen if other stakeholders are being rewarded in a disproportionate way – for example, if the management team are being rewarded excessively. If this happens, the shareholders may use their influence to remove managers as this extract from the Chartered Banker Magazine for June/July 2012 illustrates:

59%: Aviva's Boss is Forced to Quit

Andrew Moss, the Chief Executive of Aviva, the UK's largest insurer, has stepped down after some 59% of the shareholders claimed the City's largest scalp. Although Moss, who's led Aviva since 2007, offered to waive a near-5% pay rise, that wasn't enough for shareholders who have seen a 30 per cent fall in share value over the past year. Moss is replaced by incoming Executive Chairman, John McFarlane.

18.2 Managers

Managers' main concerns will be for reward and the prestige and power that go with their position. As we have seen, if it is felt that the rewards that managers are obtaining are excessive, then other stakeholders could act to have them removed.

18.3 Customers

Customers are looking for quality in the products and services that they buy, good customer service, and value for money.

It could be argued that customers are the most powerful stakeholder group as it is their business that generates the profits for the organisation. They are also the group that can find it easiest to change their allegiance – all they need to do is go to the competition. On the other hand, if an employee is dissatisfied, then they still need to find another job before they can leave.

However, this transferability of business is not always as easy as it sounds. Even in a market as competitive as financial services, some customers may still remain with the provider that they are unhappy with as it is still too much hassle to go to somewhere else, despite provisions being in place between banks to streamline this process. However, if services and quality levels fall sufficiently, then this may affect the organisation's market share.

18.4 Employees

Employees are looking for security in their employment, sufficient reward (this can be financial and fringe benefits) and job satisfaction.

They are the stakeholder group who are likely to be most dependent on the organisation – they will require the salary from their employment to sustain their lifestyle, but they have less influence over the organisation than senior managers.

Their influencing skills will be dependent upon how well organised they are as a labour force, how high the demand is for their skills and what level of importance management and shareholders place on the existence of a happy and motivated workforce.

Employees are generally not maximisers – they will often accept a lower return from their employers as they may have a high reliance on the organisation for continued employment. However, if their reward package falls below a particular level, then this may pose problems for the organisation and even if the employees do not choose to leave, this may well affect their willingness to provide high levels of service to customers, or how they interact with other stakeholder groups.

18.5 Creditors

If an organisation is not able to meet its payments to creditors as they fall due, then they have the power to put the company out of business – but this is unlikely to happen if there is a belief that the company can be turned around.

18.6 Other stakeholders

Other groups can also have an interest in the organisation – for example, the wider society, groups that the organisation supports through its Community Involvement Programme and so on.

19 Balanced objectives

As we have mentioned, no organisation should only look to one area of objective – therefore, it is preferable to perform well over a number of areas of performance rather than look to perform outstandingly in only one.

In order to achieve this balanced outlook, organisations can ensure that the various stakeholders are adequately represented in the company, by having a **mission statement** which all of the stakeholder groups can subscribe to, and have a balanced scorecard.

We will look at each of these areas in turn.

19.1 Representation

If this occurs then the organisation will not be hijacked by one group of stakeholders who are able to dominate the company and force the agenda. There needs to be an understanding and acceptance that it is to the benefit of all that the needs of the stakeholder groups are met. As a result each group can be willing to sacrifice short term pain for longer term gain.

However, whilst there is evidence of this approach being adopted in Japan and Germany, in both the USA and UK most organisations are dominated by the one stakeholder group – management.

19.2 Mission statements

An organisational mission statement is the second way in which the stakeholders can be included in the goals of the company. Most companies will now have a mission statement.

QUICK QUESTION

What is your organisation's mission statement?

Write your answer here before reading on.

The mission statement is a general statement that tells the overall purpose of the organisation. Normally it will refer directly to the stakeholders.

In general terms, the mission statement will seek to define who the key stakeholders are, and what strategy(ies) the organisation will follow to meet their needs. If there is disagreement amongst the stakeholders as to what the mission of the organisation is, then it is unlikely that the organisation is going to achieve its mission.

Mission statements have been criticised as they can appear to be so bland and wide ranging that they appear to have no useful value. However, as we have just seen, the needs of these stakeholder groups can be very diverse, therefore if we are to have a document that all can subscribe to, then it is, by definition, likely to be so. After all, the mission statement is not mean to be a specific objective – that will come later.

The mission statement will usually look to cover the following areas.

- A vision of the organisation that is likely to remain for the longer term. It can be thought of as a distant aim, or something on the far horizon.

- There should be information on the main intentions or aspirations of the organisation.

- An explanation of the main activities of the organisation and the position that it would like to hold in the market place. For the large organisation, this may mean being a market leader or within the top (say) five players in the market, for the smaller organisation it could be about providing high quality products and services within a niche market.

- There will probably be a statement of the key values of the organisation – this can cover the stakeholder groups – for example, 'year on year growth for our shareholders' or 'the growth and development of our people'.

The views that organisations have about mission statements will vary depending upon the agenda that they are operating under. For example, if the organisation is being controlled by managers who feel that the other stakeholders are a hindrance to their work, then they are likely to see little value in mission statements. If the managers see other stakeholders as collaborators with them in the future of the organisation, then they will try to use the mission statement as a way of selling the strategic direction of the organisation to them. If the agenda is being driven by other stakeholders who feel strongly that the organisation must be compliant with regulations, then any sense of mission may be lost, as the statement will get bogged down in the compliance of the organisation.

19.3 The balanced scorecard

Whilst the mission statement will contain broad objectives, these need to be focussed into more specific goals that will have specific performance measures.

Normally, these objectives , which were introduced earlier, will fall under the following headings:

- Profitability
- Growth
- Shareholder value
- Customer satisfaction

The wording of these goals will vary depending upon the business that the organisation is engaged in.

QUESTION TIME 9

Looking at these four areas, decide on what areas you think these goals may be centred on and how they will be measured:

Profitability:

Goals: *Measures:*

Growth:

Goals: *Measures:*

Shareholder Value:

Goals: *Measures:*

Customer Satisfaction:

Goals: *Measures:*

20 Measuring and managing performance

Performance management is a feature in almost all organisations now – so you will almost certainly have personal experience of this section of the study text, either as a team member or as a team leader, or even both. Whilst your organisation will have its own framework, it is likely that the main components of the framework or system will not be markedly different from that in other organisations. Also the soft skills that are necessary to help manage the performance of a team member are the same across all organisations.

We will start this section by looking at the components of most performance management systems. The next part of the chapter will then work through these components in detail. Having built up this in depth knowledge, the next step is to examine the roles and responsibilities of the parties to performance management, namely – the team leader, the individual, and the organisation's Human Resources Department. If a team leader is to be successful managing the performance of the team, then they must have strong communication skills. A popular outcome of a performance management conversation is a **coaching** session for the team member, so we will explore this topic next. Finally we will look at what actions the team leader should take to manage team members at different levels of performance.

21 The components of a performance management system

QUICK QUESTION

What do you understand by performance management?

Write your answer here before reading on.

Performance management should allow a high performance culture to exist within an organisation. It does this by enabling each member of staff to focus on carrying out the right actions and displaying the most appropriate behaviours as they do so. Performance management can also ensure that these employees are motivated and empowered to perform to their greatest potential. It allows employees to see their line of sight to the overall organisational aims – what the business is seeking to do and where it wants to be.

Performance management can achieve this through a combined process of self-appraisal and joint team leader/team member review ensuring that there is a mutual and agreed understanding of:

- What the team member should be doing
- How they should be doing it
- How well they are doing during the year
- What they should be considering for future development – either for roles they aspire to, or to improve their performance within their current role

As discussed at the start of this section, organisations design their own performance management systems – but there can be a number of common stages within these systems.

What are the major components of the performance management system in your organisation?

Write your answer here before reading on.

It is likely that your performance management system is likely to have the following components:

21.1 Planning performance (at the start of the period under review)

- To ensure that the individual understand the business goals and objectives
- To ensure understanding of the role that the individual is required to perform
- To agree what the job is in practice i.e. key roles and responsibilities for the team member
- To ensure the individual understands the priorities within job
- To agree what should be achieved, by when, and to what standard
- To agree the best way to achieve success in the role. These ideas should come primarily from the team member, but it may be that the team leader needs to input – perhaps to get the discussion going, or to have a sanity check on ideas put forward
- To agree the behaviours required to do the job in line with organisational standards and culture

21.2 Monitor and review

- Regularly review and agree ongoing performance – this should happen at regular times during the year. Best practice would suggest that the team leader and the individual should get together to discuss performance at least monthly and there should be a more formal performance discussion at least quarterly (although some organisations may do this six monthly).
- Regularly review objectives to ensure currency. If the objectives are set for a 12 month period, then in the current operating environment, it is quite possible that business needs will change during that time, therefore performance objectives would be expected to change in line with these.
- Coach the employee to maximise performance.
- Challenge poor performance.
- Identify and agree appropriate development plans.
- Support the employee's development in line with plan.

21.3 Appraising performance (at the end of the period under review)

- Formal agreement of performance appraisal and rating.
- Agreement of objectives for the forthcoming period.
- Documentation of the process.

21.4 Performance planning

A key aspect of **performance planning** is the agreeing of objectives between the team leader and the team member.

QUICK QUESTION

Why do we need to have these objectives?

Write your answer here before reading on.

It is important to agree objectives to ensure team members:

- Understand what is expected of them
- See how their individual effort relates to overall business success
- Have a baseline for effective feedback on their performance
- Are motivated to perform

QUICK QUESTION

What do you think are the key features of a good work based objective?

Write your answer here before reading on.

A good objective should be:

- Consistent with the values of the organisation

- In line with organisational and branch/departmental objectives that have cascaded down the organisation

- Clear well defined

- Challenging and stretching for the individual to achieve

- Measurable – it can be related to quantified or qualitative performance measures that are readily accessible for the team leader and the team member. These measurements should also be agreed between the team leader and the team member

- Achievable within the capabilities of the individual

- Agreed by the manager and team member

- Time-related – achievable within a defined time-scale

As you will probably be aware, objectives should fall within the '**SMART**' framework.

QUICK QUESTION

What does SMART stand for?

Write your answer here before reading on.

SMART is a mnemonic which stands for:

Specific –	Does the objective state clearly what has to be achieved?
Measurable –	Is there a clear measure for both parties to monitor progress and identify when the objective is achieved?
Achievable –	Is the objective stretching, yet attainable?
Relevant –	Is the objective relevant to the business requirements of the role?
Time based –	Is there a clear indication of when the objective must be attained and how regularly progress will be reviewed?

The agreement of objectives need not be a complicated process. The following process can be followed:

- There should be a discussion with the team member around what it is that the manager wants them to achieve.

- The manager should then explain the bigger picture – in other words, how does this objective fit into the overall goals of the business – such as those discussed in the strategy section of this chapter. This is important as it lets the individual see clearly how they are contributing towards the aims of the organisation. This can be particularly important in a large organisation as it is all too easy for staff there to feel alienated from the drivers of the business. This link between individual and organisational goals is sometimes called 'line of sight'.

- The manager should then explain why they feel that the objective(s) is/ are appropriate to that individual.

- The objective should then be drafted – ensuring that it is compliant with the SMART rule. There should then be a conversation around how the individual is going to achieve this objective. This should cover what actions are to be taken and by when. To assist with the feeling of ownership of the objective, it is important that the manager encourages the individual to think what these actions will be. A further benefit is that as the individual is closer to the technical nature of the task, it may be that they can think of ways of achieving the objective that the manager is not as aware of.

QUICK QUESTION

What factors do you think a team leader should take into account when considering which team member should work on a particular objective?

Write your answer here before reading on.

The areas to be considered here are:

- Who will find the responsibility or task useful for their development? Perhaps at a previous development planning meeting they have mentioned a particular role that they aspire to. By giving them the opportunity of working towards this objective, this may help them gain experience that will help them in this regard.

- How well does the task fit an individual's preferred role within the team? Will this objective complement their preferred ways of working – or linking to the last point, do we want to stretch the person?

- What is the competence level of the individual for whom the objective is being set? Will they be capable of fulfilling the demands of this objective?

- How confident and/or willing will the individual feel/be in relation to the task? If the person is lacking in confidence, what can the team leader do to give them the self belief necessary to meet the objective?

- Who has the time? If there are a number of completing demands on the team, then this may be an expedient and attractive option for the team leader. However, it is important that the team leader does not fall into the trap of thinking that ...'every day is a crisis'... and therefore only looks short term, thus neglecting the chance to develop team members for the longer term benefit of both the individual and the team.

QUESTION TIME 10

Look at the following objectives and consider whether they are SMART or not. If the objective is not SMART, explain what the weaknesses in it are.

Note that as these objectives do not necessarily relate directly to your current role, you may need to make some assumptions around the Achievable and Relevant headings.

1. Update customer files on a regular basis and distribute an electronic copy of the updated version to interested parties.

2. To increase the number in the green team from 25 to 75 through recruitment and selection by September 20XX.

3. Reduce the department's overtime budget by 25%

4. Spend two days per week in the role of research assistant in a forthcoming debt collection project to be responsible for the collation and interpretation of data to be provided to the project manager on a weekly basis to start 5th January 20XX.

5. To grow the customer business from 1.3 million to 2.3 million by December 20XX.

6. Present the customer registration process to all the departmental team managers by April 20XX.

7. Design and develop a Business Writing Skills programme to meet the needs of the correspondence team in the Call Centre by 30th September.

8. To compile and complete the strategic I.T. document which includes a full implementation specification, by October 20XX.

Write your answer here then check with the answer at the back of the book.

21.5 Incorporating behaviours into objectives

Many organisations now incorporate behavioural measures into objectives – thus requiring the individual not only to achieve the result specified in the objective, but also to display the appropriate behaviours when working towards the end result.

QUICK QUESTION

Why do you think some organisations now do this?

Write your answer here before reading on.

Using behavioural objectives allows a business to guard against a situation like this occurring:

A member of staff could have an objective to prepare a report on the organisation's sales effectiveness by 8 June this year. Whilst the report may be delivered by the deadline, however the business and marketing department contacts that the individual used for baseline information report that the person was uncooperative and rude and regularly late for meetings. Therefore, the end result may have been achieved, but in a less than satisfactory manner.

EXAMPLE

An example of how important appropriate behaviours are to achieving a quality output could be seen by looking at an objective for a double glazing salesperson. Their task is to sign up as many customers as possible; the individuals are targeted and can make more commission depending on how many customers are signed up.

In crude task terms you may correctly assume that the salesperson has completed a sale when the customer signs the contract. However what happens if the customer has not been given the correct information at the point of sale? What happens if the customer has been confused by the lack of (or conversely) the abundance of information the salesperson has communicated to them during their visit to the potential customer's home? The potential upshot is that the customer may ring the company to cancel their order and while the salesperson had completed the initial task the behaviours the exhibited have contributed to the sale being cancelled.

As a result the completed contracts are therefore checked for quality before a salesperson receives their commission. The indicators for a successful sale are closely linked to the number of fields that have been completed within the contract and to the absence of any customer complaints.

QUICK QUESTION

Based on the above, what would the salesperson's objective then look like?

Write your answer here before reading on.

A possible example could be:

To achieve sales target of 100 customers to replacement window products to a value of £x,000 between the 1st of January to the 31st of March while ensuring that no justified customer complaints occur as a result of your sales technique. (In order for a sale to be considered as successful all relevant customer details complete with a full signature must be entered onto the contract, and the sale must not be cancelled by the customer during the cooling off period).

In order to achieve this objective the agent will be required to demonstrate effective customer service (i.e. no justified complaints) and appropriate communication skills to ensure the customer completes the order correctly.

22 Personal development planning

Once an individual is clear what the requirements of their role is – through the agreement of SMART objectives – they are then in a position to appraise their current skill levels and decide if there are any development activities that they need to carry out to get themselves into a position where they are skilled enough to work to the objective.

QUICK QUESTION

Is there any other situation where an individual should reflect upon their development needs?

Write your answer here before reading on.

Another area where we need to consider our development is where a person aspires to a particular role, but they do not at present possess the necessary skills. They therefore need to carry out some development activities to get themselves to a position where they can apply for the desired role with a reasonable chance of success.

Personal Development Planning is about agreeing the areas of strength and areas for development for the individual firstly to maximise performance in their current role and secondly to plan development in line with their career aspirations.

Personal development planning helps individuals identify their strengths and weaknesses, focus career direction, and improve their ability to complete work objectives.

A good Personal Development Plan (PDP) should support the person's business goals and career aspirations. It also should not be limited to training. A good PDP is robust with development activities like job shadowing, professional organisation involvement, community leadership, and training or formal education.

22.1   Preparing for a PDP

QUICK QUESTION

What should an individual do when preparing for a PDP?

Write your answer here before reading on.

The person should be encouraged to collect and review any relevant documents he or she may have available that will help them determine developmental goals and actions.

Examples are:

- Performance objectives
- Past performance objectives and evaluations
- Assessments/feedback
- Past development plans
- Peer feedback or client feedback

The following questions can be useful to reflect upon when preparing a PDP:

- What individual objectives do you have to accomplish?

- What skills and knowledge would help you achieve these objectives?

- What behaviours do you need to demonstrate in order to achieve these objectives?

- What are your career aspirations?

- What are your strengths and areas for improvement?

- What skills, knowledge and competencies do you have?

- How do you learn best? Do you need to experience it, go to a traditional class/course or can you learn it on-line? Can you practice the skill?

- What are some possible developmental goals?

22.2 Personal development options

QUICK QUESTION

What options do you currently have for personal development activities?

Write your answer here before reading on.

- Mentoring
- Coaching
- Working with a civic organisation, or other external body – for example, the Princes Trust
- Studying for professional qualifications
- Studying a textbook
- Attending a formal training course
- Completing an e-learning course or module

The most effective PDPs are those completed by the individual for themselves – after all, the best placed person to know you own development areas is you.

QUICK QUESTION

What do you think is the role of the manager in the PDP process?

Write your answer here before reading on.

Within the PDP process, the role of the manager is to:

- Overview the PDP to ensure that nothing has been missed out

- Provide access to relent development opportunities – for example, signing off an application to attend a training course

- To encourage and motivate the individual to complete the activities outlined in the PDP

23 Roles and responsibilities within performance management

In this section, we will look at the roles and responsibilities of the following three parties within the performance management process:

- The manager/team leader
- The member of staff
- The HR department

23.1 The manager/team Leader

QUICK QUESTION

List what you think are the key responsibilities of a manager in the performance management process?

Write your answer here before reading on.

The manager's responsibilities include:

- Ensuring annual performance appraisals are carried out on time
- Ensuring interim performance reviews are carried out on time
- Ensuring the employee commits to objectives set during the performance review meeting
- Planning and conducting regular one to one meetings with the employee during the year
- Overviewing the development plan to ensure that it fits with the current/future role and/or relevant personal development
- Supporting the employee through their development activities
- Ensuring all supporting documentation is completed, signed off and actioned/communicated in line with organisational requirements

23.2 The member of staff

QUICK QUESTION

List what you think are the key responsibilities of the individual n the performance management process?

Write your answer here before reading on.

The individual's responsibilities include:

- Preparing for all of their performance management meetings and conversations
- Taking ownership for their performance discussions
- Taking ownership of the objectives they agree with their line manager
- Taking ownership and implementing the development plan

23.3 The HR department

The role of the HR department is to support the process in terms of:

- Ensure those responsible for operating the Performance Management System are trained

- Ensure training courses and/or materials are provided for members of staff

- Update the organisations record system on confirmation of employee rating and ensuring that any salary increases and/or bonuses are processed timeously

- Ongoing maintenance and development of the Performance Management System overall

24 Feedback skills

Why is giving and receiving feedback important?

Write your answer here before reading on.

Giving and receiving feedback is important as:

- Feedback is a way to let people know how effective they are in what they are trying to accomplish: it provides a way for people to learn how they affect the world around them. It helps them to become more effective.

- In relation to work, feedback can inform us about how other people perceive us, and we can use this information to improve the quality of our communication and interaction skills. It is important to keep in mind that others relate to us, not based on our self perception, but on how they perceive us. Even if we feel that this perception is erroneous, it is real to the other person. Fortunately, feedback can draw this to our attention and let us do something about it.

- Ideally, this should be a day-to-day process as well as a series of mini reviews leading up to the interim reviews and annual appraisal.

- This will make sure that nothing is missed, will keep the channels of communication open throughout the year and as a result, the final appraisal will be more effective.

- It is recognised that feedback directs behaviour and motivates performance at work - no matter how good or effective employees are, they can always get better or at least sustain high performance.

- Constructive feedback delivered at the right time can be highly motivating.

- Equally, if it is delivered badly and at the wrong time, it can be de-motivating and have entirely the opposite effect from the one intended.

STYLE	DESCRIPTOR	EXAMPLE - backed up by factual data
Tell	Informing	Your performance is not up to scratch and I want you to improve. Your performance is great and I'm looking at the best ways of using your talents.
Sell	Persuading	I believe your performance can improve and when it does I can see you getting the opportunity to carry out the higher-level tasks you really want. I believe your performance has improved and I am offering you an opportunity on higher-level tasks.

STYLE	DESCRIPTOR	EXAMPLE - backed up by factual data
Sample	Testing	Since your performance could be better would you consider some coaching?
		Now that you are performing really well, how would you like to tackle a higher-level task?
Consult	Sharing	How do you think we can get your performance to improve?
		How can we develop you further?

QUESTION TIME 11

Consider the following statements and write which of the styles explained above best describes it:

1. Alistair, your performance when interfacing with customers is where we hoped it would be. What can we do now to develop it further?

2. Brenda, I believe your performance on the processor could be better if you focused on a more accurate input. When your performance improves, I can see you moving on to those higher- level tasks you've been asking for.

3. Clive, once again we find ourselves speaking about getting a higher throughput from you. Do you think that coaching would help?

4. Denise, we had this conversation about your accuracy on numerous occasions yet nothing is getting better. I want you to concentrate for the next week purely on product inputs.

5. Eddie, that's you now our top performer in the first line customer charts. How would you like to tackle a more challenging range of customers?

6. Fiona, that's the quarterly results in and for the first time you're bottom of the league table in your section. How do you think we can get you back up the table?

7. Brian, you are by far and away our top sales person and I'm moving you to the new west region sales area next month.

8. Jackie, I can see that following our last discussion you have really made in roads with the weekly reports. If this continues to improve I can see you getting the employee of the month soon.

Write your answer here then check with the answer at the back of the book.

25 Coaching within performance management

How would you define coaching?

Write your answer here before reading on.

Coaching is the act of helping an individual to improve or maintain their performance level by giving them ongoing evaluation and feedback.

An adviser in a call centre may be coached by their team leader listening into their calls and then having a structured discussion on how the call went – this would include reinforcement of the things that the adviser did well, and discussing what the adviser could have done differently for those situations that were not handled so well.

Coaching is something that may happen at any time during the performance management cycle and may well be an outcome of the individual's PDP.

A model for effective coaching is called '**GROW**'. This model is based on using open questions that encourage the person being coached to say what they are aiming for, where they are now, what they could do to move forward and what they will do to improve their performance. It raises self-awareness in the person being coached and encourages them to take responsibility for, and to own, their development.

What do you think GROW stands for?

Write your answer here before reading on.

GROW is a mnemonic representing the following:

Goal	–	What do you want to achieve?
Reality	–	What is happening now?
Options	–	What can you do to improve performance?
Will	–	What will you do to improve performance?

The following diagram illustrates how to structure a coaching session:

Goal
- Establish the aim of the session
- Agree the topic for discussion
- Agree specific objectives for the session
- Assess their competence and commitment
- Assess if it is challenging for the individual and providing enough stretch

> What I'd like to do is spend the next 20 mins with you to discuss and share views...
> What is it you'd like to discuss?
> What is the objective?
> What do you want to achieve?
> Is this realistic?
> Is it aligned to business goals?
> Why are you doing it?

Reality
- Invite self-assessment
- Ask for specific examples of feedback
- Challenge misconceptions/assumptions
- Discard irrelevant history/descriptions

> What is the current situation?
> How do you feel?
> What are the implications?
> What will be the effect on others?
> What other factors are relevant?
> What have you tried so far?
> What are the measurable gaps between goal and reality?
> Who do you need to talk to?

Options
- Keep asking the individual for more possibilities
- Invite suggestions from the other person
- Offer suggestions carefully
- Help them identify role models

> How will you approach it?
> What could you do to change the situation?
> Who might be able to help?
> What opportunities are there?
> Which options do you prefer?
> What are the benefits and pitfalls of the different options?
> What factors will affect your performance?

Will
- Ensure the individual chooses to commit to action
- Identify possible obstacles
- Make steps specific and define timings
- Agree support

> How will you know how successful you have been?
> What are the next steps?
> Precisely what will you do?
> What support will you need?
> What dates are you working to?
> What are your specific measures?
> What will you do and by when?
> Who will do what?

The GROW model can be developed further:

Goal – What do you want to achieve?

- Set a context for the interaction
- Discuss and agree the objectives of the coaching session
- Identify the problem and what they want to do about it
- Ask questions to encourage them to identify a SMART goal
- Put the person at ease, reassure them, discuss confidentiality, and clear any tension
- Be specific and focus on the issue

If the aim of the session is to improve performance, there may be an end goal that is to meet the full performance target. However it maybe that this is not achievable in one session, therefore, performance goals will need to be established to build up to the end goal in achievable but challenging chunks.

Seek agreement throughout

Reality – What is happening now?

- Help the individual to understand/establish the current situation

- Ask questions to help them to raise their self-awareness of that situation

- There will be TWO realities, the team members and the coach

- Get a general sense of the issue checking to explore the current situation

- Check their reality

- This will be based around facts supported with evidence and opinions. Make sure that if they are expressing an opinion that you are clear on what it is based on

State your reality.

For example: Looking at .... your performance with regard to this issue is.......

Do you agree?

This will be based around facts supported with evidence. If it is your opinion, make sure that if you are stating an opinion, you acknowledge that it is your opinion for example: 'In my opinion, OR I think...' – this enables you to reconsider without losing face, once you state that something is a fact, it is hard to change your point of view.

Options – What can you do?

- Encourage the individual to come up with a range of feasible, realistic options for dealing with the matter

- Ask questions to get the individual to generate as many alternative courses of action as possible

- If the individual genuinely has no ideas, then ask if they would like you suggest some options. Or an alternative course of action. What to do differently or how to develop by exploring the available options

Will – What will you do?

- Encourage the individual to make things happen

- Ask questions to get them to commit to acting upon their preferred solution

- Converting a discussion into a decision based on WHAT is to be done, WHEN and by WHO requires the WILL to do it

- Be clear on who is doing what – team manager to ....   team member to ....

The outcome of the coaching session should be to:

- Agree and record an action plan with the team member

- Check understanding and buy in be asking the individual to talk through the agreed action plan to ensure that they are happy with it

26 Managing differing levels of performance

In the final section under performance management, we will look at how to manage team members who are performing at different levels. Whilst your organisation may have a range of performance levels, for the purposes of this study text we will restrict our attentions to these three performance levels:

- Staff who exceed expectations
- Staff who meet expectations
- Staff who fall below expectation

26.1 Staff who exceed expectations

The focus with this group should be on:

- Career growth
- Learning
- Development – identify employee needs and career direction
- Retention issues and actions
- Praise and recognition
- Creation of an action plan (PDP)

The team leader should:

- Seek to understand what motivates the employee

- Seek to understand the career path or paths the employee is interested in pursuing and show relevant support for it

- Stress the significance of the results the employee has achieved and his/her potential for more

- Stress the actions that you and the employee will take to prepare him/her for their next role

It is important that the team leader avoids:

- Assuming they know what's best for the employee … they should ask the individual what they would like

- Assuming the employee knows how important his/her contributions are

- Making commitments on actions which they cannot or will not follow through

It is all too easy for this group of staff to become invisible to the manager – it is easier to devote our attentions to those employees whose performance we are striving to improve, with the result that those members of the team who are exceeding expectation are merely left to get on with it.

Key questions for the team leader to explore with employees exceeding expectations:

- What can I do to help keep you challenged and engaged in your job?

- What are your next steps in your career?

- How can the company support your development? What do you need to get to your next career step?

26.2 Employees who are meeting expectations

The focus here should be on:

- Strengths
- Improvement areas
- Learning and training opportunities
- Praise and recognition
- Creating an action plan (PDP)

The team leader should:

- Provide examples of successes and achievement. Praise the employee for his or her hard work and contribution

- Review areas where he or she might improve – have specific examples ready

- Seek to understand how the employee wants to grow and develop

It is important for the team leader to avoid:

- Allowing improvement areas to overshadow the employees accomplishments
- Letting the employee leave the meeting without telling him or her about improvement areas

Key questions for the team leader to explore with employees who meet expectations are:

- What can I do to help keep you challenged and engaged in your job?
- What development opportunities would help you?
- How can the company support your development? What do you need to get to your next career step?

26.3 Employees who fail to meet expectations

The focus here should be on:

- Past/current performance vs. goals set (what are the gaps?)
- Understanding causes
- Future expectations (new goals)
- Timing
- Acknowledgement of understanding
- Follow up – creation of personal improvement plan
- If underperformance continues, the manger would need to use the formal procedures within the organisation for staff who fail to reach satisfactory levels of performance. These procedures are sometimes called 'capability programmes'

The team leader should:

- Stress the seriousness of the situation
- Be honest, sensitive and prepared to listen
- Stress that this matter is confidential
- Give specific examples when describing the problems or issues
- Confirm that the employee understands what has just happened
- Follow up on agreed actions

The team leader should avoid:

- Being overly harsh towards the employee
- Letting the employee get the team leader off track
- Apologising for their actions
- Blaming others for the actions being taken – own it

27 Managing change

Change is something that happens to us all in our personal and working lives and the pace of this change has quickened in line with technological innovations. Can you imagine life without mobile phones or e-mail? Yet 25 years ago, we may not have heard of e-mail and mobile phones were too bulky and pricey for most of us.

As managers, we are often expected to implement and lead organisational changes. The success or failure of these changes is likely to hinge upon how motivated our colleagues are and yet people may not respond to change positively – at least not in the first instance. An analysis of the transition many of us go through when faced with change was described by JM Fisher below.

The Process of Personal Transition

27.1 Anxiety

This refers to the awareness that events lie outside one's range of understanding or control. Fisher believes that the problem here is that individuals are unable to adequately picture the future. They do not have enough information to allow them to anticipate behaving in a different way within the new organisation.

27.2 Happiness

This is the awareness that one's viewpoint is recognised and shared by others. The impact of this is two-fold.

At the basic level, there is a feeling of relief that something is going to change, and not continue as before. Whether the past is perceived positively or negatively, there is still a feeling of anticipation, and possibly excitement, at the prospect of improvement.

On another level, there is the satisfaction of knowing that some of your thoughts about the old system were correct (generally no matter how well we like the status quo, there is something that is unsatisfactory about it) and that something is going to be done about it.

In this phase we generally expect the best and anticipate a bright future. However one of the dangers in this phase is that we may perceive more to the change, or believe we will get more from the change than is actually the case. The organisation needs to manage this phase and ensure unrealistic expectations are managed and redefined in the organisation's terms, without alienating the individual.

27.3 Fear

People may need to act and behave in a different way and this will have an impact on both their self-perception and on how others externally see them.

27.4 Threat

Here people perceive a major lifestyle change; one that will radically alter their future choices and other people's perception of them. They are unsure as to how they will be able to act/react in what is, potentially, a totally new and alien environment - one where the 'old rules' no longer apply and there are no new ones established as yet.

27.5 Guilt

This is the awareness of dislodgement of self from one's core self-perception. Once the individual begins exploring their self-perception, how they acted/reacted in the past and looking at alternative interpretations, they begin to re-define their sense of self. This, generally, involves identifying what are their core beliefs and how closely they have been to meeting them. Recognition of the inappropriateness of their previous actions and the implications for them as people can cause guilt as they realise the impact of their behaviour.

27.6 Depression

This phase is characterised by a general lack of motivation and confusion. Individuals are uncertain as to what the future holds and how they can fit into the future world. The resultant undermining of their core sense of self leaves them adrift with no sense of identity and no clear vision of how to operate.

27.7 Disillusionment

The awareness that your values, beliefs and goals are incompatible with those of the organisation. The pitfalls associated with this phase are that the employee becomes unmotivated, unfocused and increasingly dissatisfied and gradually withdraws their labour, either mentally (by just going through the motions, doing the bare minimum, actively undermining the change by criticising/complaining) or physically by resigning.

27.8 Hostility

Continued effort to validate social predictions that have already proved to be a failure. The problem here is that individuals continue to operate processes that have repeatedly failed to achieve a successful outcome and are no longer part of the new process or are surplus to the new way of working. The new processes are ignored at best and actively undermined at worst.

27.9 Denial

This stage is defined by a lack of acceptance of any change and denies that there will be any impact on the individual. People keep acting as if the change has not happened, using old practices and processes and ignoring evidence or information contrary to their belief systems.

It can be seen from the transition curve that it is important for an individual to understand the impact that the change will have on their own personal construct systems; and for them to be able to work through the implications for their self-perception. Any change, no matter how small, has the potential to impact on an individual and may generate conflict between existing values and beliefs and anticipated altered ones.

One danger for the individual, team and organisation occurs when an individual persists in operating a set of practices that have been consistently shown to fail (or result in an undesirable consequence) in the past and that do not help extend and elaborate their world-view. Another danger area is that of denial - where people carry on operating as they always have denying that there is any change at all. Both of these can have detrimental impact on an organisation trying to change the culture and focus of its people.

27.10 Implementing change

Change can happen at an industry, organisational or local level. These pointers will help you in the implementation of change.

Know why you are making the change

Make sure you understand why you are making the change and that it is really necessary. Be prepared to explain to people who are affected.

Involve people in the change

Sell the change to people and involve them. Being part of the planning gives people a sense of control. Ask for opinions at all stages. Use surveys and discussion groups.

Put a respected person in charge

All change needs a leader. Select someone with integrity and who is respected.

Acknowledge and reward people

Identify and acknowledge those who have made it happen. Many people take personal risk to help towards success – this should be acknowledged and rewarded.

Manage the stories

Use anecdotes of where change has brought about positive results.

Look for outside help

Often an outsider, with no axe to grind provides good, neutral advice. Use this to reinforce the direction in which you want to go. This person may be referred to as a 'change agent'.

Create teams

You need to motivate and encourage people together – provide an official route to do this.

Provide training in new values and work methods

People need help. Training brings people together and it allows them to air their concerns.

Be dogged and persistent

Changed organisations can easily slip back to the old ways – be vigilant.

Walk the talk

Be seen to change and do things differently from the past.

KEY WORDS

Key words in this chapter are given below. There is space to write your own revision notes and to add any other words or phrases that you want to remember.

- Interpersonal roles

- Informational roles

- Decisional roles

- Span of control

- Formal team

- Informal group

- Belbin's team roles

- Trait approach

- Style approach

- Contingency approach

- Stages of team development

- Theory X

- Theory Y

- Action centred leadership

- Strategic fit

- Strategic stretch

- Strategic analysis

- Strategic choice

- Strategic action

- Stakeholders

- Mission statement

- Performance management system

- Performance planning

- SMART

- Personal development planning

- Coaching

- GROW

REVIEW

Now consider the main learning points that were introduced in this chapter.

Go through them and check that you are happy that you fully understand each point.

- Managers need to achieve organisational objectives in a changing environment. They need to maintain a balance of efficiency, effectiveness and equity, whilst obtaining the best return that they can from limited resources, by working with and through other people.

- Management is about the control of resources, whilst leadership is concerned with direction, movement, progress and change.

- The functions of management are to plan, organise, problem solve, coordinate, control and communicate.

- Both formal and informal groups exist within organisations.

- The common factors in effective teams are: goals, roles, size, supportiveness, process, relationships and cohesiveness.

- Effective teams will have members with a complimentary set of characteristics. These were developed by Dr Meredith Belbin.

- Tuckman identified the four stages of team development as forming, storming, norming and performing.

- The three main approaches to leadership effectiveness are trait, style and contingency.

- An important aspect of leadership is the ability to manage conflict.

- Strategic decisions are concerned with the longer term direction of an organisation.

- The three stages of strategic management are strategic analysis, strategic choice and strategic action.

- Objectives are used to give an organisation a sense of direction, a focus for decision making, to motivate and energise employees and to control.

- Objectives tend to be set in the following areas: profitability, growth, shareholder value and customer satisfaction.

- Stakeholders are those groups who have an interest in an organisation.

- A performance management framework will consist of performance planning, monitoring/reviewing, and appraising performance.

- The process of transition through change can be explained by Fisher's model.

chapter 6

REGULATION

Contents

BPP
LEARNING MEDIA

Learning outcomes

On completion of this chapter you should be able to:

- Analyse the framework that regulates the activities of the activities of the retail banking sector
- Identify the implications of the FSMA for individuals operating in the retail banking sector
- Examine the significance of international regulation in retail banking
- Explain the key aspects of employment legislation that affect retail operations

Introduction

In this chapter we will examine the current regulatory regime facing retail banks in the UK. In particular we will focus on:

- The Financial Services and Markets Act 2000 Treating Customers Fairly
- Banking Conduct of Business Sourcebook
- The Lending Code
- Mortgage Regulation
- The Regulatory Bodies
- The Consumer Credit Act
- Money Laundering Regulations
- The Data Protection Act
- The Equality Act/Health and Safety at Work/Employment Law

Regulation is the system through which governments impose mandatory standards to which organisations must comply in order to ensure that they operate in the best interests of certain stakeholders and for the benefit of society as a whole. Within the financial services sector and at the macro level, government has to ensure that financial institutions operate within adequate safety margins, avoiding the likelihood of insolvency. Banking institutions have failed in the past, and sometimes depositors have lost some or even all of their money. As you will be aware, some of the UK Banks came perilously close to this during the banking crisis that started in 2007. Such events are thankfully rare, but in the most significant cases governments have responded by bringing in new regulations or reinforcing existing ones. Another reason that governments have to be concerned about the financial sector is that the activities of retail banks have a direct effect on the level of consumer demand, which in turn can affect macro-economic policy targets. At the micro level, governments seek to protect the interests of customers of financial institutions. Before the Financial Services and Markets Act 2000 came into force, micro level regulation mainly applied to staff fulfilling certain roles in financial services organisations. The main focus of legislation was on those engaged in 'investment business'. This related to sales of products that were long-term in nature with some risk attached to the capital investment, such as company shares, collective investments such as unit trusts and investment trusts, some life assurance products and pensions. For those in customer facing roles, it was necessary under the provisions of the Financial Services Act 1986 to be qualified and signed off as competent to advise on a regular basis. The 1986 Act made no provisions in respect of senior executives, who continued to be governed by the general principles of company law, or in the case of mutual organisations, legislation specific to those organisations.

Although all financial institutions must be authorised by the Financial Conduct Authority before they can do business with the public, not all staff are regulated. The 2000 Act has however broadened the scope of regulation, with separate conduct of business rules now applicable to those selling mortgages and general insurance products – as discussed in Chapter 2. In addition, the Act also introduced an approved persons regime, which requires those occupying certain statutory, management or risk functions to be registered.

1 The Financial Services and Markets Act 2000

The purpose of the Financial Services and Markets Act 2000 was to simplify and rationalise the regulatory system, whilst broadening its scope to ensure an appropriate level of protection. The Act introduced a completely new regulatory system under the overall control of the Treasury and implemented through the Financial Services Authority (FSA). As a result of the Independent Commission on Banking, the FSA is no longer in existence. The new regulatory landscape is discussed in the next section.

1 The UK Regulatory Landscape

1.1 The UK regulatory framework

The UK Regulatory Landscape

Under this heading, we will consider the work of the following three bodies:

- The Financial Conduct Authority (FCA)

- The Prudential Regulation Authority (PRA)

- The Financial Policy Committee (FPC)

The Financial Conduct Authority

The **FCA** is responsible for the regulation of the UK financial services industry. The aims of the FCA are to:

- Regulate and supervise firms

- Protect consumers

- Ensure that customers are treated fairly

- Promote healthy competition

- Enforce change in the behaviour of firms where necessary

In order to achieve these aims, the FCA has the power to make rules and issue guidance, investigate and to enforce its rules.

The FCA will intervene if it feels that customers are not being treated fairly, or where they feel that a firm is acting in a way that risks the integrity of the market. The FCA does not supervise every firm in the sector in the same way, rather the approach taken with each firm reflects its size and what they do – this is called a 'risk-based approach' and is discussed in more detail later on in this chapter.

The FCA also works with firms to ensure that the fight against financial crime is ongoing. To do this, they ensure that firms protect themselves against fraud and that they have suitable anti-money laundering policies and procedures. Firms are also aware that the FCA will take action against them if they are corrupt, or use unethical practices.

The organisation has also made it clear to firms that if they breach the rules, then there will be significant consequences. The view of the FCA is that enforcement can happen through suitable deterrence. In order to do this, the FCA has:

- Brought enforcement cases and pressed for penalties for infringements of rules to reset conduct standards

- Pursued cases against individuals and holding members of senior management accountable for their actions

- Pursued criminal prosecutions, including those for insider dealing and market manipulation

- Taken action to tackle unauthorised business – this is business that a firm has transacted where it has no regulatory authority to do so

- Continued to prioritise compensation for consumers

FCA policy is set by its Board – but as with any large organisation, the day-to-day decisions are made by management and staff who report to the Executive Committee. The FCA is responsible to the Treasury and so to Parliament.

Funding comes from the member firms, which are subject to regulation.

The Prudential Regulation Authority (PRA)

The **PRA** is responsible for the prudential regulation of the UK financial services industry. It is part of the Bank of England. The PRA works alongside the FCA – although the FCA is not part of the Bank of England.

Prudential control is concerned with ensuring that financial institutions adopt policies that will achieve an appropriate balance between risk and reward. As you know, the business of banking is primarily concerned with the management of risk. Without taking risks it is not possible to generate returns to the owners of the business – a bank could have a zero figure for bad debts if it chooses not to lend to borrowers, but such a course of action would mean that the bank was not making any profit. Conversely, by taking risks financial institutions can threaten the wealth of their owners – if a bank is not profitable, it cannot pay dividends and the value of its shares inevitably falls.

From a regulatory perspective, the key to achieving this balance is to adopt prudential standards that will ensure that commercial activities are backed by appropriate levels of capital. Capital is made up of shareholders' funds, which comprise equities (or shares) plus retained profits (retained profits are sometimes referred to as 'reserves'). These funds represent the inherent worth of the organisation. They serve as a buffer against unforeseen losses as well as a means of maintaining the confidence of investors. The various commercial activities of banks have differing risk profiles. For example, a secured loan is less risky than an unsecured loan.

Historically, residential mortgages have witnessed much lower default rates than other types of bank lending. From these lessons it is possible to estimate the level of capital that should back the various activities of any organisation.

The PRA has two statutory objectives:

- To promote the safety and soundness of firms

- Secure an appropriate degree of protection for policyholders and investors

To carry out its role, the PRA focuses on the harm that firms can cause to the stability of the UK financial system, and so makes judgements based upon the risks posed by firms to its statutory objectives.

Regulated firms must maintain certain Threshold Conditions, which include maintaining appropriate capital and liquidity, along with having suitable management.

The tools used by the PRA are regulation (the setting of standards that firms must meet), and supervision (assessing the risks that firms pose to its objectives).

To carry out this regulation and supervision, the PRA's approach has three characteristics:

- A judgement based approach: where the PRA uses judgement when determining the soundness of firms and whether insurers provide appropriate protection for consumers. This approach is also used when determining if a firm has met the Threshold Conditions.

- A forward looking approach: where the PRA assesses firms against both current and possible future risks. Should intervention be deemed necessary, then the PRA will attempt to do this at an early stage.

- A focusses approach: where the PRA will focus on those areas posing the greatest risk.

The PRA's approach to supervision is not to operate a 'zero failure' regime. However, should a firm fail; the PRA will seek to ensure that this happens in a way that avoids significant disruption to the supply of critical financial services.

Significant decisions are made by the Board, which comprises the Governor of the Bank of England and the Deputy Governor for Financial Stability, the CEO of the PRA and the Deputy Governor for Prudential Regulation, and independent non-executive members.

The Board of the PRA are accountable to Parliament.

The Financial Policy Committee

The **FPC** is a Committee of the Bank of England.

Its primary objective is to identify, monitor and take action to remove or reduce systemic risks in the UK financial system, with the aim of enhancing the resilience of the system.

The role of the FPC is to identify risks and weaknesses in the UK financial system. The Committee has 10 members – five are appointed by the Bank of England and the remaining five are appointed by the Chancellor of the Exchequer. The FPC meets at least quarterly and every six months it publishes its 'Financial Stability Report'. This Report states the FPC's assessment of the risks it has identified in the financial system and the measures it is taking to address them.

1.2 Authorisation

Before any financial institution can commence operations, it must obtain permission from the FCA. This gives them **authorisation** to operate. It is a criminal offence to offer services to the public without being authorised. Prior to the 2000 Act, different bodies authorised different categories of financial institutions. Now the only route to authorisation is through the FCA.

1.3 Approved persons

The 2000 Act broadened the scope of regulation considerably. The Act requires persons in defined areas of activity to be approved.

An **approved person** is an individual who has been approved by the FCA and/or the PRA to perform one or more controlled functions on behalf of an authorised firm. In order to become an approved person, the individual must:

- Satisfy the FCA that he or she can meet and maintain the criteria for approval. This considers honesty, integrity, and reputation; confidence and capability; financial soundness.
- Perform the controlled function in a manner that is consistent with the Statements of Principle and Code of Practice for Approved Persons.

1.4 Risk-based approach

The Financial Services and Markets Act 2000 requires that the regulators provide an appropriate level of protection for personal customers. In practice, some financial institutions have very simple businesses with little risk attached to them, while others are highly complex. In addition, the nature of the risks is very different from business to business. For example, larger organisations may be exposed to the risk of computer fraud whereas in small deposit taking businesses the risk is of a member of staff walking out of the office with cash.

The UK regulators adopt a risk-based approach to regulation and supervision. This entails identifying potential risks, prioritising these risks and then applying the tools of regulatory management to reduce or eliminate the risks. Once such tools have been applied, feedback can be generated from which new insights into risk identification are gained.

The risk-based approach is summarised below.

Risk assessment/prioritisation ⟶ Regulatory response

Identification of risk

Allocation of resources

Performance evaluation ⟵ Application of regulatory tools

2 Regulated activities

As stated above, not all functions in a financial institution are regulated. In fact, the vast majority of counter transactions in banks and building societies may be carried out by anyone with suitable training. It is also permissible for anyone to give factual information to a customer, provided this is not extended to giving advice.

The regulatory regime demands that those occupying certain functions be competent to do so. They include:

- Giving advice, dealing, arranging or managing investments on any form of investment previously regulated under the Financial Services Act 1986, including long-term assurance products, pensions, unit trusts, investment trust shares, open-ended investment company (OEIC) shares, company shares and loan capital, futures, options, warrants and swaps.

- Advising, arranging, managing or administering regulated mortgage contracts as defined in the **Mortgage Conduct of Business (MCOB) rules.**

- Advising on general insurance contracts as defined in the Insurance Conduct of Business (ICOB) rules.

Individuals who advised on mortgages and general insurance products were previously regulated under the Mortgage Code and the General Insurance Standards Council code of practice. While these were regarded as binding by providers of these services, they were in fact voluntary codes. ICOB and MCOB are statutory regimes under the FCA's powers. They are therefore legally binding.

2.1 The FCA and PRA Handbooks

Specific rules have been developed to provide a framework within which each type of financial services provider must operate. These are incorporated into the handbooks issued by both the FCA and the PRA as a definitive source of guidance for financial services providers.

Sourcebooks set down more detailed rules. These are either general or specific in nature - they may apply to all institutions or to a specific set of institutions.

3 Treating customers fairly

The **treating customers fairly** initiative is enforced by the FCA in order to reinforce compliance with the spirit of the high level principles, particularly principle six Customers' interests which we will look at shortly.

QUICK QUESTION

Whilst we have all heard about TCF, write down what your understanding of the initiative is.

Write your answer here before reading on.

Fundamentally the concept of TCF is that firms should carry out their business in a way that ensures that the customer gets fair treatment. TCF was set up in response to the growing concerns of customers that they were being mis-sold financial products and services. TCF covers all of the activities of financial services firms – covering branches, agencies, contact centres, publicity material and website content.

3.1 Expectations of firms

Firms must be able to demonstrate that they are consistently delivering fair outcomes to consumers and that senior management are taking responsibility for ensuring that the firm and staff at all levels deliver the consumer outcomes relevant to their business through establishing an appropriate culture. Firms should:

- Be able to demonstrate that senior management have instilled a culture within the firm whereby they understand what the fair treatment of customers means; where they expect their staff to achieve this at all times; and where firms promptly identify (a relatively small number of) errors, put things right and learn from them

- Be appropriately and accurately measuring performance against all customer fairness issues materially relevant to their business, and be acting on the results

- Be demonstrating through those measures that they are delivering fair outcomes

- Have no serious failings

However, it is useful at this juncture to consider what TCF is NOT:

- Firstly, TCF is not about creating a satisfied customer – a customer may have had a credit request turned down by their bank and feel that they have been treated unfairly. However, it may well be that the firm has treated the customer fairly and that the reason they declined the request was because the customer was not able to demonstrate that they could repay the loan. In this situation, had the bank had agreed to lend the money, then it could be argued that this sanction was treating the customer unfairly, as the customer is not in a position to repay the borrowing.

- Secondly, TCF is not about each firm providing an identical level of service – all financial services organisations are different and have different levels of resources, so they will go about providing their customer service in their own way.

- Lastly, TCF is not about taking customers' decision making powers away from them, nor is it about removing the responsibility for decision making away from the customer. What firms are expected to do is ensuring that customers have enough information to make an informed and educated decision.

3.2 TCF behavioural drivers

The FCA has not dictated how TCF should be applied in each firm – rather it is up to each organisation to make that decision. What the FCA has done though is to identify six behavioural drivers which they feel have a significant effect on whether or not a firm will meet the requirements of TCF.

- **Leadership** – senior management should provide middle management with sufficient direction and ensure that adequate controls are in place to monitor. A firm's business plan should provide the ongoing development of policies, management information and procedures.

- **Strategy** – TCF should be incorporated into any changes that are made to the business. For example, a bank's mission statement could state that the bank will treat its customers fairly. Also procedures could be put in place to ensure that all of the changes implemented by the bank have had an earlier analysis of TCF – for example when designing a new complaints procedure, or implementing new documentation. It would be expected that before a change is delivered, whoever in the bank has responsibility for the final sign off of this change should ensure that TCF requirements have been embedded in this change.

- **Decision making and challenge** – the firm should encourage staff to challenge anything they see which contradicts TCF. This could involve the establishment of focus groups to review both new and existing processes and procedures to question and challenge how they meet TCF expectations. Firms should communicate to their staff that each individual has the responsibility to satisfy themselves that TCF is being considered in everything that the organisation does. An approach such as this will ensure that a TCF culture is embedded throughout the business.

- **Controls** – firms should identify, interpret and use relevant management information which will allow them to monitor TCF effectively and show that the firm is treating its customers fairly. Relevant management information could include customer surveys, mystery shopper results, complaints returns and so on. Any issues or concerns that come out of this management information should be investigated fully and any necessary actions taken. This type of information could also be used by a firm to demonstrate that they are complying with TCF. For example, customers could make an increasing number of enquiries about how long it should take for a payment to clear and as a result, the bank may include a clearing timetable on its website.

- **Performance management** – staff should receive performance management objectives that demonstrate what TCF means for the particular role carried out by that member of staff – both in terms of what they should do (their actions) along with the way in which they should do this (their behaviours)

- **Reward** – firms should consider how targets can be met whilst still treating the customer fairly. This requirement will guard against the likelihood of a member of staff treating a customer unfairly simply to achieve a performance management objective. An example of this would be selling a customer a credit card that they had no need for in order for the member of staff to reach their personal sales target.

The FCA has also defined six customer outcomes that they expect firms to demonstrate that they have achieved in their dealings with customers. These outcomes are:

OUTCOME 1: Consumers can be confident that they are dealing with firms where the fair treatment of customers is central to the corporate culture.

OUTCOME 2: Products and services marketed and sold in the retail market are designed to meet the needs of identified consumer groups and are targeted accordingly.

OUTCOME 3: Consumers are provided with clear information and are kept appropriately informed before, during and after the point of sale.

OUTCOME 4: Where consumers receive advice, the advice is suitable and takes account of their circumstances.

OUTCOME 5: Consumers are provided with products that perform as firms have led them to expect, and the associated service is of an acceptable standard and as they have been led to expect.

OUTCOME 6: Consumers do not face unreasonable post-sale barriers imposed by firms to change product, switch provider, submit a claim or make a complaint.

Compliance with TCF will be monitored and regulated as part of the FCA's routine assessments.

QUICK QUESTION

With whom in a firm do you think that responsibility for TCF rests ultimately?

Write your answer here before reading on.

3.3 Senior management responsibility

The responsibility for ensuring that a firm demonstrates that it is consistently delivering fair outcomes to consumers belongs to senior management, including the board of directors where appropriate. It is they who must ensure that the firm and staff at all levels deliver the consumer outcomes relevant to their business through establishing an appropriate culture.

The FCA expects firms to:

- Demonstrate that senior management have instilled a culture within the firm whereby they understand what the fair treatment of customers means; where they expect their staff to achieve this at all times; and where firms identify errors promptly, put things right and learn from them

- Appropriately and accurately measure performance against all customer fairness issues materially relevant to their business, and act on the results

- Demonstrate through those measures that they are delivering fair outcomes

- Have no serious failings

4 Implications of the Financial Services and Markets Act 2000 for individuals

As we have seen, the provisions of the Act are far reaching and apply not only to those selling financial products but also those in certain defined functions.

Approved persons must be fit and proper for their roles and competent to discharge their duties. The regulators monitor the performance of firms through its risk-based approach, either by desk-based activities or field operations, such as review visits to firms. If it is apparent that a function is not being discharged properly they are likely to require that action be taken to correct this. If action is not taken, powers of enforcement can be used.

For those in customer-facing roles, the conduct of business rules lay down minimum standards that must be observed. This is particularly important in the sales cycle.

4.1 The Banking Conduct of Business Sourcebook(BCOBS)

The **BCOBS** was introduced with effect from November 2009 to regulate certain banking services. The regulations set out in the sourcebook are legally binding under the authority conferred on the FCA. It is important to consider BCOBS not in isolation but within the overall framework of regulation. Therefore, the regulations should be considered alongside the eleven high level principles for business (PRIN) that apply to all regulated firms and the rules set out in related legislation such as the Payment Services Directive of the European Union.

Prior to the introduction of BCOBS, banking business was subject to a voluntary regulatory regime under the Banking Code Standards Board (BCSB). This body provided the platform for self-regulation and was administered by the banking industry itself.

The two main sources of reference under the former regime were the Banking Code and the Business Banking Code. The former set out minimum commitments agreed by the Code's signatories to personal customers while the latter set out minimum standards that could be expected by small businesses. The Codes were originally reactive in nature, having been introduced at a time when retail banks were facing increasing criticism in the national media. However, the BCSB has been pro-active in progressively updating the provisions to the codes to take account of market and environmental changes. For example, when the codes were introduced in the early 1990s there was much less emphasis on the then fledgling internet banking services. By the time they were withdrawn, they had been amended significantly to reflect the expectations of the growing number of customers accessing banking services through this channel to market.

The changeover to BCOBS was implemented in November 2009, at which point the Banking Code and the Business Banking Code ceased to be operational.

The regulations do not address every aspect covered by the Codes. For example:

- Standards in respect of lending services, such as mortgages, loans and credit card products continue to be self-regulated to some extent under the provisions of **the Lending Code**, which captures the salient features of the former codes and builds on them.

- Most residential mortgage products are regulated under the Mortgage Conduct of Business (MCOB) rules.

- Most non-mortgage consumer lending products such as personal loans, credit cards and some overdrafts are regulated under the **Consumer Credit Acts** 1974 and 2006, with the Office of Fair Trading bearing responsibility for oversight of the provisions of these Acts.

- Communications with customers may be subject to the provisions of the Credit Institutions (Protection of Deposits) Regulations 1995.

At various points in the BCOBS regulations, reference is made to legislation governing unfair terms in contracts. These include the Unfair Terms in Consumer Contracts regulations 1999. The regulations also refer to the usefulness of the Code of Conduct for the Advertising of Interest Bearing Accounts when designing promotions. This Code is published by the British Bankers Association and the Building

Societies Association. BCOBS applies to firms that accept deposits from banking customers and that are subject to regulations under UK territorial jurisdiction. The application section of the regulations states that the regulations do not apply to activities regulated under the payment services regulations

The regulations lay down a general principle that communications must be clear, fair and not misleading. This is the same term used in sourcebooks developed earlier, including the MCOB rules that apply to mortgages and equity release products. Firms should also take account of how information is provided in the context of the recipients' needs. For example, information provided for a consumer may need to be presented in a different way and have different content to that provided for a banking customer who is not a consumer.

The regulations remind firms of the need to comply with the provisions of the Senior Management Arrangements: Systems and Controls (SYSC) sourcebook in relation to rules on past and future performance, direct offer financial promotions and systems and controls and approving/communicating financial promotions. Misleading statements and practices may under certain circumstances be treated as a criminal offence.

Communications to banking customers must:

- Include the name of the firm (this can be a short or trading name, provided the customer can identify the firm)

- Be accurate and not emphasise the benefits of a retail product without giving a clear indication of relevant risks

- Not disguise, diminish or obscure important information, statements and warnings

Any omissions of information should take account of the possibility that such omission may make the communication insufficient, unclear, unfair and misleading.

When communicating with customers, the firm should take account of:

- The nature of the service
- The customer's likely or actual commitment
- The likely information needs
- The role of the communication or promotion in the sales process

Where a communication refers to the Regulators and also to any matters not regulated, it should be made clear that these matters are. When financial promotions refer to interest rates or tax treatment of a product, they should make clear the extent to which these factors may change in the future. They must also clarify the extent to which such factors are dependent on the circumstances of the customer. This information must be provided via a durable medium in good time before any commitment to enter into a contract arises.

Distance marketing information must include prescribed facts relating to the firm, the service, the contract and redress. The commercial purpose of the communication must be made clear and pay due regard to principles of good faith and legal principles governing the protection of certain groups in society, such as young persons. For voice telephony contacts, the identity of the firm and the purpose of the call must be made clear at the beginning of the conversation. Information on contractual obligations that is communicated before a contract comes into force must be consistent with the obligations that will arise if the contract is completed, and must be communicated in good time. Any conclusion of a contract is subject to the customer's approval. Where there is no initial service agreement but several operations of the same nature are concluded over time, the disclosure rules apply to the first operation, unless there is a gap between operations of a year or more. For voice telephony communications, the firm may provide abbreviated distance marketing information as prescribed in the regulations, but the full information must be provided in a durable medium before the contract is concluded. However, under certain circumstances, the information may be provided after the contract comes into force, provided the consumer consents to this. Consumers are entitled to paper copies of marketing information.

Except in the case of tacit renewal of a contract, a firm may not attempt to enforce any obligations in respect of unsolicited services or those provided without consent. This rule may not be waived.

For e-commerce activities, the firm must make appropriate disclosures in relation to its name, address, status and FCA Register number – this is also called the 'firm register number (FRN)'. Additional disclosures apply to regulated professional firms. References to prices must be clear and unambiguous, and where appropriate must refer to whether the price is inclusive or tax and delivery terms or not. Commercial communications must identify the person on whose behalf it is issued and make the nature of the communication clear. For example, offers, competitions and games must be identifiable as such. Any unsolicited commercial communication must state that this is the case. The regulations lay down detailed provisions in respect of placing and receipt of orders. However, these do not apply to orders placed exclusively be exchanges of emails.

In order to assist customers in making informed decisions, a firm must provide appropriate information. This must be communicated in good time, in an appropriate medium and in easily understandable language that is in a clear and comprehensible form. In deciding on appropriateness, the firm must pay due regard to the importance of the information in taking a decision and the timing that will be most useful to the customer. For example, if terms and conditions will apply, these must be made available in good time for the customer to consider them.

If material changes are to be made, such as changes in terms and conditions, charges or rates of interest, these must be notified in good time, providing reasonable notice. Firms should also consider the notice requirements for terminating the contract. If a change in interest rate is to the detriment of the customer, the firm must refer to comparable products offered, any right to switch and that they will assist the customer in transferring to the alternative product. If a product offers special rates with an end date, the firm must provide reasonable notice of their expiry.

The appropriate information rule insists that information is provided ahead of any commitment to enter into a contract. The general information provided should state:

- The name of the firm
- The services offered, unless the customer has specifically stated that particular information is not required
- Terms and conditions and any changes, including rates of interest, charges, matters relating to timing of transactions (including time scales for payment clearing), right of cancellation, right to complain and compensation arrangements

Statements must be provided for customers at appropriate intervals. However, this does not apply to customers who have passbooks as a permanent record of transactions, those who can access statements through electronic means, those who have chosen not to receive statements and those for whom the address is in doubt. Charges may not be made for statements unless they are requested by the customer and agreed. Such charges must be reasonable and reflect the administrative costs involved.

BCOBS sets out detailed requirements in relation to post-sale service:

- Service must be prompt, efficient and fair.

- Customers must be treated fairly (specific references are made to the need to consider the order in which payments are processed and the requirement to deal with customers experiencing financial difficulties fairly).

- Requests to move to another provider must be treated promptly and fairly, including all the processes and formalities associated with terminating the service, such as cancellation of electronic mandates.

- Firms must assist customers to trace dormant accounts and obtain access to them.

- If a customer denies having made a transaction, the onus is on the firm to prove that he or she has done so.

- Where transactions have not been authorised, the firm must reinstate the account to the position that existed prior to the transaction within a reasonable time.

- The maximum liability of a customer is £50 in respect of unauthorised transactions following loss or theft of a passbook, or failure to preserve the secrecy of personalised security features.

- The liability of the customer may be greater if the loss is due to gross negligence on the part of the customer or fraud.

- Except where deposits are made by paper cheque, the value date for calculating interest must be the date the funds are credited to the account of the firm, or the date of receipt of cash (if this is in the same currency as the account).

- Where a customer claims that a transaction has not been properly executed, the burden of proof lies with the firm.

- In relation to incorrect payment routing, it is up to the firm to take reasonable steps to recover the funds, and any charge imposed for doing so must accurately reflect the costs involved.

With some exceptions (such as fixed rate deposits), customers have a right to cancel contracts within 14 days of conclusion of the contract. Effectively, this provides a cooling off period for the majority of retail deposit related banking services. The right to cancel must be notified to the customer in good time. For his or her part, the customer must notify the desire to cancel within the specified period, and this notification will be deemed to have been given if despatched before the expiry date. Records of cancellation must be retained for at least three years.

Any payment due to be made by the customer to the firm on cancellation must be proportionate to the service received and cannot be levied as a penalty. No charge can be made unless the customer has been made aware of it. Any transactions made to close down the relevant account must be completed within 30 days of cancellation.

The main implication of BCOBS is that a voluntary, self-administered system is replaced by a mandatory one. As the regulations are legally binding, the FCA can use its powers of enforcement to hold regulated firms to account through the imposition of financial penalties and the right to order regulated firms to act or desist from acting in a prescribed manner.

Despite the fact that the BCSB has some powers of enforcement, this change gives the mandatory regime a finer cutting edge than the Codes. It was believed that enforcement powers have a deterrent effect that the voluntary system lacked. Certain specific aspects of BCOBS address issues that were dealt with inadequately in the past.

Switching accounts

BCOBS requires regulated firms to provide a prompt and efficient service in helping customers to switch accounts. This gives a broader commitment to customers than the former Codes, .

Provision of information

Under the former Codes, regulated firms were committed to providing information to customers when they formed the initial relationship with the firm. BCOBS focuses on the provision of information before

BPP
LEARNING MEDIA

this stage, requiring information to be given when the customer is considering entering into a relationship with the financial services provider. This helps customers to make informed and timely decisions, enabling them to decide which account is best and how it will be used.

Longer-term service commitment

Building on the overarching provisions of the 'Treating Customers Fairly' requirements, BCOBS compels regulated firms to maintain this commitment over the whole duration of the customer relationship. Service must remain prompt, efficient and fair as long as the person remains a customer. The rules contained in BCOBS contain an explicit commitment to fair treatment in respect of customers experiencing financial difficulties and when processing payments.

5 The Lending Code

The Lending Code is the most important remaining feature of the former self-regulatory framework administered by lending organisations. Its provisions are not legally binding. The Lending Code sets minimum standards of best practices that banks, building societies and credit card providers should follow when dealing with personal, micro-enterprise customers and small charities. Micro enterprises are small businesses employing less than 10 persons and with an annual turnover or balance sheet value of less than €2 million. A small charity is one with an income of less than £1M.

The Lending Code was introduced on 1 November 2009. It is independently monitored and enforced by the Lending Standards Board. The organisations responsible for creating this framework are the British Bankers Association, the Building Societies Association and the UK Cards Association.

The Code is based on the provisions that related to lending within the former Banking Code. The Banking Code was withdrawn following the introduction of the Banking Conduct of Business rules in 2009.

The Lending Code applies to:

- Loans
- Credit cards
- Lending to micro-enterprises and small charities as defined above
- Current account overdrafts

Most residential mortgages are regulated under the provisions of the FCA's Mortgage Conduct of Business (MCOB) rules. In addition, most personal lending products are regulated by the Consumer Credit Acts 1974 and 2006. The Lending Code provides a platform for establishing good voluntary lending practices operating within the legal context.

There are 11 sections in the Code.

6 Key commitments

The Key Commitments are generic statements of best practice.

They are amplified in the subsequent sections of the Code.

Subscribers will act fairly and reasonably in all their dealings with customers by, as a minimum, meeting all the commitments and standards in the Code. The key commitments are shown below.

Subscribers will make sure that advertising and promotional literature is fair, clear and not misleading and that customers are given clear information about products and services.

Customers will be given clear information about accounts and services, during and after the point of sale including how they work, their terms and conditions and the interest rates that apply to them.

Regular statements will be made available to customers (if appropriate). Customers will also be informed about changes to the interest rates, charges or terms and conditions.

Subscribers will lend money responsibly.

Subscribers will deal quickly and sympathetically with things that go wrong and act sympathetically and positively when considering a customer's financial difficulties.

Personal information will be treated as private and confidential, and subscribers will provide secure and reliable banking and payment systems.

Subscribers will make sure their staff are trained to put this Code into practice.

Communications and Financial Promotions:

Throughout this section of the Code, references are made to legal obligations in respect of the Data Protection Act 1998 and regulations made there under.

The overarching requirement is that information disseminated to potential and existing clients will be clear, fair and not misleading, as well as compliant with relevant laws. For direct sales of credit cards, communications and promotions will comply with best practices issued by the UK Cards Association.

For some unsecured lending products, information will be provided in summary boxes in standard format, set out in an appendix to the Code.

In deciding whether promotions meet the clear, fair and not misleading test, lenders will pay due regard to:

- The need to avoid technicalities and jargon by using plain language
- The method of communication to be used
- The type and complexity of the product and the responses that might be elicited
- The intended audience

Microenterprise customers will be provided with a copy of the BBA Statement of Principles. This is included as an appendix to the Code.

Lenders cannot pass on personal information without the consent of the customer. This section of the Code elaborates on ways in which such consent might be obtained. When information is passed to subsidiary companies, it should be made clear if appropriate that the company is a separate legal entity.

Customers have the right to opt out of receiving marketing information and should be reminded of this right every three years.

Lenders must consider carefully whether the aim of a communication is operational or promotional. An offer of free add-on travel insurance is not a promotion.

However, offering a new credit card under new terms and conditions would be a promotion.

7 Mortgage regulation

The Mortgage Conduct of Business (MCOB) rules came into effect in October 2004. These lay down minimum regulatory requirements that must be followed by mortgage lenders, advisers, administrators and arrangers. The MCOB rules apply to:

- Regulated mortgage contracts – loans by way of first legal mortgage to individuals or their relatives secured on residential land (where at least 40% of the property is used for residential purposes).

- Regulated lifetime mortgage contracts – there are mainly loans to older borrowers for equity release purposes, usually repayable on death of the borrower or sale of the property. These products were discussed in Chapter 2.

Not all mortgages are regulated contracts. The MCOB rules do not apply to second mortgages or commercial mortgages. However, since the introduction of the MCOB sourcebook, home reversion plans were added to the range of products subject to regulation.

The MCOB rules lay down detailed requirements in relation to sales and marketing, documentation to be issued through the sales process, at offer stage and after the mortgage is completed. There are also provisions setting out requirements for calculating the Annual Percentage Rate (APR), principles of responsible lending and handling customers experiencing financial difficulties.

Although mortgages are generally less complex than some regulated investments, the rules lay down specific descriptions of products and interest rate calculation methods (for example, discounted, capped, fixed, stepped, etc.) that must be used in any documentation. The rules are also much more prescriptive on the format and content of documents that must be issued to the customer.

During the sales and application process, any customer who is likely to do business with the firm must be issued with:

- An initial disclosure document (IDD) at the outset, which gives basic information on the firm, details of the FCA, the level of service to be provided and information on fees.

- A key facts illustration (KFI) , which is used once the customer decides on a mortgage and sets out the technical features, benefits and drawbacks of the product, fees and charges that will be incurred and any risks associated with entering into the contract.

The IDD specifies the level of service that the firm is offering. Although lenders are not subject to the polarisation rules, they do have to state whether advice will be given or simply information provided. If the latter applies, the adviser may ask questions to help the customer narrow down the borrowing options, provided the questions used are scripted in advance by a suitably competent person. If the firm does not give advice, the customer must not be influenced in respect of the actual product that should be purchased.

The rules specify the precise wording to be used in various risk warnings and the exact terms that must be used to describe certain fees. This is very important from an advisory perspective – for example, a fee for paying back the mortgage early must be called an 'early repayment charge', and a fee for purchasing mortgage indemnity insurance must be called a 'higher lending charge'. Failure to use the prescribed terms may be a breach of the rules.

The regulations require the adviser to help the customer understand the implications of taking out a mortgage for debt consolidation purposes. For example, by doing so, the borrower may be converting unsecured borrowing into secured borrowing, thereby putting the family home at risk, and of course, rescheduling existing borrowings over a longer period usually means that the borrower will pay more interest overall.

The MCOB rules also govern documentation that must be issued to existing borrowers and those experiencing financial difficulties.

8 Regulatory bodies in the European Union

8.1 The European Banking Authority

The **EBA** was established in 2011 as a regulatory body serving all European Union countries. It succeeded the Committee of European Banking Supervisors.

The EBA seeks to contribute to the creation of a European Single Rulebook in banking. These aim to have a single set of harmonised rules for financial organisations throughout the UK.

In pursuit of this, the EBA has developed and implemented a common reporting framework to be used by all authorised firms. The content of reports include own funds and capital adequacy ratios and various risks, including credit risk, market risk and operational risk.

The EBA carries out stress test analyses in order to increase transparency and identify weaknesses in banks domiciled in member states.

Theoretically, the EBA can overrule regulatory authorities in member states if they fail to take the appropriate steps to regulate firms under their jurisdictions.

8.2 European Systemic Risk Board

This organisation was founded in 2010 in response to the credit crisis. For its first few years of operation, its operations are supported by the European Central Bank.

The Board has responsibility for oversight of the financial system within the EU, and identifying and where appropriate mitigating systemic risks. These are risks that threaten the whole financial system, as opposed to individual organisations or groups of organisations.

8.3 European Securities and Markets Authority

The Authority was established in 2011 as a successor body to the Committee of European Securities Regulators.

The aims of the Authority are to improve the functioning of financial markets and to strengthen investor protection across the EU.

8.4 European Securities and Occupational Pensions Authority

The Authority was founded in 2010 as a successor body to the Committee of European Insurance and Occupational Pensions Supervisors.

EIOPA's core responsibilities are to support the stability of the financial system, transparency of markets and financial products as well as the protection of insurance policyholders, pension scheme members and beneficiaries.

9 International regulation

The operations of financial services organisations often span many countries or even continents, and the markets in which they operate are global. This means that domestic regulation can only be partially effective in ensuring that financial services organisations comply with universally accepted standards of behaviour.

The UK government cooperates with several international organisations in order to monitor and sometimes control the activities of financial institutions. Some arrangements aim to increase the efficiency of financial markets, while others promote competition and reduce the risks arising from financial crime.

9.1 International Monetary Fund

The IMF was originally founded by the Bretton Woods agreement in 1946, with the primary aim of facilitating international monetary cooperation between member states. From its foundation until 1971 it operated the fixed exchange rate system that pegged currencies to the US dollar, the value of which was linked to the price of gold.

Over many years, the IMF has provided financial support to governments experiencing financial crises. In the most recent financial crisis the IMF has provided support to economies struggling to deal with capital outflows. It has also helped to broker rescue packages for the governments of Greece and Ireland, working with the European Central Bank and European Union institutions.

9.2 G20

G20 was established in 1999. It brought together 20 of the largest economies in the world with a view to stabilising global financial markets. G20 represents more than 20 countries, as the European Union is considered to be one member alongside 19 other sovereign states.

Under the auspices of G20, the head of central banks and finance ministers come together twice each year to discuss matters of global concern, and since 2008 it has held special conferences to consider the ramifications of the global credit crisis.

According to G20:

The concerted and decisive actions of the G20, with its balanced membership of developed and developing countries helped the world deal effectively with the financial and economic crisis, and the G20 has already delivered a number of significant and concrete outcomes:

First, the scope of financial regulation has been largely broadened and prudential regulation and supervision have been strengthened. There was also great progress in policy coordination thanks to the creation of the framework for a strong, sustainable and balanced growth designed to enhance macroeconomic cooperation among the G20 members and therefore to mitigate the impact of the crisis.

Finally, global governance has dramatically improved to better take into consideration the role and the needs of emerging of developing countries, especially through the ambitious reforms of the governance of the IMF and the World Bank.

Building on these important progresses, the G20 has now to adapt to a new economic environment. It must prove that it is able to coordinate the economic policies of major economies on an ongoing basis

Specifically, G20 has pursued its objectives through:

- Promoting transparency in fiscal policies of member states
- Facilitating exchanges of information in relation to taxation in member states
- Coordinating policies to reduce the risks arising from **money laundering** and terrorist financing

9.3 Bank for International Settlements

The BIS was founded in 1930 as a supra-national organisation representing central banks. In the context of regulation, its most important role is the creation and regular revision of capital adequacy requirements for banking organisation through the 'Basel Accords'.

The BIS lays down minimum capital requirements in relation to basic capital (shareholders' funds) and the different types of assets held by banks. The latter are 'risk weighted' according to the perceived level of safety of engaging is specified types of business activity. Generally, the higher the risk, the higher the proportion that must be backed by capital.

The Basel Accords comprise three sets of agreements, in 1988, 2004 and 2010. The last of these sets out capital requirements in relation to capital as follows:

- A minimum common equity requirement of 4.5% (increased from 2%)
- Tier 1 capital of 6% (increased form 4%)
- A capital conservation buffer, met with common equity, of 2.5%
- A discretionary countercyclical buffer of up to 2.5%, determined by national conditions
- Basel III introduces a minimum 3% leverage ratio and two required liquidity ratios

You will study these concepts in more detail in the risk management study text of the Chartered Banker programme. For the detail of what comprises the different forms of capital, you should visit www.bis.org.

10 The Consumer Credit Act 1974

The Consumer Credit Act 1974 was enacted to protect private consumers who enter into certain types of consumer credit agreements. It also consolidated several other pieces of earlier legislation, including the Hire Purchase Act 1964, the Moneylenders Act 1900 and the Pawnbrokers Acts of 1872, 1922 and 1960.

The Act is **enabling legislation** which permits the regulations to be changed. Since the Act came into effect, it has been updated several times, mainly through secondary legislation. However, important supplementary legislation in the form of the Consumer Credit Act 2006 changed some of the rules as well as creating new safeguards for consumers. The 2006 Act is described in the next section of this chapter.

The 1974 Act lays down rules covering the following:

- The form and content of credit agreements – agreements must be in writing and contain at least the minimum information specified in the regulations

- Advertising loans

- The calculation of the Annual Percentage Rate

- Procedures in relation to early repayment

- Procedures that must be followed when agreements are breached and the lender wishes to recover the loan

- Extortionate credit bargains

The threshold that determined whether a loan is regulated or not was £25,000:

- If the loan exceeded £25,000 it was unregulated.

- If the loan was of £25,000 or less it was regulated or exempt.

Exemptions included:

- Family arrangements where there is no intention of entering into a legal relationship

- Loans for the purpose of improving, repairing or enlarging a private residence by way of further advance.

   Loans secured on a private dwelling are regulated if the lender is a party other than the holder of the first legal charge (mortgage), such as a second or subsequent mortgage. Loans that are regulated mortgage contracts or regulated lifetime mortgage contracts are exempt from the Consumer Credit Act 1974 but regulated under the MCOB rules.

Only consumer loans are regulated under the Act. A consumer can be an individual or an unincorporated business such as a sole trader or partner in an unlimited partnership.

10.1 Regulation of Consumer Credit Agreements

Consumer credit is regulated by the Office of Fair Trading (OFT) . Those who wish to create consumer credit contracts cannot do so without obtaining a consumer credit licence. This applies not only to businesses whose mainstream business is lending but also traders who make credit available to purchase their goods and services. Lending without a licence is a criminal offence.

10.2 Content of Credit Agreements

Agreements must always be in writing. The regulations made under the Act specify the minimum required information:

- A prominent statement at the head of the document that the agreement is regulated by the Consumer Credit Act 1974 – you will see this on any application form for a personal loan or credit card

- Names and addresses of the parties to the agreement

- If appropriate, the security to be provided by the borrower

- The amount of the loan

- The total charge for credit, the APR, the total amount payable (unless the interest rate is variable) and the frequency and amount of repayments

- Any charges payable on default

- Statutory notice of rights under the Consumer Credit Act 1974

- Signature in prescribed format – the agreement is binding on both parties once this is completed, subject to any cooling off period

- Cooling off period if applicable

- Date

10.3 Types of agreement

There are three types of regulated agreement:

Running account credit: This is where the contract enables the debtor to draw down credit from time to time, usually subject to a maximum credit limit. The best examples of this are credit cards and current account overdrafts. Some contracts of this type provide a stand-alone means of increasing the credit, such as a credit card. Any device of this type is called a 'credit token'.

Fixed sum credit arises where the agreement is for a specific sum to be repaid over a period of time, usually by instalments. An example of this is a personal loan.

Restricted and **unrestricted** use credit: A restricted use agreement is where the creditor has control over how the funds are used, such as a second mortgage. It is not necessary for the contract to define how the funds will be used – the agreement is restricted use if the creditor keeps control of the credit.

Unrestricted use credit is where the debtor can use the funds in any way he or she chooses.

Debtor-creditor-supplier and debtor-creditor: This can take two forms:

- The creditor supplies the goods or services to the debtor, such as a retailer offering finance at its own risk.
- The creditor has a pre-agreed arrangement with the supplier of goods or services in the knowledge that credit can be used to finance the purchase, such as where a retailer has an agency agreement with MasterCard or VISA.

Cancellable and **non-cancellable** agreements: Cancellable agreements are those where face-to-face discussions are held with the customer about the credit arrangements but where the customer does not sign the agreement on trade premises. Agreements where there are no face-to-face discussions, or where the agreement is signed on the trade premises, are non-cancellable.

Cancellable agreements have a cooling off period starting on the day the customer signs. For goods purchased through a mail order catalogue the period is 14 days. Otherwise it is 5 days from when the customer receives either a second copy of the agreement or a separate copy of a notice of cancellation rights. The second copy must be provided at least 7 days after the first copy.

10.4 Annual percentage rate (APR)

The Annual Percentage Rate (APR) must always be quoted when offering credit and entering into a credit agreement. It is calculated using a formula laid down under the regulations. The main purpose is to enable consumers to compare the costs of taking out credit using different products.

> The formal definition of the APR is:
>
> '...the effective annual compound interest rate at which the sum of the present values of the repayment of the loan and associated charges equate to the amount of the loan'.

The APR is calculated using the total charge for credit. This takes account of the interest rate to be charged, the intervals on which interest will be calculated (for example, daily interest or annual) and the setting up costs, such as fees and charges incurred or specified before the contract is completed.

The APR does not include all fees and charges that may be incurred after the lending agreement has been signed. It excludes arrears charges, early repayment charges and part capital repayment charges. Any pre-agreed charge for discharging the contract at the end of the term is included.

The Act requires that the APR be quoted in any consumer credit advertisement other than a simple advertisement. It must be as prominent or more so than any headline rate quoted by the provider and expressed to one decimal place. Many lenders now quote just the APR rather than confusing the customer with a headline rate and an APR.

10.5 Advertising

The advertising of consumer credit products is governed by the Consumer Credit (Advertisements) Regulations 1989, secondary legislation enabled by the Consumer Credit Act 1974. The purpose is to ensure that customers are fully aware of the nature and cost of credit terms offered.

There are three types of advertisement defined in the regulations:

- Simple – these are basic advertisements that usually promote an image of the lending institution and do not refer to specific lending products, so there is no requirement to quote the APR.

- Intermediate - the advertisement may be more detailed but is subject to restrictions and some information is prohibited, though the customer must be informed that a quotation may be requested.

- Full – these are detailed advertisements will full information on the loan, fees and charges, interest rate and security required, and usually include an illustration.

10.6 Default and recovery

The Act prescribes the period of notice that must be served on the borrower and also the form it must take if the lender wishes to enforce the agreement before the end of the term of the credit agreement.

The usual reason for this is if the borrower is in default.

When a borrower is deemed by the lender to be in default, it may issue a 'Default Notice' to the customer, stating the nature of the default, how if may be remedied and the time limit by which action must be taken. If the debtor fails to take the necessary action, the creditor can apply to the court for an enforcement order.

10.7 Implications of the Consumer Credit Act 1974

Failure to comply with the precise requirements of the Act can make the loan unenforceable and therefore create a loss-making situation for the lending institution.

As the legislation is relatively complex, most lenders have information systems in place to ensure they meet the compliance requirements fully. For example, the system does not usually permit the loan application to move forward unless time limits imposed by the legislation has passed.

Special care is needed in respect of cooling off periods. As some sections of credit agreements often have to be processed manually to take account of special features of individual loans, it is possible for errors to occur. This can be especially significant where the loan is subject to a cooling off period, as one copy of the agreement is issued before the cooling off period starts and a duplicate copy is sent at the end of the period. Unless these copies provide identical information they are not compliant with the provisions of the Act.

During the cooling off period, it is not permitted to contact the applicant in any way. The purpose of cooling off is to permit the customer time to change their mind free from any influence from the lender.

Therefore, even a telephone call to ask if the applicant requires any further information may be a breach of the Act.

In organisations that quote a headline rate of interest and an APR, this may give rise to confusion. It is never desirable to try to explain the complexities of calculating compound interest formulae unless the customer specifically wishes to do so. The best way of describing the APR is to inform the customer that it is a standard formula required by the government and used by all financial institutions to enable the customer to make a comparison of the relative costs of borrowing from different finance providers.

Although the Act does not regulate giving advice, it is important that bank staff should guide applicants on the full implications of taking out loans, especially when they already have existing borrowing. For example, it is rarely best practice to borrow more when experiencing financial difficulties.

11 The Consumer Credit Act 2006

The 2006 Act amended the Consumer Credit Act 1974 in order to create a fairer and more competitive credit market. Most of the substantive changes came into effect in Spring 2008.

One major purpose of the Act is to improve consumer rights and redress, in order to empower consumers. The new Act introduced a mechanism for more effective resolution of disputes, bringing consumer credit agreements within the jurisdiction of the Financial Ombudsman Service. It also replaced the previous 'extortionate credit' test with a new test based on unfairness.

The Act should improve the regulation of consumer credit businesses by strengthening the licensing regime to enable the Office of Fair Trading (OFT) to keep rogue lenders out of the credit market. There are two ways that it seeks to achieve this aim:

- Extending protection to all consumer credit by abolishing the financial limit that caps protection at loans of £25,000
- Introducing a more proportionate approach to the enforceability of defective agreements

As discussed in the previous section, under the 1974 Act, any amount borrowed on credit above the limit of £25,000 was not regulated by the Act. From 6th April 2008, this limit was removed, thus, any amount borrowed will be subject to the provisions of the 2006 Act unless specifically exempted. This is to ensure that all loans including mortgages are regulated. Previously, the majority of mortgages were unaffected by consumer credit legislation.

Exemptions: Loans will be exempted from the 2006 Act where:

- The debtor has a high net worth.
- The loan exceeds £25,000 and is entered into for business purposes.

To qualify for exemption as a high net worth debtor the agreement must include a declaration made by the person that he/she agrees to forego the protection of a regulated agreement.

If the agreement is for credit exceeds £25,000 and it is entered into by the debtor wholly or predominantly for business purposes it will be outside the ambit of the Act.

11.1 Scope of protection

The 1974 Act regulated consumer credit agreements between a creditor and an individual. The definition of individual only covered private individuals, partnerships and other unincorporated bodies, which meant that agreements with individuals or partnerships could be regulated but not agreements with a limited company. The definition of an individual has now been altered by the new Act: only small partnerships (with two or three partners, most of which are not bodies corporate) are now covered.

11.2 High net worth debtors and hirers

The Secretary of State has the power to allow to create exemptions within consumer credit and consumer hire agreements for private individuals who are high net worth debtors and hirers. A declaration must be included by the debtor/hirer in the exemption agreement stating that they agree to forego the remedies and protection otherwise afforded by the Act. To receive this exemption, the debtor/hirer must provide a recent statement of net worth confirming that in the previous financial year his net income or net assets were above a specified amount.

11.3 Statements

The Act requires creditors in regulated fixed-sum credit agreements to provide debtors with annual statements in the specified form, the first of which is required within one year of the day after the date on which the agreement was made. If this is not provided, the creditor cannot enforce the agreement and the debtor is not liable to pay interest during the period of non-compliance. Under the 1974 Act, it is required that creditors give annual statements of required information. The Secretary of State can require more information to be submitted in addition to the annual statements.

11.4 Arrears and default

The Act requires the Office of Fair Trading to prepare and publish information sheets for debtors and hirers about arrears and default.

Under the 2006 Act creditors must give notice of arrears to debtors/hirers in respect of regulated agreements that are fixed sum credit agreements or hire agreements. This notice must be in a standard form and must be supplied in certain circumstances. Briefly, these are triggered when two instalments are due on agreements with payment intervals of more than one week, or when four instalments are due on agreements with payment intervals of a week or less.

If the creditor does not give the correct notice of sums in arrears, then during this time it cannot enforce the agreement and the debtor is not obliged to pay interest for the relevant period.

When a debtor/hirer breaches a regulated agreement they can be required to pay default sums (such as a late payment fee or additional interest). Under the 2006 Act, the creditor must give notice to the debtor/hirer when default sums are due to be paid. A creditor or owner may only require a debtor or hirer to pay interest in connection with a default sum 28 days after the day the notice was given to the debtor or hirer. If the creditor or owner fails to give a notice to the debtor or hirer then the agreement cannot be enforced until such notice is given. A creditor may only require simple interest to be paid in respect of default sums owed by the debtor/hirer, including sums payable under non-commercial or small agreements. The period of grace for debtors who have been issued with a default notice is now 14 days, increased from seven days previously applicable under the 1974 Act.

The Court now has complete discretion in determining whether agreements are enforceable, irrespective of breach by the creditor.

The 1974 Act enabled a debtor or hirer to apply to the court for a time order. This is an order in which the court may reschedule any payments due under the regulated agreement. Under the 2006 Act, this has been amended to enable the debtor/hirer to apply for a time order not just in that case but also after they have been served with a notice of sums in arrears. If this is the case, the debtor/hirer must notify the creditor of their intention to apply for the time order.

When interest is applied to a judgement debt by virtue of a term in the credit agreement, a creditor is required to provide information to the debtor/hirer in a prescribed form. Such interest only accrues on a judgement debt if the notice requirements are satisfied.

Unfair relationships: As we have seen, the 1974 Act enabled the courts to re-open extortionate credit agreements. This part of the Act has been altered significantly to deal more effectively with loan sharks.

The court can now consider the relationship between the creditor and the debtor/hirer to be unfair on the grounds of the terms of the agreement or the way that the creditor operates the agreement. The court can take into account all matters deemed to be relevant with regard to the agreement and has access to a wide range of solutions to remedy the unfairness.

11.5 Licence requirements

Under the 1974 Act, consumer credit licences were required for consumer credit and hire businesses, credit brokerages and credit reference agencies. This list is now widened to include debt administration and credit information services. Additionally, an agreement cannot be enforced by a person who is not licensed or who was required to hold a license when the agreement was made (although that person can apply to the Office of Fair Trading for a retrospective order to treat him as if he was licensed at the time).

In judging whether an applicant is a fit person to hold a licence, the Office of Fair Trading assesses the experience and knowledge of the applicant and his staff and the practices and procedures that will be implemented. It also considers whether:

- The applicant has committed an offence involving fraud or violence.
- The 1974 Act or the Financial Services and Markets Act 2000 (so far as it relates to consumer credit) have been contravened in the past.

- The applicant has practiced discrimination.

- The applicant has engaged in business practices which appear to be deceitful, oppressive, unfair or improper (whether or not actually illegal).

The Office of Fair Trading has the power to impose requirements on licensees where it is dissatisfied with the business conducted. It can serve notice specifying the matters with which it is dissatisfied and requiring the licensee to ensure the same matters do not arise again. The Office of Fair Trading has to inform the licensee of its reasons for imposing requirements, and these may be appealed.

Licence holders must allow an enforcement officer to enter the premises (on reasonable notice and at a reasonable time) to observe the business and inspect documents. For serious cases, a search and entry warrant may be obtained from the court.

12 Money laundering

Money laundering is the process through which the financial proceeds of criminal activities (dirty money) are cleansed by filtering them through the financial system. It enables the perpetrators to disguise the origin of such funds, often over long periods of time.

The proceeds of crime include money obtained, inter alia, through extortion, sales of counterfeit products, robbery, terrorism, drug trafficking and tax evasion. These activities are not the exclusive preserve of those with large balances to invest. It is obvious that a bank robber will try to place several large deposits in different banks: less obvious perhaps is the case of a small trader who seeks a loan from a bank and states that his financial accounts 'do not tell the whole story'. That is an indication, or at least implication, of tax evasion and is therefore a reportable money laundering incident. So too is the regular banking of monies obtained from street sales of illicit compact discs.

Organised money operations normally involve three stages:

- **Placement** – where the funds that have been obtained by criminal means are placed in bank deposits, building society shares, life assurance policies or other investments, thereby enabling conversion (at integration stage - see below) to take place by withdrawals of cash and cheques.

- **Layering** – where the illegal funds are processed through multiple transactions in order to conceal their origins, often using false identities, by using the funds as collateral or by taking out life assurance policies then surrendering them at some date in the future.

- **Integration** – the final stage at which the funds are converted into apparently legitimate cash or bank accounts.

The money laundering regulations are laid down in the Proceeds of Crime Act 2002. Under the Act, offences may be committed in relation to:

- Possession and obtaining criminal property
- Assisting money launderers to retain the laundered funds
- Advising launderers that they are subject to investigation (tipping off)
- Failing to report suspicions as soon as practicable
- Failure of a compliance official, such as the Money Laundering Reporting Officer, to take appropriate action once a report has been made

The criminal liability falls on both the financial institution and the individual employee. Offences are punishable by fines on the individual and the organisation. Breaches of the regulations by individuals may also render the guilty person liable to a custodial sentence.

The regulations are updated regularly. Recent regulations are the Money Laundering Regulations 2012. They required organisations:

- To take all practical measures to comply with the regulations in relation to identification, keeping appropriate records and adherence to reporting procedures
- To establish internal control and communication procedures
- To make employees aware of their obligations and to provide appropriate ongoing training

The Money Laundering Regulations 2012 came into force in October 2012.

The HMRC website explains that all businesses that are covered by the new regulations have to put in place suitable anti-money laundering controls.

All financial institutions must have formal written procedures to reduce the prospect of money laundering through their accounts. They must also have an officer specifically responsible (the Money Laundering Reporting Officer) for compliance with the money laundering regulation.

It is the institution's responsibility to ensure that staff are trained in anti-money laundering measures and procedures. They must also ensure that subsequent ongoing training is provided so that existing staff are updated on a regular basis. Therefore training must be delivered not only at induction stage for new employees but for existing employees at regular intervals. You have no doubt completed such training along with the associated assessment.

Of special importance are the following:

- New customers – the identity of new customers should be checked and ratified - most institutions require at least two pieces of identification, at least one of which should include a photograph (such as a passport) and the other verifying the permanent address of the customer.

- Changes of name – proper documentary evidence should be provided by the customer (this can be difficult for the customer when, for example, the children adopt a new name when a parent takes a new partner).

- Childrens' accounts – these can be used ostensibly as a 'nest egg' for the children but sometimes disguising the origin of the funds.

- Suspicious transactions – where movements on an account are inconsistent with the profile of the customer.

- Lump sum investments – where there is no obvious reason for the customer to have such funds.

- Frequent but irregular investments from overseas, possibly indicating tax evasion.

A specific offence under the regulations is 'failure to report'. Reporting of suspicions of money laundering is required to be made as soon as is practicable. Under earlier regimes it was necessary to report whenever there was knowledge or suspicion of money laundering. This has been replaced by the more onerous requirement to report when there are reasonable grounds for suspicion. Any doubt in relation to the letter or spirit of these regulations were dispelled by several fines being levied on well-known financial institutions in 2003 and 2004. The reporting of such a suspicion does not breach the banker's duty of confidentiality discussed in Chapter 2.

Verification requirements are specifically laid down for transactions exceeding 15,000 Euros. These also apply where a related or linked series of transactions totalling or exceeding 15,000 Euros are made.

However, many financial institutions have now implemented tighter (lower) limits than those prescribed by the regulations.

It can be seen from the above that the money laundering regulations should be applied strictly, with no exceptions. An individual is not absolved from responsibility if the customer is well known or even related.

Having stressed the importance of compliance, reporting means just that. The person who makes the report should not make the customer aware of it (this would amount to 'tipping off' the individual and it is highly unlikely that the person will be specifically identified to the customer as the source of the report.

The Chartered Banker programme offers an optional Money Laundering Module within its examination structure to enable students to study this important subject in greater depth.

13 Data protection

The purpose of data protection legislation is to provide protection for private individuals in relation to personal data held by individuals and organisations so that their personal rights are not infringed.

There have been two major pieces of data protection legislation in the UK:

- The Data Protection Act 1984 regulated personal data held mechanically and electronically but not hard copy or manual records.

- The Data Protection Act 1998 repealed the earlier Act but introduced similar (reinforced) measures in relation to all data, whether held electronically, mechanically or in hard copy form.

Under the legislation:

- A data subject is a living individual on whom personal data is held.

- A data controller or user is the person or organisation that holds personal data.

- A data processor is any person or organisation that processes information on behalf of a data controller.

- A recipient is any person or organisation to whom personal data is disclosed.

The 1998 Act affects all persons and individuals who hold personal data. As well as most organisations, therefore, this includes private individuals who maintain details of personal data in the course of their work. Such persons have to register and pay the relevant fee, stating the purpose for which data is held or processed.

The government official responsible for regulating the provisions of the Data Protection Act 1998 is the Information Commissioner.

13.1 Main provisions of the Act

The Act states that data may only be held for lawful purposes and that these purposes must be registered with the Information Commissioner.

Processing of data must be fair and lawful: data must be both accurate and up-to-date. Data users must comply with the principles of data protection as laid down in the Act.

As well as users of data, the Act sets out provisions in relation to different types of data, distinguishing between 'personal data' and 'sensitive' personal data. Personal data may relate to any facts about an individual, whilst sensitive personal data concerns matters such as ethnicity, political views, religion, health, sexual orientation or worker affiliation (such as trade union or staff association membership).

It should be noted that the Act also regards criminal prosecutions as sensitive personal data. Additional responsibilities apply here under the provisions of the Rehabilitation of Offenders Act 1965, which sets down limits on how long data may be retained in relation to spent convictions.

Obtaining and recording sensitive personal data requires the express consent of the data subject. This means that the data subject must be informed of the exact manner in which the relevant data will be processed and must give express permission - usually formally recorded in writing.

The Act also makes special provisions in relation to data bureaux whose actual business is concerned with the processing of data.

13.2 The principles of data protection

The Act sets down eight principles of data protection with which all data controllers must comply. These are set out below.

The eight principles of data protection

Principle	Provision
1	Personal data may not be processed unless the controller complies with the conditions for fair and lawful processing in relation to personal data and sensitive personal data. These conditions are reinforced by a fair processing code of practice.
2	Data must be obtained in relation to its specific lawful purpose and processed in a manner that is compatible with this purpose.
3	Personal data must be adequate, relevant and not excessive, consistent with the specified purpose.
4	Personal data must be accurate and up-to-date.
5	Personal data must not be retained for longer than necessary. The Act does not specify what is a 'reasonable' period, however, as this often depends on the characteristics of the user and the data itself. Many credit bureaux retain data for a maximum of six years - this is a matter of policy and not a legal requirement.
6	Processing of personal data must be carried out in a manner consistent with the rights of the data subject.
7	The data controller must keep personal data secure against unlawful processing and accidental loss, with the degree of security appropriate to the nature of the data and the potential resultant damage or harm.
8	Where data is transferred outside the European Economic Area (EEA) the data controller must ensure that the recipient state has a comparable standard of data protection.

13.3 Rights of the data subject

The data subject has several rights:

- To have access to information on personal data held by data controllers and to be informed of whether data is being processed, the nature of the data, its purpose and to whom it is disclosed

- Where data is inaccurate, to demand that the data be corrected - in addition, the Act empowers the data user to apply to the court for rectification, blocking, erasure or destruction of the data

- To compensation for loss resulting from breaches of the Act

- To prevent processing if the personal data is likely to cause damage or loss to the data subject or to a third party

- To contact the Information Commissioner to determine whether personal data processed on the data subject is compliant with the legislation.

To those who feel plagued by junk mail and unwanted e-mails, the Data Protection Act may not go far enough. The Act falls short of a blanket prohibition on contacting potential customers through these media, though there are facilities in place such as the Telephone Preference Service that can reduce such communications.

In 2003 the European Union enacted further legislation to outlaw illicit e-mails (commonly referred to as spam), though such controls may be less than effective given that many of these are originated from outside the European Union.

14 The law and the employer

There are many Acts of Parliament that have been passed in relation to employment in the last fifty years.

This section of the study text is limited to providing you with a brief overview of the more important laws.

14.1 Contracts of employment

An employee should be provided with written particulars of the employment within two months of the starting date. This is usually set out in a contract of employment that sets out the respective rights and obligations of the employer and the employee.

Even if the employer fails to provide these written details, a contract normally comes into existence by the implied behaviour of both parties.

The written particulars should set out:

- Names of the parties
- Job title and main responsibilities
- Commencement date
- Hours of work
- Remuneration and basis (weekly or monthly)
- Leave entitlement
- Sickness entitlement (whether remuneration will be paid in the event of sickness and for what minimum period)
- Grievance and discipline procedures
- Termination conditions, including period of notice to be served
- Signatures of parties
- Date

Those engaged by the organisation under a contract for service as independent contractors are not affected by these provisions, though in some instances the courts have regarded independent contractors with just one client as being employees for the purposes of employment law.

14.2 Trade Union membership

Employees have a right to join a trade union or staff association. If an individual is dismissed because he/she has joined a union, or because he/she refuses to join a union, this is regarded in law as automatically unfair dismissal.

14.3 Whistleblowing

Whistleblowing occurs when an employee reports malpractice or the inappropriate behaviour of another person in the workplace. Examples of matters that may be reported include crime, negligence and other civil offences, miscarriages of justice, dangers to health and safety and attempts to conceal these activities.

Those who blow the whistle are protected by the provisions of the Public Interest Disclosure Act 1998. As well as full-time employees, it covers trainees, agency staff, home workers, and public sector employees. It does not apply to the self-employed, voluntary workers, the intelligence services or the armed forces.

Disclosures can be made to appropriate persons in the organisation or to relevant external bodies, such as the police, the media, Members of Parliament or the Health and Safety Executive. A disclosure in good faith is protected under the legislation. External disclosures are protected subject to three conditions:

- If the employee had reason to believe he would be victimised by referring the matter to an internal person or prescribed regulator

- If the person believes that a cover up is likely and there is no prescribed regulator

- If the matter has already been raised internally or with a prescribed regulator

If a person is victimised or dismissed as a result of blowing the whistle on malpractices that have either occurred or are likely to occur, the individual can refer the matter to the Employment Tribunal. The Tribunal can make an order for compensation, or where the individual is in danger of losing his job, make an interim order preventing dismissal.

The Act makes any gagging clauses that are included in a contract of employment null and void.

14.4 Discrimination

The Equality Act 2010 came into force in 2011 with the aim of consolidating the many pieces of primary legislation, and some statutory instruments, in relation to various forms of discrimination. The Act is also a response to the European Union's Equal Treatment Directives, which compel member states to bring their provisions into force through domestic legislation.

The Act requires equal treatment for individuals in respect of their access to public and private services as well as in the employment market. It goes beyond the scope of previous laws in that it forbids discrimination (except where specific exemptions apply) not only in relation to sex, race and disability but also age, gender reassignment, marriage, civil partnership, religion and belief.

The Act also corrects some of the idiosyncrasies of the laws it replaced. For example, the Sex Discrimination Act 1975 forbids discrimination against married persons but not against single persons.

The main provisions of the legislation are set out in table below:

Legislation on discrimination

Previous statute	Principal provisions
Equal Pay Act 1970 (amended 1983 and 1986)	Employment terms to be at least as favourable regardless of gender; equality clause in contract.
Sex Discrimination Act 1975	Forbidden to discriminate on grounds of gender. Introduced the concepts of direct and indirect discrimination and genuine occupational qualification. Cannot discriminate against married persons
Race Relations Act 1976	Set up the Commission for Racial Equality. Cannot discriminate on the grounds of race, but exceptions relating to entertainment, art, photography, personal services, ethnic authenticity. CRE Code of Practice - advisory only. Remedy for discrimination is through Employment Tribunal.
Disability Discrimination Act 1995	Similar rights to the above for disabled persons. Introduced the Disability Rights Commission. Employer must make reasonable adjustments in the working environment. Remedy through Employment Tribunal.

Discrimination can be direct or indirect. For example, a job advertisement for male applicants only is obviously direct discrimination. A job advertisement that requires applicants to be 'at least 5' 11' tall' may be indirectly discriminatory, as women are on average shorter than men.

When recruiting new staff, it is important to ensure that any questions asked are appropriate irrespective of the gender of the applicant. Equally important, it should not be assumed that disability is automatically going to impede an individual from doing the job.

14.5 Maternity and paternity

The law sets down minimum rights in relation to maternity leave and statutory maternity pay.

Fathers are now also entitled to leave as a statutory right. Dismissal of an individual on the grounds of being pregnant is regarded as unfair in virtually all occupations.

The rights of expectant mothers are:

- A right to paid leave for ante-natal care
- Protection against dismissal
- An entitlement to statutory maternity leave
- A right of return to work – notice of intent is required, except in firms with less than five employees and where the job is redundant (if so, equivalent employment must be offered)

Paternity rights are an entitlement of fathers who have 26 weeks continuous service ending with the 15th week before the week the baby is due.

14.6 Unfair dismissal and wrongful dismissal

The concept of unfair dismissal was introduced in the 1960s. It can apply to any employee with more than one year's continuous service.

A worker is unfairly dismissed if the reason for dismissal is inappropriate. The law acknowledges several grounds for fair dismissal:

- Wilful disobedience of a lawful and reasonable instruction
- Misconduct
- Fraud and dishonesty
- Habitual neglect of duties
- Any other common law ground

An Employment Tribunal usually hears cases for unfair dismissal. If proven, the Tribunal may award compensation, reinstatement or re-engagement, though it is unusual to make any award other than compensation.

Wrongful dismissal occurs where there is a breach of contract. Cases are dealt with by either the Employment Tribunal or the County Court.

Wrongful dismissal occurs when the worker is either summarily dismissed without appropriate notice or pay in lieu of notice, or constructively dismissed, where the worker is forced to resign by the unreasonable conduct of the employer. If proven, wrongful dismissal normally results in damages being awarded by the court.

All those involved in recruiting staff or with responsibility for staff should be familiar with these issues. Failure to do so can have serious financial consequences for the organisation as well as the inevitable negative impact on the reputation of the organisation among the workforce and the community at large.

14.7 Redundancy

Redundancy occurs when a job no longer exists. This may be caused by the changing nature of work such as the introduction of new technology, reorganisation or where the organisation merges or closes down.

Any employee with two years or more continuous service is entitled to redundancy payments based on minimum levels set down by the government. Entitlement to redundancy payments is based on a sliding scale with reference to age of the employee and a multiple of pay.

It is permissible to make redundancy payments in excess of the minimum requirements.

15 Health and safety at work

15.1 Health and Safety at Work Act 1974

The Health and Safety at Work Act 1974 was introduced as a radical legislative initiative created to make employers and employees accountable in law for matters relating to health and safety in the work place.

The Act requires all employees to pay due regard for their own safety as well and the safety of others.

There are two very significant features of the legislation:

- The Act criminalises breaches of health and safety requirements, with offenders punishable by fines and imprisonment rather than being subject only to civil remedies.

- The Act limits the doctrine of vicarious liability – whilst the employer may be liable for a whole range of actions taken by its employees in the normal course of employment, both the employee and the employer may be criminally liable under the Act.

Offences are committed if the individual has breached the Act through consent, connivance or neglect.

The objectives of the 1974 Act are:

- To secure health, welfare and safety for people at work
- To protect others from risks arising at work
- To control the use and storage of dangerous substances
- To control the emission of noxious or offensive substances into the air

The general responsibility of employers is:

> ...to ensure as far as is reasonably practicable the health, safety and welfare of all...not only employees, but those affected by products or plant.

Under the Act, employers must:

- Provide information, training and supervision
- Issue a policy statement
- Consult trade unions where applicable
- Establish safety committees

The Act also confirms that employees have a role to play, as safety at work cannot be achieved without the interest and support of employees. Employees have a duty to take reasonable care for their own safety and that of others.

The Act established two enforcement bodies:

- The Health and Safety Executive has the right to enter premises, examine the premises and question employees in pursuit of health and safety objectives.

- The Health and Safety Commission is responsible for issuing codes of practice and new regulations as well as carrying out general research.

15.2 The Occupier's Liabilities Acts 1957 and 1984

These Acts impose civil liability on occupiers of premises. An occupier is any person who has control or possession of the premises. Importantly, the occupier does not have to be the legal owner of the premises.

The 1957 Act established that occupiers have a duty of care to all visitors to ensure that visitors are reasonably safe when using the premises for the normal purpose for which the visitors are present. This is not an all-embracing responsibility in that visitors should be aware of the need to guard against special risks. For example, a worker repairing the roof of the building occupied by the bank would be expected to be aware of the risks specific to the work to be done.

The occupier can fulfil its responsibility to visitors by giving adequate warnings and by employing specialists to carry out work to mitigate risk.

The 1984 Act extended the provisions of the earlier law by conferring responsibilities on occupiers to persons other than visitors. The occupier may owe a duty of care to any person on the property if:

- The occupier is aware of the danger.
- He knows that persons may come into the vicinity of the danger.
- It is reasonable that the occupier should be expected to protect the person against the risk.

Liability is limited to injury to the person and not to the person's property, although separate action could be taken in this respect out with the provisions of the Acts.

The Acts have implications for all financial services providers. The premises do not actually have to be owned – they can be leased offices or even temporary premises.

KEY WORDS

Key words in this chapter are given below. There is space to write your own revision notes and to add any other words or phrases that you want to remember.

- Enabling legislation

- Authorisation

- Approved person

- Prudential control

- Treating Customers Fairly (TCF)

- Banking Conduct of Business Sourcebook (BCOBS)

- The Lending Code

- Mortgage Conduct of Business rules

- Financial Policy Committee

- Prudential Regulation Authority

- Financial Conduct Authority

- European Banking Authority

- Consumer Credit Act

- Running account credit

- Restricted credit

- Unrestricted credit

- Cancellable agreement

- Non-cancellable agreement

- Money laundering

- Whistleblowing

REVIEW

Now consider the main learning points that were introduced in this chapter.

Go through and check that you are happy that you fully understand each point.

- All financial services providers in the UK are regulated. There are several different levels of regulation.

- Regulation is effected through legislation, regulatory bodies, voluntary codes and statements of practice and the policies and procedures of financial services providers themselves.

- The Financial Services and Markets Act 2000 reformed the system of regulation in the UK.

- All financial services providers have to be authorised before they can commence business. It is a criminal offence to offer most financial services without being authorised.

- The Act introduced the 'approved persons' regime, which requires designated persons to be 'fit and proper' as well as competent to discharge their functions properly.

- The regulatory and supervisory framework is laid down in the eleven Key Principles and more detailed sourcebooks.

- Detailed statutory regulations for investment, mortgage and insurance providers are set out in the conduct of business rules applicable to each.

- The Bank of England has overall responsibility for regulation through an oversight body called the Financial Policy Committee.

- The Prudential Regulatory Authority is responsible for regulation and supervision of firms. It focuses on authorised firms having an appropriate level of expertise to formulate and implement appropriate strategies, as well as having robust systems of control in place to ensure there is reasonable assurance that objectives can be met.

- The Financial Conduct Authority is responsible for facilitating market efficiency and choice, whilst providing an appropriate level of protection for consumers.

- The Consumer Credit Act 1974 requires credit providers to be licensed by the Office of Fair Trading and to adhere to statutory practices and procedures relating to the selling and administration of loans. The 2006 Act removed the £25,000 limit, increases the powers of the Office of Fair Trading and imposed greater transparency requirements on providers of credit.

- The money laundering regulations are aimed at reducing the prospect of criminals being able to 'cleanse' the proceeds of crime by filtering money though the financial system. There are three main crimes defined in the legislation: laundering; failure to report; tipping off.

- The Data Protection Act 1998 requires all data controllers (users) to register and comply with minimum statutory principles in relation to personal data.

- There are many Acts of Parliament that govern the relationship between the employer and the employee. The relationship is usually defined in a contract of employment. Subject to conditions, the law protects the employee by providing an entitlement to monetary compensation if the employee is wrongfully dismissed, unfairly dismissed or made redundant.

- The Health and Safety at Work Act 1974 requires all employees to pay due regard for their own safety in the workplace as well and the safety of others.

SOLUTIONS TO QUESTION TIMES

SOLUTIONS TO QUESTION TIME QUESTIONS

Question Time 1

1. The banker-customer relationship is one of debtor and creditor. Any money paid in is the bank's to do with as they wishe as long as they repay that money when demanded.

2. (a) The bank was liable because, having responded to the bank's advertisement; Woods became a customer of the bank.

   (b) Woods became a customer when the bank accepted his instructions to make the first investment.

Question Time 2

1. The banker should ensure that he/she is not acting negligently. Therefore full checks should be carried out to ensure that there have been no errors made that have resulted in the balance of the account being incorrectly stated in the bank's books – for example, a countermanded cheque could have been paid in error, or a credit made by the customer could have been lodged to the wrong account.

2. The banker may be liable for breach of contract and defamation of character.

3. Until the *Kpoharor v Woolwich Building Society* case in 1995, the courts did differentiate as to the amount of damages that could be claimed (non-traders could only claim substantial damages if they could prove special loss, whereas business customers could recover substantial damages without actual damages being proved or alleged), but since this case it is unlikely that this will be the case in future. In the court's view a presumption of some damage arises in every case.

4. Apologise to the customer, correct the mistake, and inform the payee that the bank had made a mistake and request re-presentation.

5. The bank was unsuccessful in the claim that the customer is under is duty to examine bank statements in order that the customer may recognise where their cheques had been forged.

6. The bank was not liable as Greenwood knew his signature was being forged by his wife, yet he did not inform the bank.

7. MacMillan and Arthur failed to take care in the drawing of cheques.

Question Time 3

- Are you here for the Festival? – Why are you visiting the city just now?
- Have you booked a holiday this year? – Where do you plan to go on holiday this year?
- Are you working in the theatre? Where do you work?
- Are you happy with our product range? What do you think about our product range?
- Do you work locally? How far is your daily commute?
- Did you hear about us though a colleague? How did you hear about the bank?

Question Time 4

Cash is convenient to use – particularly for small payments. However it is costly to handle and presents a security problem for those holding it.

Cheques are convenient to use and are reasonably safe – although many consumers are dissatisfied with the length of time it can take for a cheque to pass through the clearing system. Fewer and fewer personal customers use cheques on a daily basis.

Question Time 5

(a)   These cards can be used to make payments for goods and services at the point of sale or elsewhere. They can also be used to withdraw cash at ATMs, bank branches, etc.

(b)   A debit card generates a debit entry in the customer's account after the transaction has occurred. The card may also be used to make cash withdrawals. When the customer uses the card, they must have sufficient available funds in the account.

A credit card transaction is repayable up to 56 days after the transaction has occurred. This credit period may be extended should the cardholder choose not to repay the balance in full. The card will have a maximum limit, beyond which the balance of the account must not go.

Credit card cash withdrawals are subject to interest from the time of withdrawal.

(c)   Safety.

Convenience.

If cash is lost, it cannot be replaced, but a card can.

They are useful for making internet payments.

Question Time 6

1.   James is not really acting as a team leader. But is it his fault? Has the role of the team leader been explained? Has he had feedback from his line manager?

2.   To help James to improve, you could:

- Explain his role to him
- Agree performance standards
- Discuss appropriate leadership styles
- Advise him to match style to situation
- Delegate work
- Ask that he trains team members
- Counsel on oral and written communication
- Monitor and give feedback
- Explain to him the consequences if there is no improvement

Question Time 7

Management success can be seen in the way that a manager performs different roles.

Interpersonal	<ul><li>Good with staff, managers, peers and clients</li><li>Dealing with conflict successfully</li><li>Motivating</li><li>Dealing with stress and pressure in self and helping others cope with this</li></ul>
Decisional	<ul><li>Effective in decision making</li><li>Problem solving</li><li>Innovation and creativity</li><li>Management of alternatives</li></ul>
Informational	<ul><li>Motivating the organisation</li><li>Technical and financial control</li></ul>

Question Time 8

1. George Boxer is using one of a range of styles in the categories:

    Tells Sells, Consults Joins

    The characteristics of the 'tells' style as used by George are that the leader sets goals, tells people what to do, expects obedience, and supervises closely, so that little initiative is left to individuals; it is a punishing rather than a supportive style which does not encourage participation in decisions.

    The consequences of this style of management are that, although everyone knows who is boss and things get done, the work is often uninteresting as George does not delegate, people do not innovate or take risks because of fear of punishment, and this can result in low motivation and a high turnover of staff.

2. The other possible styles of management here are:

    'Sells', which is a disguised form of telling; the leader uses persuasion rather than direct orders; it is more supportive than 'tells', and dependence on the boss is emphasised.

    'Consults' – the problem solving style – where the manager sets goals but employees are involved in decision making through consultation in matters affecting them; opinions are sought; open discussion is encouraged and employees are given freedom to make their own decisions on what to do and how to do it within an agreed framework.

    'Joins', where the group (including the manager) makes the decision, the manager defines the problem, the group members jointly solve it, and decisions reflect the majority opinion.

    You should explain to George the advantages of the different styles and point out the need for flexibility in styles so that the most appropriate is chosen for each situation.

Question Time 9

Profitability:	
Goals:	*Measures:*
Liquidity	Cash flow
Profits	Profit and Loss A/C/Management A/Cs

Growth:	
Goals:	*Measures:*
Turnover	Profit and Loss A/C
Number of employees	Payroll records
Spread of organisation	Geographical coverage
Size of organisation	Market share

Shareholder Value:	
Goals:	*Measures:*
Earnings	Dividend payment, Return on shareholders' funds, Earnings per share
Capital Appreciation	Share price

Customer Satisfaction:	
Goals:	*Measures:*
Customer approval	Customer survey results, repeat business, referral business

Question Time 10

Objective 1 – not SMART: what are the specific customer files, who are the interested parties and what is meant by regularly?

Objective 2 – SMART – although it may be necessary for the objective to state more clearly the roles that the new recruits are required to fill.

Objective 3 – not SMART: there is no time frame mentioned and what is the base figure that the reduction is to be measured by?

Objective 4 – not SMART: there is no indication of what the data to be provided to the project manager is, or the time in the week when it should be provided.

Objective 5 – not SMART: the objective should state whether these are new customers, or if it is possible to sell more products to existing customers to meet the objective.

Objective 6 – not SMART: the objective should state more clearly either what is to be covered by the presentation, or what the outcomes of the presentation should be – for example, is it intended merely to make the departmental team managers aware of the registration process, or should they be able to implement the new process?

Objective 7 – not SMART: the objective should either specify what the needs of the training population are, or where this information may be sourced.

Objective 8 – SMART.

Question Time 11

1. Alistair, your performance when interfacing with customers is where we hoped it would be. What can we do now to develop it further? – *consult*

2. Brenda, I believe your performance on the processor could be better if you focused on a more accurate input. When your performance improves, I can see you moving on to those higher- level tasks you've been asking for. – *sell*

3. Clive, once again we find ourselves speaking about getting a higher throughput from you. Do you think that coaching would help? – *sample*

4. Denise, we had this conversation about your accuracy on numerous occasions yet nothing is getting better. I want you to concentrate for the next week purely on product inputs. – *tell*

5. Eddie, that's you now our top performer in the first line customer charts. How would you like to tackle a more challenging range of customers? – *sample*

6. Fiona, that's the quarterly results in and for the first time you're bottom of the league table in your section. How do you think we can get you back up the table? – *consult*

7. Brian, you are by far and away our top sales person and I'm moving you to the new west region sales area next month. – *tell*

8. Jackie, I can see that following our last discussion you have really made inroads with the weekly reports. If this continues to improve I can see you getting the employee of the month soon. – *sell*

GLOSSARY

Glossary

Action centred leadership	Theory developed by Adair to describe the leader's three areas of responsibility – task, team and individual.
Active listening	The process by which the receiver of verbal communication shows the sender that they are listening to them.
Annual percentage rate (APR)	The true rate of interest charged on a loan.
Approved person	An individual approved by the FCA to carry out one or more controlled functions on behalf of an authorised firm.
Authorisation	The permission given by the FCA to a financial firm to allow it to trade.
Automated telephone service	A service that allows customers to access basic information without the need to talk to an advisor.
Banking Conduct of Business Sourcebook (BCOBS)	The binding rules set out by the FCA to regulate certain banking services.
Belbin's Team Roles	The description of 9 different roles that need to be carried out in a successful team. These were developed by Dr Meredith Belbin
Brainstorming	A free flowing creative thinking technique designed to generate a number of ideas from a group of participants.
Building Society	A mutual organisation that accepts deposits and lends funds for house purchase.
Business process re-engineering	The rethinking and redesign of business processes to achieve dramatic improvements.
Buyers' remorse	The feelings of doubt that many customers experience after making a major purchase.
Buying signals	Signs from the customer that they are ready to take the product being offered.
Cancellable agreement	Credit agreements regulated by the Consumer Credit Acts where face-to-face discussions are held with the customer about the credit arrangements but where the customer does not sign the agreement on trade premises. The borrower has a cooling-off period in which they can cancel.
Cause and effect diagram	A tool that helps identify, sort and display possible causes of a problem
Clayton's case	The case of Devaynes v Noble, 1816 which established the first in, first out principle for running accounts regarding the appropriation of payments.
Closed question	A question that can be fully answered with either a 'yes' or 'no' response
Coaching	The process of helping a person maintain or improve their performance through ongoing evaluation and feedback
Consumer Credit Act	Legislation to protect consumers entering into certain credit agreements.

Contingency approach	The concept that leaders must adopt their style to meet the situation they face.
Credit scoring	An automated method of assessing credit applications.
Credit union	A mutual organisation offering savings and loan products.
Decisional roles	Mintzberg's description of the role of a manger in making decisions that impact on the future of the organisation and/or their department.
Distribution channels	A range of ways by which organisations and customers interact.
Electronic purse	A plastic card that is topped up to pay for goods and services with a particular organisation.
Empathy	The ability to understand how another person is feeling.
Enabling legislation	Legislation that allows regulation to be changed and updated without the need for fresh legislation.
European Banking Authority	A regulatory body covering all EU countries seeking to maintain common regulatory standards.
Exchequer account	The government's account at the Bank of England
External customer	The end user of an organisation's products and services – for example, an account holder.
Faster payments service	A service that offers the facility for an automated payment to reach the beneficiary's account within two hours.
Financial intermediation	The function of a bank where it acts as a link between savers and borrowers.
Financial Policy Committee	The area of the Bank of England responsible for protecting the stability of the UK financial system
Financial Conduct Authority	The body responsible for the regulation of retail and wholesale markets.
Formal team	A group created by the organisation to help achieve the organisation's goals
GROW	Mnemonic for the coaching process – grow, reality, options and will
Independent Commission of Banking	Commission set up under Sir John Vickers as a result of the banking crisis. It considered and made recommendations on reforms to the UK banking system to promote stability and enhance confidence.
Individual Savings Account (ISA)	A tax free savings product, subject to annual limits.
Informal group	A group formed by the informal relationships within the organisation and is formed to satisfy needs beyond those of doing a job.
Informational roles	Mintzberg's description of the mamager's role where they are communicating within the organisation
Internal customer	A member of staff in an organisation who has needs served by colleagues.

Interpersonal roles	Mintzberg's description of those managerial roles that require the manager to interact with others
Irrevocable mandate	The security taken for a bridging loan, whereby the customer's solicitor undertakes to remit the free proceeds from the sale of the customer's house to the bank.
Investment Bank	A wholesale bank that offers specialist services to large organisations.
Lender of Last Resort	A function of the Bank of England where it may lend funds to a bank suffering urgent liquidity shortfalls.
Lending Code	A voluntary code setting out best practice for banks when dealing with personal and small business customers.
LIBOR	London Inter Bank Offered Rate. The rate of interest used for inter-bank loans on the London interbank market.
Lien	The right implied by law to retain the movable property belonging to another person until a debt is paid.
Limiting factors	Aspects of an organisation's products or services that do not compare favourably to those offered by competitors.
Manual underwriting	The process of assessing a credit proposal by a lending official as opposed to using an automated credit scoring procedure.
Mission statement	A general statement outlining the purpose of an organisation.
Money laundering	The process of converting money obtained from illegal purposes into money that appears to come from legitimate sources.
Money transmission	The process and systems used to facilitate the transfer of money from debtors to creditors.
Money transmission account	Another name for a current account.
Mortgage Conduct of Business rules (MCOBS)	The rules stating the minimum regulatory requirements to be followed by mortgage lenders, advisers, administrators and arrangers.
National Savings and Investments (NS&I)	Part of the UK Treasury that offers savings products (often with some tax benefits). The funds raised are used by the UK government.
Nominal group technique	A structured form of brainstorming.
Non-cancellable agreement	Agreements regulated by the Consumer Credit Acts where there are no face-to-face discussions, or where the agreement is signed on the trade premises. The borrower cannot cancel such an agreement.
Non-verbal communication	Those aspects of communication that are not spoken – for example, eye contact, facial expression, body movement, etc.
Open question	A question starting with who, what, where, when, why, or how. It cannot be answered with a 'yes' or 'no' response.

Operational risk	The risk of direct or indirect loss resulting from inadequate or failed internal processes, people and systems or from external events.
Outsourcing	A third party organisation that provides services to an organisation.
Personal development planning	The stage of the performance management framework whereby the manager and employee agree on the relevant development activities for the employee
Performance management system	An organisation's process for managing the performance levels of its employees.
Performance planning	The first stage of the performance management process whereby the goals for each employee are agreed and plans put in place to facilitate the attainment of these goals
PEST analysis	A tool used to assess the external environment, covering the following factors – political, economic, social and technological
Primary bank	A bank that operates the payments mechanism and offers money transmission accounts
Prudential control	Ensuring that firms have policies with an appropriate balance of risk and reward.
Prudential Regulation Authority	A subsidiary of the Bank of England that supervises deposit takers, insurers and some significant investment firms.
Quality circle	A work group that meets regularly to discuss work problems and seeks to overcome these.
Quantitative easing	The process of injecting funds into the economy by the Bank of England buying securities on the market
Queue management	The process of reducing queues by offering customers alternative and quicker ways to carry out their business.
Restricted credit	Credit where the lender has control over how the funds are used
Regulated products	Those products that only appropriately qualified staff cab give advice on.
Repayment vehicle	The source of repayment for an interest-only loan.
Risk acceptance	Where the risk is taken on – possibly as the potential rewards are so attractive.
Risk avoidance	Where the risk is assessed as so high, the organisation chooses not to participate in the activity.
Risk management	The sum of all the actions taken to reduce risk to an acceptable level.
Risk management lifecycle	Risk identification, assessment, mitigation and monitoring.
Risk reduction	Actions to reduce the possibility of the risk event occurring or the impact of the risk event should it occur.

Risk retention	Where the risk is accepted, but plans are in place should the risk event occur.
Risk sharing	Where risk is shared with another party – for example, through a joint venture
Risk transfer	Where either the risk itself or the financial consequences of the risk is transferred to another party – for example, by subcontracting
Running account credit	An account where the debtor can draw down credit from time to time, subject to a maximum limit – for example, an overdraft.
Secondary bank	A bank that does not operate the payments mechanism
Service level agreement	A negotiated agreement between two parties regarding the services to be provided from one to another.
Set off	The practice of combining the balances of accounts in the same name to determine whether or not the customer has sufficient funds to pay an item presented.
Share dealing	A service offered by a bank where they take a customer's instructions to buy or sell shares and execute the transaction through a broker.
Six sigma	An approach to quality that seeks to achieve as near to zero defects as possible
Six thinking hats	Concept designed by Edward de Bono to look at situations from a range of perspectives.
SMART	A framework for the drafting of objectives
Span of control	The number of people who report to the one manager.
Stages of team development	Theory developed by Tuckman that describes the stages that a team moves through from inception to maturity.
Stakeholders	These groups that have an interest in an organisation
Strategic action	The third stage of the strategic management process where the strategic plan is put into action.
Strategic analysis	The first stage of the strategic management process, where consideration is given to the external environment, resources and the needs of stakeholders.
Strategic choice	The second stage of the strategic management process where consideration is given to which strategic options the business should pursue
Strategic fit	Matching the activities of an organisation into its environment.
Strategic stretch	When the organisation seeks to stretch its resources to gain competitive advantage.
Style approach	The argument that suggests that there is a range of approaches and behaviours a manager can use when dealing with their team.
Switching service	The service offered by banks to streamline the transfer of an account from one bank to another.

SWOT	Strengths, Weaknesses, Opportunities and Threats.
Theory X	The description of an autocratic manager developed by McGregor
Theory Y	The description of a democratic manager developed by McGregor
Third party payments	Payments made through a bank to another person
Total quality management	Techniques used to improve the efficiency and effectiveness of a business
Trait approach	The argument which suggests that some people have certain inherent qualities that mark them out to be leaders.
Treating Customers Fairly (TCF)	The FCA initiative designed to protect customers' interests.
Undue influence	Where a stronger party influences a weaker party to a course of action that the weaker party would not otherwise have undertaken.
Unrestricted credit	Credit where the borrower can use the funds for any use he/she wishes
Ways and means advance	Temporary finance provided to the government by the Bank of England
Whistleblowing	Where an employee reports another employee for inappropriate behaviour or malpractice.

INDEX